APOCALYPSE MAN

APOCALYPSE MAN

THE DEATH DRIVE AND THE RHETORIC
OF WHITE MASCULINE VICTIMHOOD

CASEY RYAN KELLY

THE OHIO STATE UNIVERSITY PRESS

COLUMBUS

Library of Congress Cataloging-in-Publication Data
Names: Kelly, Casey Ryan, 1979– author.
Title: Apocalypse man : the death drive and the rhetoric of white masculine victimhood / Casey Ryan Kelly.
Description: Columbus : The Ohio State University, [2020] | Includes bibliographical references and index. | Summary: "Examines white masculine victimhood by looking at the rhetoric of gender-motivated mass shooters, white supremacists, online misogynist and incel communities, survivalists and doomsday preppers, gun culture and political rallies, and political demagogues"—Provided by publisher.
Identifiers: LCCN 2019044295 | ISBN 9780814214329 (cloth) | ISBN 9780814277775 (ebook)
Subjects: LCSH: Mass media—United States—History—21st century. | Men, White, in mass media. | Masculinity in mass media. | Death instinct in mass media. | Identity (Psychology) and mass media—United States. | Rhetoric. | Men, White—United States—Attitudes. | Mass media—Political aspects—United States. | Masculinity—Political aspects—United States. | Identity politics.
Classification: LCC P94.5.M432 U654 2020 | DDC 305.809—dc23
LC record available at https://lccn.loc.gov/2019044295

Cover design by Susan Zucker
Text design by Juliet Williams
Type set in Adobe Minion Pro

CONTENTS

ILLUSTRATIONS

ACKNOWLEDGMENTS

I AM PRIVILEGED to have a network of generous friends and colleagues who have supported this project in one way or another. Whether they know it or not, my thinking throughout writing this book has been influenced by our informal conversations, spontaneous riffs, and moments of commiseration. I am also fortunate enough to have the institutional support of my department, university, and national association. In short, this book would not have materialized were it not for the invaluable support of others. I would be remiss if I did not acknowledge at the outset my gratitude to Tara Cyphers and The Ohio State University Press. Their enthusiastic support for this book was indispensable, and I am proud that this book is part of their growing library of critical rhetorical scholarship. A book about the compulsions of white masculinity is not for the faint of heart, and I have been fortunate enough to work with a press and reviewers who were willing to go down the rabbit hole with me. I also wish to acknowledge those who have provided financial support for this book. Namely, the College of Liberal Arts and Sciences and the Department of Communication Studies at the University of Nebraska–Lincoln as well as the National Communication Association's Karl R. Wallace Memorial Fund.

My departmental colleagues at Nebraska have been extraordinarily supportive throughout the various stages of this book. I am indebted to the support of my department chair Dawn Braithwaite, and colleagues Chuck Braithwaite, Allison Bonander, Kathy Castle, Aaron Duncan, Kristen Hoerl, Jody Koenig Kellas, Justin Kirk, Kathy Krone, Ron Lee, Angel Maldonado, Angela Palmer-Wackerly, Bill Seiler, and Jordan Soliz. I cannot imagine a more supportive and intellectually nourishing place to work. I am also fortunate to have wonderful graduate advisees (Chase Aunspach, Jennifer Rome, Mallory Marsh, and Will Sipe) whose work remains a continual source of inspiration.

This book also took shape through conversations with brilliant people in communication studies. I draw inspiration not only from their published work and academic presentations, but also from their willingness to share ideas, offer feedback and suggestions, read drafts, write together, or simply commiserate. I am also thankful for the opportunity to present early versions of this project to colleagues at Texas A&M University, University of Utah, University of Arkansas, and Wake Forest University. I have had the great fortune to get feedback on this project from supportive friends and colleagues. I wish to thank Claire Sisco King, Joshua Gunn, Leslie Hahner, Calum Matheson, Lisa Corrigan, Bryan McCann, Eric King Watts, Kirt Wilson, Damien Pfister, Michael Lee, and Ryan Neville-Shepard for their feedback on various versions of this project. I am especially grateful to my writing group partners Paul Johnson, Jennie Keohane, and Kelly Jakes not only for helping me with the final push to finish this book on schedule but also for being supportive friends. Finally, the voice of dear friend Matt May has been with me throughout this project. May your recovery be swift, my brother—the world is a better place with you in it.

My spouse and colleague Kristen Hoerl deserves special recognition for her willingness to look into the abyss with me as I completed this book. I could accomplish nothing without her love and support. I cannot adequately express how much her support, as well as the support of her family means to me. Thank you to my parents, Diane and Marvin, for teaching me that masculinity can be something other than what it has been in the past and might become in the future. Finally, thank you to my late canine companion Roxie, who provided the best unconditional moral support I could ever ask or deserve.

A few select parts of the introduction were previously published as Casey Ryan Kelly, "The Wounded Man: *Foxcatcher* (2014) and the Incoherence of White Masculine Victimhood," *Communication and Critical/Cultural Studies* 15, no. 2 (2018): 161–78. Portions of chapter 1 were previously published as Casey Ryan Kelly, "The Man-poclypse: *Doomsday Preppers* and the Rituals of Apocalyptic Manhood," *Text and Performance Quarterly* 36, no. 2 (2016): 95–114. Small segments of chapter 3 were published as Casey Ryan Kelly, "The Rage Network: Toxic Masculinity in Digital Space," in Carol Winkler (ed.), *Networking Argument: Selected papers for the 19th Biennial Conference on Argumentation* (London: Taylor & Francis, 2018).

The Apocalyptic Male

ON AUGUST 11–12, 2017, a coalition of white supremacists, neo-Nazis, and other white ethnonationalist organizations occupied the streets of Charlottesville, Virginia, in protest of the removal of a monument to Confederate General Robert E. Lee. Dubbed by its organizers the "Unite the Right" rally, the event began with a parade of white men carrying lit tiki torches and chanting in unison "Jews will not replace us."[1] The following day, far-right protestors engaged in violent attacks against a growing group of opponents, resulting in dozens of injuries and the death of one counterprotestor.[2] Particularly striking was the macabre nature of the protestor's performance: white men bearing an assortment of Nazi and neo-Nazi uniforms, torches, automatic rifles, skull facemasks, gas masks, white hoods, KKK robes, paramilitary and guerilla uniforms, homemade weapons, pro-Trump regalia, and quasi-ironic signs featuring the smirking icon of online hate groups, Pepe the Frog. The rally served as a stage for a series of arresting performances in which aggrieved white men consummated the fantasy of violently terrorizing, if not upending, a society nominally committed to the progressive goals of race and gender equality. The protest was a ghoulish image event that presented social progressives with a chilling vision of the death of liberal democracy. Above all, the protest announced the new smirking public face of white nationalism, a movement that revels in taboo performances, nihilism, sadism, masochism, death, lawlessness, and cathartic acts of violence. Moving from the fringes of internet culture to the main stage of public life, the Charlottesville protest previewed an emerging form of white male identity politics that far exceeded the boundaries of white nationalism. The event represents a politics that seeks to radically deterritorialize liberal democracy and openly embraces cruelty and creative acts of destruction as its organizing principles. At its extremities, this rendition of white masculinity strives not for political reform but instead a cataclysmic remaking of the social order that would restore white men to their entitled place in society.

The events at Charlottesville serve as a representative anecdote for what I have deemed the "apocalyptic turn" in white masculinity, "an embodied model of masculinity that seeks a permanent resolution to immanent crises of the male self in the imminent collapse of feminized society."[3] With their perennial pronouncements of the so-called crisis of white masculinity, a network of men's rights organizations, online hate groups, and like-minded aggrieved men have generated a powerful narrative of victimization in which white men have been emasculated by the family court system, affirmative action programs, man-hating feminists, gold-digging ex-wives, political correctness, job-taking immigrants, the social acceptance of queer intimacy, and even television situation comedies that satirize oafish working-class fathers.[4] This powerful script of white male victimization was amplified during the 2016 presidential election. The Trump presidential campaign decried the loss of white male status to immigrants and foreign competitors and embraced the hypermasculine virtues of zero-sum competition, subjugating one's opponents, and boastful pride in both self and nation.[5] Ostensibly, the call to "Make America Great Again" hailed a melancholic subject beseeched by an intoxicating fantasy of return to an imagined past before feminism, the Black freedom struggle, and queer activism fundamentally questioned cisgender heterosexual white men's primacy in all aspects of public and private life. Popular articulations of wounded white masculinity reflect the rise of a reactionary politics of white male resentment that seizes tropes of victimhood and marginalization even as it celebrates white male primacy. While the economic, social, and political status of white men remains comparatively undisturbed, the rhetoric of white male victimhood nonetheless asserts that relative gains by women, people of color, immigrants, and GLBTQ movements threaten white men's social status and upward mobility.[6] Aggrieved by feminism, multiculturalism, secularism, and demands for structural equality, the reactionary posture of white male victimhood brackets the historical context of male dominance and violence in an effort to position men as the forgotten casualties of identity politics.[7] The character of contemporary white masculinity is increasing bellicose, particularly where white men view themselves as besieged by others. This particular expression of white masculinity engenders an unconscious desire for a social cataclysm that will permanently return white men to prominence.

This book examines how and why contemporary white masculinity is increasingly animated by images of death, mayhem, destruction, and the apocalyptic as a response to demands for inclusion that might otherwise augment white men's structural privilege. Exemplified by President Donald J. Trump's slogan "Make American Great Again," white masculinity has become organized around melancholic attachments to an imagined past when white men were supposedly whole. In addition to being incapable of moving forward, white masculinity is haunted by a destructive impulse to publicly restage the scene of its traumatic loss. In turn, this investment in loss ultimately sutures white male subjectivity to its wounds. Consequently, the enactment of trauma becomes the very condition of possibility for the recovery of white masculinity. This compulsive return to loss is characteristic of what Freudian psychoanalysts refer to as the *death drive,* or the subject's enjoyment of a symbolic regression to an imagined state, prior to the formation of the subject, and therefore prior to its traumatic entry into subjectivity. The compulsion to repeat constitutes a performance of mastery aimed to give the subject a coherent image of the self. As Sigmund Freud astutely inquired, "How is it then that in melancholia the superego can become the gathering-place for the death instinct?"[8] In responding to this question, this book contends that there is something about white men's inability to experience and address social change as anything other than a catastrophic loss that aggregates those destructive aspects of the drive(s) that are antithetical to the subject's self-preservation.

In their crude mimicry of racial and gender identity politics, some white men are increasingly drawn to narratives of victimhood and persecution and, in turn, are invited to violently deflect the death drive outward in response to perceived injuries. While violence has long been an attribute of hegemonic masculinity, the so-called crisis of masculinity is increasingly organized around a *thanatopolitics,* a politics of death, that seeks to extinguish that in society that threatens the white male ego—not just women and people of color, but institutions that represent the threat of emasculation, including government and the mass media among others.[9] To understand the violent implications of this apocalyptic turn in masculinity, this book examines the textual, mediated, and performative nuances of contemporary white male backlash rhetoric, including that of gender-motivated mass shooters, white supremacists, online misogynist communities, survivalists and "doomsday preppers," pro-gun activists, and political demagogues. To capture the scope and diverse character of apocalyptic manhood, I explore a wide variety of textual forms including manifestos, networked media, public performances, image events, and unconventional genres of political address that craft a composite image of aggrieved white masculinity. Here my aim is not to address white masculinity or white men as empirical phenomena, but instead to treat the masculinity crisis as a signifier or cultural figure that circulates widely and speaks loudly. Hence, this book is not a critique of flesh-and-blood subjects, but rather a series of discourses and images that address white men as if they are victims. I contend that proclamations of crisis particularly resonate in US public life as a consequence of a media system and digital culture that privileges shrill voices, grotesque image events, manufactured controversy, and the exploitation of lived pain.[10] This book considers how white masculinity is enacted and how white male subjects are addressed in a media culture that is addled by fear, outrage, and cruelty.

Taken together, I argue, the texts that convey an image of white men in crisis construct a version of white masculinity that is consummated through the destruction of civil society and liberal democratic publics, as well as antisocial and destruction behaviors, taboo and even sadomasochistic performances. At the intersections of critical rhetoric, media studies, and performance, this book illustrates how death and fatalism have come to underwrite representations and expressions of white masculinity. Preoccupied with fantasies of victimization, a mosaic of discourses and images invite aggrieved white men to think of themselves as structurally oppressed and, in turn, to "take their country back" even if it means tearing apart the social fabric of liberal democracy. Although white masculinity is not reducible to an essence, and it is true that white men suffer alongside others, this book investigates how texts that construct what it means to suffer as white and male enlist their audiences in the fraught reproduction of cultural melancholia and the death drive.

In the remainder of this chapter, I offer a guiding theoretical framework to make sense of the melancholic and self-destructive tone that characterizes contemporary white masculinity. This framework historically situates the proverbial "crisis of masculinity" as white men begin to constitute their identities not solely through primacy—strength, individualism, and self-sufficiency—but also through marginalization. Next, drawing from Freudian psychoanalysis, I theorize the relationship between white masculine victimhood, cultural melancholia, and the death drive. Here I argue that death and trauma have become the organizing tropes of white masculinity—both of which are underwritten by the compulsion to repeat and revisit without adequately mourning the past. In this way, white male victimhood constitutes a politics of death in the name of life. Finally, I sketch an approach to unfurling the constellation of diverse texts and psychical structures that constitute the scope of white masculine victimhood and attend to the affordances of different rhetorical forms that constrain and enable how white masculinity can be represented and enacted in the present political moment.

WHITE MEN AS VICTIMS?

In the 1999 adaption of Chuck Palahniuk's *Fight Club*, the anonymous protagonist (Ed Norton) laments being part of a generation of men raised by women in the absence of their fathers. Further emasculated by consumer culture and wage slavery, his generation of men had become soft. Speaking with (and through) his alter ego Tyler Durden (Brad Pitt), the two come to the conclusion that "we are a generation of men raised by women. I wonder if another woman is what we need?" Their creation of "fight club" was an attempt to deliver men from the phoniness and femininity of late capitalism to the raw violent masculinity of the primal past.[11] Hence, the two adopt an ethos of self-destruction to counteract the demands of a feminized society. "Hitting bottom," as Durden characterizes it, means achieving self-actualization by abandoning the artifice of self-improvement, consumer lifestyles, and social conformity. Smirking at advertisements featuring the perfectly sculpted bodies of Calvin Klein models, the protagonist asks Durden, "is that what a man looks like?" to which Durden replies, "self-improvement is masturbation, now self-destruction . . ." The inquisitive tone that precedes the ellipses invites audience to an open-ended consideration of male masochism as a response to emasculation. While self-improvement equates to feminine narcissism, self-destruction dismantles the ornamental façade of an emasculating culture that, in Durden's words, has men "chasing cars and clothes, working jobs we hate so we can buy shit that we don't need." The film portrays self-destruction as a creative and liberatory act, the last resort for men who see themselves as structurally oppressed—mere "slaves with white collars."

Fight Club indexed an array of millennial masculine anxieties that have culminated in the present dark and nihilistic phase of the so-called crisis of masculinity.[12] Whereas *Rambo: First Blood* (1982) resonated with white male baby boomer's feelings of displacement and victimization following America's defeat in Vietnam, *Fight Club* suggests that the total feminization of society by consumerism, and what Joshua Gunn and Thomas Frentz refer to as the "cultural decline of the father figure," has left contemporary white men with no nation to "take back" or *re*masculinize.[13] Seemingly, white men's only alternative is to divest themselves of the concept of a liberal society altogether. Put another way, *Fight Club* consummated a fantasy of male autarky wherein white men embrace destruction and homosociality to render themselves independent of and invulnerable to women.[14] The film marked the broader cultural development of a more elusive, diffuse, and fragmented form of white masculinity that Claire Sisco King calls "abject hegemony."[15] Reveling in masochism and self-destruction renders the male body abject by making it bear grotesque wounds that threaten the borders of subjectivity. Blood and other bodily wastes are material that must be expelled to establish the subject as fully symbolic so that it bears no trace of its relation with nature.[16] In King's estimation, "white masculinity prevails not by expelling that which is Other, but by sacrificing its own fictions in order to absorb, assimilate, and make room for Otherness, offering up, for instance, cherished narratives of masculine strength, aggression, and invulnerability in order to indulge in femininity, passivity, and lack."[17] Diffuse and amalgamated, abject white masculinity benefits from being able to accommodate "a multitude of incarnations of what the 'white' and the 'masculine' can be."[18] Although masochism places the male body in what Freud called a "characteristically female situation," this interpretation of abject masculinity suggests that masochism enables men to disavow that hegemonic masculinity still ultimately structures society.[19] Hence, self-destruction is but a creative reservoir of strategic advantages for white men as they address the present iteration of the so-called crisis of masculinity.

Bearing one's wounds—physical or emotional, real or perceived—has become a powerful way of articulating white masculinity in American culture. Abject white masculinity is underwritten by a powerful script of victimization that blames feminism and multiculturalism for white men's dwindling social and economic privileges. When one lives a life of entitlement, even the most modest demands for equality can be perceived as an assault. This book suggests that the apocalyptic turn in the rhetoric of white masculinity is the by-product of a nearly forty-year effort to position white men as victims of identity politics and policies mandating formal equality. Sally Robinson contends that following decades of social upheaval in which white men were asked to share their social and economic privileges with women and people of color, "post-sixties American culture produced images of a physically wounded and emotionally traumatized white masculinity."[20] In addition to new antidiscrimination laws and affirmative action programs, deindustrialization and the decline of American manufacturing and family farming undermined male primacy in America's labor force.[21] The transition from an industrial to a service economy untethered hegemonic masculinity from its long-standing association with professions that required physical skill.[22] As Susan Faludi argues, in an "ornamental culture," the necessity of male labor was replaced by "celebrity and image, glamour and entertainment, marketing and consumerism."[23] In addition, America's military defeat in Vietnam emasculated a nation whose collective identity was premised on a hypermasculine war culture that venerated military heroes and celebrated American exceptionalism.[24]

Besieged by these socioeconomic forces, some white men began to speak about themselves as victims and blamed women and minorities for their woes. Despite the fact that white men still outpaced every other demographic in economic opportunities and social privilege, mere exposure to the kind of structural precarity experienced by women and minorities provoked a reactionary response from certain demographics of white men.[25] In contrast to the stoic masculinity of the 1950s, the post–1960s white man put his suffering on public display. That he no longer seemed invulnerable to economic and social precarity was evidence of not only white men's share in structural oppression but also the systematic displacement of white men altogether.

Invoking victimhood seems counterintuitive if it is the case that hegemonic masculinity is defined by attributes such as physical strength, virility, self-reliance, independence, and self-confidence.[26] Yet, victimhood is a powerful trope in American culture that elevates the moral status of the subject who suffers. John Mowitt's notion of "trauma envy" and Wendy Brown's theorization of "wounded attachments" illustrate how a preoccupation with victimization can forge political communities solely on the basis of shared trauma.[27] Thus, Bryan McCann underscores the importance of distinguishing between therapeutic and material victimhood, the former an appropriation of victim status as a means of acquiring credibility and the latter a tangible experience with structural oppression.[28] Masculine victimization is more characteristic of the former, and thus serves as a "convenient strategy by which publics can deflect blame and insist upon their own moral purity by being a victim or sympathizing with one."[29] Masculine victimhood encourages white men to speak about common human vulnerability as if it were systemic structural oppression. Hence, narratives of white masculine victimhood conflate material and therapeutic victimhood to destabilize the social conventions by which justice is adjudicated.

In part, victimhood's appeal is owed to its long-standing relationship with the political genre of melodrama. Melodrama foregrounds agonistic moral polarities, the spectacular yet virtuous suffering of innocent victims, heroic acts of redemption, and overwrought pathos and sentimentality. Elisabeth Anker argues that the generic conventions of melodrama have found their way out of novels and films and into post–9/11 political discourse. Melodramatic political discourse, she writes, "depicts the United States as both the feminized, virginal victims and the aggressive, masculinized hero in the story of freedom, as the victim-hero of geopolitics."[30] Inviting the public to ruminate on their injuries, political melodrama legitimizes violence and the consolidation of state power as necessary components of national healing. On account of the genre's cultural work, men's rights discourse has taken up many of these melodramatic qualities, including virtuous suffering, unjust persecution, innocence, and a call for heroic salvation. Suffering of any kind, for that matter, seems to underwrite white men's efforts to lay claim to the status of the victim-hero. Victimhood unmoored from the materiality of justice can be an intoxicating discourse that can lead otherwise caring and thoughtful individuals to feelings of resentment and animosity.

While white supremacist and men's rights groups take the claim for granted, how is it that objectively privileged white men have come to understand themselves as victims? Michael Kimmel offers perhaps the deepest historical account of white male victimhood in which he argues that the pre–World War II masculine archetypes such as the self-made man and artisan hero were undone by the emasculating forces of mass culture and the rise of a service economy. The resultant *masculine mystique* was based on a recognition that male archetypes that embodied unassailable strength, rugged individualism, and stoicism not only were fraudulent but were quite literally killing men who were unable to escape a vicious pattern of overwork, emotional repression, and self-medication.[31] While factory workers felt powerless and isolated, white-collar organization men felt that they were cogs in the corporate machine. America's failure in Vietnam further demonstrated that the American warrior archetype was no longer a reliable foundation for white masculinity. A new generation of baby boomer men rebelled against the stoic masculinity of their fathers. Even Betty Friedan suggested that masculinity oppressed men too, noting that "it seems to me that men weren't really the enemy—they were fellow victims, suffering from an outdated masculine mystique that made them feel unnecessarily inadequate when there were no bears to kill."[32] The idea of men's liberation drew strength from the other liberation movements of the period, even harboring potential for identification and coalitional politics with the feminist movement, the civil rights movement, and gay liberation. At the outset Warren Farrell, now a prominent antifeminist, convened NOW's taskforce on the male mystique and ran consciousness-raising groups for men. By the early 1970s there were a litany of key writings that suggested that men, too, suffered from the "problem without a name" and also endured lives of quiet desperation.[33]

Men's liberation adopted a victimization narrative when it took a hard right turn in the 1980s and became enveloped in the antifeminist backlash that was part and parcel of the Reagan Revolution.[34] Early aspirations toward solidarity with other liberation movements were dashed by white men's newly found vigor for frontier manhood and avenging action heroes.[35] Moreover, despite the downward trajectory of the working class, men were exhorted to invest in the same marketplace myths used to deindustrialize American cities and ship jobs overseas. The decade's backlash against entitlement programs, affirmation action, and political correctness all took aim at feminists (also called "feminazis") as the source of men's victimhood.[36] Antifeminists characterized feminism and other liberationist causes as a demand for special rights that unfairly advantaged women and minorities over white men.[37] Men's liberation proponents began to speak about men as victims of family courts and divorce proceedings, domestic abuse, falsified sexual harassment and rape allegations, and affirmative action programs. Farrell even proposed a men's Bill of Rights to enshrine protections against feminism.[38] Others such as Robert Bly, Robert Moore, and Douglas Gillette offered therapeutic correctives that sought out the mythopoetic foundations of manhood as an alternative to renegotiating the gender division of labor. Bly's *Iron John* (1990) and Moore and Gillette's *King, Warrior, Magician, Lover* (1990) presented a softer boutique image of manhood dredged from ancient archetypes. Yet, this less aggressive form of men's liberation ultimately affirmed that men had been led astray by modernity and that there was an innate social order that affirmed men's birthright to power.[39] Bly also echoed the belief that men have been unjustly accused by feminism and should not accept the blame for patriarchy. In short, they disavowed the need for social change in favor of changing men's emotional expectations.

As those who have written about mass shootings and white extremism have observed, guns and paramilitary culture, militias, online hate groups, and conservative talk radio also offered sanctuary to white men who felt dispossessed by demographic shifts and identity politics.[40]

Much like the aforementioned scholars, Douglas Kellner's historicization of contemporary white male victimization begins with the vast social upheaval of the 1960s in which feminism, gay liberation, and the counterculture transformed the institutions, practices, and values that white men once took for granted.[41] This transformation in social values also coincided with an inflationary economy and the global restructuring of capital that put downward pressure on wages and led to the decline in traditionally male professions such as manufacturing. The combination of social change and downward economic pressure caused white men to reconstruct their political identities, some retreating to apocalyptic fantasies and extremist violence. In response to the dizzying pace of social change, these institutions provided men both a narrative that made sense of their feelings of alienation and an affirmation that white male identity was a distinct and vitally important aspect of American culture. Kellner writes that "this situation gave rise to a new strain of white male identity politics fueled by intense rage, resentment, paranoia, and apocalyptic visions, often exploding into violence and finding solidarity with militia movements, right-wing hate and extremist groups, Christian fundamentalism, survivalist sects, and talk radio and Internet subcultures."[42] He calls the new white male identity politics a kind of "postmodern pastiche," as it often blended Christianity, white supremacy, and other militant beliefs into a shallow and psychotic identity characterized by paranoia, anxiety, and antimodernism.[43]

The contemporary men's rights movement is a heterogeneous mixture of formal and ad hoc communities, many of whom gather adherents through networked media. The men's rights message varies widely depending on the community they target, ranging from divorced dads and pickup artists to white supremacists and male separatists. Although some groups identify as pro-feminist men's organizations or therapeutic emotional support groups, the more vitriolic and increasingly visible organizations are those that speak to white male victimhood and constantly cycle rage into public life.[44] For instance, *Voice for Men* founder Paul Elam uses a victimization narrative to justify spousal rape as well as domestic battery as a form of self-defense. In a particularly nauseating piece of "satire," he explains, "women, please listen to Whoopi Goldberg. If you don't want to be slapped, backhanded, punched in the mouth, decked or throttled keep your stinking hands off of other people. A man hitting you back after you have assaulted him does not make you a victim of domestic violence. It makes you a recipient of justice. Deal with it."[45] Matt Forney, a writer for the men's rights website *Return of Kings,* often publicly fantasizes about gender violence. He argues that "women should be terrorized by their men; it's the only thing that makes them behave better than chimps."[46] All couched in a smirking irony, these passages exemplify the kind of violent fantasies fomented in a series of online portals dedicated to decrying the victimization of white men.

While men's rights can be easily dismissed as a fringe movement, hundreds of thousands of men (and some women) visit these sites annually. As of January 2018, Reddit.com's Red Pill subreddit—a page populated with violent misogyny—has 245,500 subscribers.[47] The men's rights subreddit also has over 175,000 subscribers. Elam's website generates 20,000 to 30,000 visitors per day.[48] Canadian psychologist and virulent men's rights activist Jordan Peterson's Youtube.com lectures have received over forty million views.[49] Other sites that devote a significant attention to men's rights topics include *Infowars,* which has averaged twenty million visitors per month since 2013,[50] and *Breitbart News,* which surged from approximately eight million to eighteen million visitors per month following Donald Trump's presidential campaign announcement in the summer of 2015.[51] As this significant amount of web traffic suggests, the message of white male victimhood has attracted a very large audience.[52] This audience will continue to grow as men's rights websites cross-pollinated with alt-right groups such as the National Policy Institute. Chris Cantwell, one of the organizers of the Unite the Right Rally at Charlottesville, is a prominent example of how men's rights activists have been enlisted in the cause against "white genocide." What both groups share—and the similarities are many—is the belief in the ongoing persecution of white men and, in R. W. Connell's words, an "apocalyptic awareness of the historicity of masculinity itself defined the political goal."[53] The synergy between alt-right, white supremacy, and men's rights organization explains both the visibility and the intensity of the rhetoric of white male victimhood. If white men are to believe that they are not only marginalized but at war for their very survival—then extreme acts of spectacular violence seem all the more rational. Of course, I read much of men's animosity as misguided and misplaced. Hence, my focus is on verbal, mediated, and embodied discourses that address white men as victimized subjects rather than on white men themselves. This book is interested in the recent apocalyptic tone in the rhetoric of white masculinity and what kinds of anxieties it tends to circulate. At this moment, the narrative of persecution seems to hold the attention of white men more than any other discourse. In light of this, the next section offers a psychoanalytical framework to understand the connection between victimization, melancholia, and the death drive.

MASCULINITY, MELANCHOLIA, AND THE DEATH DRIVE

This book traces how white masculine victimhood is underwritten by the perverse effects associated with what Freud called the "death instinct," which has been subsequently reformulated as the death *drive*. I am concerned with how the death drive is externalized or deflected into public life toward external persecutors to stave off and defend against threats to the ego that germinate from within.[54] In other words, the rhetoric of white male victimhood constructs an external tormentor onto which its audience can project those fears and anxieties that are generated from the internal desires of the subject. Projection, then, does less to address specific imminent needs than it does existential dread, or the *immanent* and recursive crises of the white male subject. The *apocalyptic man*, then, is beseeched to invest in imagery and narratives of death and lawlessness to address the subject's unending anomie and project a fantasy of self-mastery. For Joshua Gunn and David Beard, such ritualistic behavior constitutes the terrain of the "apocalyptic sublime" that "replaces the traditional sense of impending cataclysm (an 'ending') with a sense of never-ending crisis."[55] For those white men who consider themselves persecuted victims, the apocalypse is nigh: their institutions have been taken over by their enemies, their rights and freedoms have been dispossessed, their reign at the top of the socioeconomic ladder has been deposed, their society has collapsed. This is the message emanating from conservative talk radio, paramilitary culture, and networked media.[56] Hence, the white male subject repetitively gazes backward toward an imagined time and place where he was supposedly whole. In their view, the present cannot nor should not be reconstructed but instead discarded altogether. But white male victimhood belies the multitude of ways in which the existing social order is still organized around hegemonic masculinity. In one sense, white male victimhood is a response to external threats such as demographic shifts and policy changes that have forced men to sacrifice some of their entitlements—albeit very few.[57] In another sense, white male victimhood is also a deflection of an internal persecution in which a perceived trauma is disavowed and suffering kept at bay through the compulsion to repeat and domesticate past experiences. The failure of white men to adequately address the confounding effects of rapid social change has produced a state of cultural melancholia wherein white men's feelings of absence are addressed as if they were genuine loss recurring in the present. In turn, that imagined loss is incorporated into a subject haunted by and preoccupied with death and mayhem, some intent on inflicting suffering on others.

Freud identifies the death drive with those aspects of the mental apparatus that do not protect life or preserve pleasure.[58] Whereas Eros represents the life instinct that strives toward well-regulated pleasure and survival, Thanatos represents the subject's drive toward equilibrium or quiescence that preceded its existence. Freud's initial inquiry found that the death drive is often muted and otherwise repressed, sublimated, or externalized by the ego. But the death drive is neither merely innate preparation of organic life's inevitable return to inorganic matter nor the termination of life, but instead a *symbolic* regression of the subject to a state absent of tension and antagonism between the libido and the ego (which strives for self-preservation). Characterized as a *drive,* we find in Freud not a biological argument but a cultural concept that symbolic life is inherently regressive. Joan Copjec observes that Freud's writings about death and regression are incomprehensible if we take *instincts* to be the same as *drives,* which are the product of the pleasure principle and, thus, social reality. For Freud, the subject undergoes two deaths; the "first is the real death of the biological body, after which there is usually another, the second, exemplified by the various rituals of mourning that take place in the symbolic. It is with this second death that we are concerned when we speak of the Freudian concept of the death drive."[59] In other words, while our biological life moves forward, our symbolic life continually looks backwards and can be best characterized by the compulsion to repeat and disavow the loss that is subjectivity. Hence, Copjec surmises that "the death drive and the compulsion to repeat are thus the inevitable corollaries of *symbolic* life."[60] Our psyche and our social life are both unwritten by this mechanism of regression that forces the subject to repeat in order to bind its existence.

In *Eros and Civilization,* Herbert Marcuse elaborated further on the symbolic rituals of death and mourning when he argued that "the death instinct is destructiveness not for its own sake, but for the relief of tension. The descent toward death is an unconscious flight from pain and want. It is an expression of the eternal struggle against suffering and repression."[61] While Freud's earlier work argued that all mental phenomena are governed by repression (the pleasure principle), his later observance of clinical responses to trauma found that subjects felt compelled to repeat past traumas rather than remember them as happening in the past. The subject relives traumatic events as a way of binding those experiences, and so integrating them into their psyche.[62] For instance, Freud observed in his grandson Ernst a refusal to be undone by the trauma of his mother's absence by staging a game in which he threw a tethered toy, exclaiming "fort!" (gone!) and upon its retrieval declaring "da!" (there!).[63] Through repetition, Freud's grandson tamed the displeasure of loss by shifting from passive to active agent in relation to trauma.

The trouble with reading the compulsion to repeat as the ego's mastery of trauma is that the death drive's radical unbinding of the subject cuts against the possibility of its domestication.[64] In one sense, the compulsion to repeat trauma is actually a form of *unbinding* in which traumatic subjects revisit without mourning loss (melancholia). Yet, in another sense, the compulsion to repeat is part of fulfilling the subject's need for mastery. Freud's theorization of the death drive is incompatible with the claim that repetition fulfills the subject's need for control. As Kaja Silverman explains, "the death drive seeks to reduce the organism once again to nothingness, and so poses a radical challenge to the organization of the psyche. If repetition is indeed to be located at the level of the drive, then it must be understood to subvert rather than consolidate control."[65] In other words, we must "differentiate the death drive from these other types of repetition so as to arrive at a clearer understanding of the role that is plays within historical trauma, and its subset, war trauma."[66] Hence, we might distinguish how the ego insulates itself from the death drive differently than it does the libido. In the latter, the threat of the libido is sublimated into erotic activity whose effect might be characterized as release. The libido is managed but is by no means inimical to the coherence of the ego. The death drive, however, confronts the subject with its own feigned coherence, and its effect is to shatter or unbind the ego. In other words, the repetition associated with mastery is the same repetition that forces the subject to experience object loss as ego loss. The compulsion to repeat for the sake of taming displeasure also forces the ego to experience without mourning loss; hence, the ego re-experiences threatening trauma while never fully achieving mastery. Unlike the libido, the death drive is never fully sublimated and, as such, is projected as aggression toward others. The subject is caught in a perpetual re-enactment of fort/da.

White men's attachment to loss—real and imagined—explains both why white men refuse to move forward and their preoccupation with catastrophe.[67] That is to say that the fantasy of return is accompanied by a confrontation with the ego-shattering void upon which white masculinity must be feigned and belabored. Silverman notes that white masculinity is particularly vulnerable to the unbinding implications of the death drive because it is premised on the fantasy of self-mastery and control—neither of which repetition fully achieves. Hence, white masculinity remains oriented toward and within the past, ceaselessly unbinding itself while attempting to recover its unicity. The masculinist slogan "Make America Great Again" is premised on the fraught construction of a meridian between "before" and "after," or that there was a time at which male subjectivity was whole.[68] But, as scholarship on cultural trauma illustrates, subjectivity is itself feigned and fragmented, yet must constantly seek some underlying yet illusory anchor.[69] As Dominick LaCapra suggests, the difference between *absence* and *loss* provides clues to how traumatic male subjects have become haunted by melancholia.[70] Whereas loss refers to specific events such as the death of a loved one or a traumatic historical incident, absence is a transhistorical and inchoate sense of lack. Speaking to the significance of this distinction, LaCapra writes:

> When absence is converted into loss, one increases the likelihood of misplaced nostalgia or utopian politics in quest of a new totality or full unified community. When loss is converted into (or encrypted

in an indiscriminately generalized rhetoric of) absence, one faces the impasse of endless melancholy, impossible mourning, and interminable aporia in which any process of working through the past and its historical losses is foreclosed or prematurely aborted.[71]

Put differently, because one can never recover what one never had, conflating the historicity of loss with the transhistoricity of absence mistakes lack for a specific traumatic event or violent interruption of the psyche. Thus, the general precarity common to human existence can be reinterpreted as a discrete traumatic event that is more characteristic of loss than of lack.

Freud's distinction between melancholia and mourning provides an additional explanation of how white men are encouraged to read the presence of difference and uncertainty through the lens of trauma.[72] Freud distinguishes mourning and melancholia as different responses to loss, or in this case, when absence is mistaken for loss. While mourning is the process by which the conscious mind grieves a traumatic injury, melancholia entails an inability to fully register the loss of an object. Melancholia is a perverse form of nostalgia in which the narcissistic ego disavows a traumatic wound by psychically internalizing the existence of a lost object. Judith Butler argues that melancholia characterizes "those identifications which are formed from unfinished grief [and] are the modes in which the lost object is incorporated and phantasmatically preserved in and as the ego."[73] If the lost object cannot exist in the external world, it is made to exist within the psyche "to disavow that loss, to keep it at bay, to stay or postpone the recognition and suffering of loss."[74] For white masculinity, melancholia explains the fixation with remaking the present in the image of a time before men were supposedly wounded. As this lost object can longer exist, or never existed, it must be internalized. Thus, object loss is experienced as ego loss. At the same time, melancholia is also accompanied by feelings of ambivalence concerning the lost object. The subject cannot overcome or move past their grief because they are conflicted—if not guilty—for perhaps desiring loss even if they felt attached to the lost object. Either way, the notion of wholeness is a feigned form of subjectivity that can never be recovered because the lost object never existed. While white masculinity is strategically framed in terms of loss, it is more fitting to conceptualize it as a *lack*: an illusory sense that the white male self, or subjectivity for that matter, was ever whole. The ambivalence that accompanies melancholia, in part, explains white masculinity's incoherence: men seek to overcome their traumatic feelings of loss, and yet it is loss they require to make the case for masculinity's recovery.

Finally, the odd consonance between melancholia and the death drive highlights why white masculinity is so closely aligned with masochism. There is something about the inability to grieve (or unfinished grieving) that aggregates those aspects of the drive that are antithetical to the subject. In part, this is the case because melancholia represents both a similar regression and a disavowal of loss that postpones suffering. As Butler explains, "where melancholy is the refusal of grief, it is also always that incorporation of loss, the miming of the death it cannot mourn."[75] Put differently, the very death that melancholia disavows becomes incorporated into the subject through the repetition. As the death drive constitutes the regressive striving of the psyche toward equilibrium—the melancholic (and cruel) superego makes efficient use of such regression. Hence, white masculinity has come to embody a regressive posture that revels in self-abasement and masochistic fantasies of persecution. The death drive produces masochistic attachments by compelling the subject to repeat unpleasant experiences.[76] Following Silverman, David Savran observes that in his writings on female masochism, Freud actually names a distinctly masculine pathology in which the male sufferer is positioned as female.[77] When Freud observed female masochism it was in men "being pinioned, bound, beaten painfully, whipped, in some way mishandled, forced to obey unconditionally, defiled, degraded."[78] But, as noted earlier, masochism does not unsettle the polarity of gender identification but instead functions, according to King and Gunn, as a "valorization of the suffering of men-as-womanly objects."[79]

In another sense, white male masochism also converges with the death drive in the operation of surplus repression, in which Marcuse suggests we invest in our own subjugation in pursuit of the performance principle. Marcuse's Marxist uptake of Freud suggests that the drives are shaped by historical forces; that under advanced capitalism, repression has outlived its necessity for civilizational survival. Capitalism, therefore, requires surplus repression so that subjects invest in domination and toil and sublimate their desires into productive enterprises. Repressive desublimation channels the erotic and creative energies of the libido into commodified forms of leisure.[80] Capitalism also makes use of Thanatos by transforming death into "an instrument of repression" or a "token of unfreedom."[81] That is to say that death might be valorized as a sacrifice that alleviates our collective guilt or threatened in a way that compels those of us who toil to surrender to life. It is the death drive that animates life under capitalism, or rather that capitalism's ideological manipulation of drives is to locate loss, suffering, and recuperation outside the subject. Masochism and surplus repression resist the theoretical possibility that Eros might liberate us from an *unnecessarily* repressive society. The question remains: to what extent is liberation even a possibility if it is the case that subjectivity is inescapably underwritten by object loss and compulsive repetition?

White men's peculiar fascination with death and destruction reflects how oblivion has been incorporated into the psyche of the melancholic white male subject. In this book, I am interested in how the death drive has been mobilized to extinguish those ideas and attachments that align themselves with Eros. Liberation of the libido—even if illusory—is the enemy of contemporary men's rights groups who identify feminist and queer movements as the culprits responsible for their suffering.[82] Doomsday preppers, survivalists, mass shooters, men's rights activists, pro-gun activists, demagogues, and white supremacists alike cling to life in the name of death. Their apocalyptic fantasies are organized around compulsive repetition, masochism, and melancholia— they carry death with them everywhere they go. As a rhetorical critic, I am primarily concerned with the symbolic life of the death drive, or how discourses and performances of white masculine victimhood propel the death drive into public culture by playing out repetitive scenarios of trauma, victimization, and persecution. This form of white male identity politics disrupts our conventional connotations of justice and equality—even disarticulating them from life-affirming expressions of hope and replacing them with profound pessimism. As Hamilton Carroll summarizes, "white masculinity turns to a reactive strategy under which it redefines the normative by citing itself as a marginal identity."[83] White male victimhood rehearses the same politics of identity that white men believe dispossessed them of their birthright. Yet, the rhetorical performance of victimhood brings neither mastery nor wholeness, merely an interminable and recursive encounter with lack. In this way, white male victimhood becomes an unending and cyclical politics of death in the name of life. It is no surprise, then, that white men who identify as victims also demonstrate a proclivity for apocalyptic fantasies and imagery of death: they are quite literally haunted by the symbolic life of the death drive.

RHETORICAL CRITICISM, PSYCHICAL STRUCTURES, AND FORM

This book is concerned with how the compulsive repetition that characterizes the death drive manifests itself *culturally* in an array of different rhetorical forms. To wit, neither does this book provide a critique of individual neuroses nor is it directed against individual men who adhere to the rhetoric of victimhood. My concern instead is with the figural—the signifiers, public personae, and subject positions that are constituted in language and circulated through different forms and genres of public discourse, often with an idealized audience in mind. Though at points my critique highlights the symbolic activity of particular men, I attend to white men as cultural figures who necessarily serve as conduits for bigger things. As such, I am not concerned with hidden internal conditions of the mind that are obfuscated by signifiers but with what Gunn calls "psychical structures" that denote "recurrent strategies and defenses that are culturally derived."[84] I read repetition not as a symptom to be diagnosed but rather as a performance of control and habitual sense-making activity that attempts to domesticate radical contingency. As Edwin Black illustrates in his comparison of rhetorical criticism and psychoanalysis, both are less invested in distinctions between appearance and reality than "the premise that appearances have real consequences."[85] Motives and investments are conveyed as much, if not more so, through what is said than what is concealed.

Repetition can be characterized as a form of *enjoyment,* a concept that names the subject's investment in a fantasy that nonetheless organizes, accumulates, and provides a sense of mastery over the subject's world. Jacques Lacan contends that durable social formations are the product of the Symbolic's (language) necessary failure to mediate the Real.[86] The Real is not reality but instead a material and mind-independent realm that is accessible to us only through mediation.

Despite conditions of impossibility—the vast chasm between the Symbolic and the Real—the subject labors and invests in reality to obtain a sense of coherence, however feigned. Christian Lundberg explains that "enjoyment is the compulsion to repeat as to give coherence to the subject's world by investing it with identity and a set of predictable habituated relationship with the world."[87] Enjoyment, however, should not be conflated with pleasure. It's very unlikely that compulsive iterations of victimhood or simulations of world-ending doom bring subjects anything akin to joy or happiness, yet subjects nonetheless express desire or a deep investment in attaining a hypothetical object. Calum Matheson summarizes the relationship between repetition and enjoyment as such:

> This is the repetition compulsion, in which the subject tries again and again to attain something that eludes its grasp . . . There is jouissance in repetition not because speaking subjects necessarily enjoy the possibilities of destruction or rebirth in and of themselves, but because repetition gives a sense of mastery over the contingency of the world. Jouissance isn't happiness or joy. Rather, it is an investment in something, a kind of attachment that may very well be painful but is nonetheless compelling.[88]

Hence, repetition creates the conditions of possibility (Imaginary) for the making and unmaking of enduring social arrangements. It is in the persistent reiteration of victimhood and rebirth—its melancholic longings for hypothetical objects that the subject never possessed—that accounts for adherence to and consummation of masculinist fantasies of death and rebirth.[89] Marcuse reminds us that the drives are both psychological and historical, meaning that they are, in part, both motor and by-product of cultural forces.

As a rhetorical critic invested in understanding the cultural entailments of psychical structures in the context of a manufactured crisis of white masculinity, my mode of inquiry concerns how patterns of public discourse take form and organize a subject's encounters with and investments in those socially durable arrangements that constitute reality. This approach also entails creating a cultural map of victimhood attachments so as to track how and to what effect masculinist fantasies traffic across a variety of textual forms, media, genres, embodiments, and networks. How might an array of texts organize white men's encounter with victimhood and court particular investments in such a painful proposition? Drawing from Black, I ask: what would these different forms have their audience become?[90] Herein, the act of rhetorical criticism attends not to hidden patterns or idiosyncrasies that link a series of diverse texts, but instead to both the singular and cumulative *affordances* of rhetorical forms and the content that populates them. For Caroline Levine, the concept of affordance engenders both the potential uses latent in particular sociological or textual forms and the modes of thinking and characterizations of reality that are constrained and enabled by reliance on particular forms.[91] By *form* I mean any pattern of experience or arrangement of elements that order, shape, and configure content according to an implicit or explicit organizational structure. For instance, whereas a form like a binary imposes rigid and mutually exclusive categories onto content, a hierarchy imposes a top-down structure that by nature ranks and subjugates lesser values.

Further, we might also consider how a textual form like narrative orders information according to rising action or a genre such as melodrama imposes moral polarity and a preoccupation with the persecution and redemption of innocent victims. Hence, I am also concerned with the rhetorical entailments of particular *genres* of public discourse, which are themselves distinct types of forms that organize and arrange discourse in response to recurring situations.[92] Although not all forms are genres, all genres are forms and, as such, tend to organize content according to recognizable patterns. But, as Karlyn Kohrs Campbell and Kathleen Hall Jamieson explain, "a genre does not consist merely of a series of acts in which certain rhetorical forms recur . . . Instead, a genre is composed of a constellation of recognizable forms bound together by an internal dynamic"[93] Genre is neither a label for a text nor a description of particular elements that reside in a text, but rather a description of recognizable forms that recur in the public imaginary. In any case, attention to form tells us how a pattern imposes order onto content and dictates how audiences are invited to understand and relate to particular messages. Such an approach might enable critics to grasp "both the particular constraints and possibilities that different forms afford, and the fact that those patterns and arrangements carry their affordances with them as they move across time and space."[94]

This approach to criticism suggests that it is the nature of form to impose its own particular and arbitrary sense of order onto content, and, therefore, that a privileging of form accounts for how different texts elicit different modes of identification and degrees of investment. In this way, form imposes order in a manner similar to psychical structures. Thus, in the chapters to come, I argue in a general sense that the affordance of repetition is that it privileges a backward gaze, habitual re-enactment, and re-experience of past as both present and prologue. An inflection on form stresses the importance of patterns that structure content and, therefore, how audiences are invited to take up and make sense of that content. But I am also concerned with the affordances of specific forms of mediation and symbolic action such as reality television, Reddit, online manifestos, public performances, political rallies, and tweets in which appeals to white masculine victimhood are made manifest yet are also constrained by the unique structure demanded by each platform.

This book is invested not in what hidden meanings are unearthed when texts are subjected to critique but rather in what texts *do to* and *do for* aggrieved white men. I argue that each form anchors its imagined audience to reality in distinct ways and thus constrains and enables the audience's relationship to politics. For instance, where the techniques for producing reality television impose authoritative (though impossible) unmediated access to the Real (chapter 1), digital platforms that support men's rights rhetoric afford intimacy, self-disclosure, and a magical sense of agency over users' so-called social programming (chapters 2 and 3). By contrast, chapter 4 focuses on the affordances of guns and the white male body as co-extensive of state sovereignty and how embodied paramilitary performances affirm white male authority. This insight gives way to the final chapter's analysis of the affordances of other modes of political address, including President Trump's embrace of melodrama as a genre of political discourse to amplify his electorate's suffering as well as his use of unconventional platforms (political rallies, Twitter) to speak to his electorate without the pesky conventions of empathy and rejoinder. Each form establishes another way in which the content of victimhood is arranged, organized, and enacted.

As Rita Felski suggests, quite often the impulse in criticism (critique, to be more accurate) in the humanities has been to interrogate hidden meanings and thus narrow and relegate the function of texts to either obscuring or occluding systems of power.[95] I myself am no less guilty of indulging this impulse. But we might take Felski's polemic as an occasion for thinking about other functions of both texts and professional criticism. For instance, it might behoove rhetorical critics to consider how form asserts an agency all unto itself. Such an approach would be consistent with Kenneth Burke's statement on form as "the creation of an appetite in the mind of the auditor, and the adequate satisfying of that appetite."[96] Form modulates audience attitudes toward ideas that populate particular texts and cultivates enjoyment, expectation, and identification with a desired object. Hence, I take Felski's directive as an opportunity to explain the rhetorical pull of form in activating particular relationships between the speaker, audience, and content. As Felski explains, "once we take on board the distinctive agency of art works—rather than their imaged role as minions of opaque social forces or heroes of the resistance—we cannot help orienting ourselves differently to the task. Such a shift is desperately needed if we are to do better justice to what literature does and why such doing matters."[97] The goal of criticism herein is to explain how the rhetoric of white masculine victimhood is neither a rhetorical delusion nor an obfuscation of white male power. Such an incredulous approach would risk merely blaming individual men, leaving us with an anemic understanding of how and why this rhetoric cultivates such toxic identifications. A more provocative question would be to ask what makes such a discourse seem so plausible in the face of so much evidence to the contrary? What is the structure of enjoyment that enraptures white men, cultivates macabre attachments, and enlists them in a project of remaking the world with fantasies of the end in mind? Criticism can illustrate rhetorical functions beyond obfuscation, including registers such as enjoyment, conversion, reconfiguration, transformation, identification, and subjectification—all of which explain the affective force of white masculine victimhood in terms of both the present cultural context and the endurance of psychical structures.

To account for the diverse range of discourses explored in this book, it is important to distinguish between the rhetorical effects of mediation, performance, and political address. In the first three chapters, I address two unique forms of media that developed in conjunction with one another over the past two decades: reality television and networked media. As Marshall McLuhan surmised, transformations in media necessarily "alter the pattern of interdependence among people."[98] Taken together, both forms afford connectivity and blur boundaries between the private and the public self. Both privilege speed and accessibility to platforms, information, celebrities, and the private lives of others. As Nick Couldry notes, "the most puzzling aspect of this whole landscape is the notion that the media provide a 'central' space where it makes sense to disclose publically aspects of one's life that one might not otherwise disclose to anyone."[99] Reality television and networked media encourage audiences to conflate access to mediated personas with encounters with the unmediated subjectivity of others.[100] While neither platform can provide unmediated access to the Real, they can certainly plug subjects into circuits that connect them with a compelling portrait of an authentic expression of one's personhood. Of concern here is the darker side of the democratization and accessibility of new media—that television and networked media are often devoid of space for empathy and time for critical reflection. For instance, Brian Ott and Greg Dickinson observe that the media ecology of social media platforms affords narcissism, simplicity, carelessness, and even cruelty toward others.[101] Reality television scholars have similarly observed the same behaviors, values, and attributes valorized in popular reality programming—all of which are delivered with a wink of dissociative irony.[102] In chapter 1, I begin with an inquiry into how the techniques of producing reality television have helped lend authenticity and political credibility to the taboo and hypermasculine ethos of doomsday prepping. Examining the National Geographic program *Doomsday Preppers*, I argue that the reality format helps recast the apocalypse as an opportunity to demonstrate the necessity of male skills against a cultural moment seemingly enraptured by misandry.

Chapter 2 shifts attention to men's rights discourse on websites such as Reddit, Return of Kings, and a Voice for Men by attending to the narrative structure of the manosphere—a constellation of online forums, blogs, and news sites steeped in tales of white male victimhood. This chapter is concerned with how patterns of discourse within online platforms court particular investments in users that tends to cycle negative emotions into public life. I argue that networked men's rights activism takes on a perverse form of consciousness-raising—co-opting a feminist form—that seeks to awaken men to their supposed subjugation by women so that they can turn the tables on feminism. I suggest that networked media afford men space for personal confessions and intimate diatribes even as it relieves them of obligations to demonstrate empathy. Networked men's rights discourse organizes male attention economies around an ascendant mythology of "men who sit at screens": a previously untenable network of aggrieved men seeking to literally reprogram reality. Building on the networks explored in the previous chapter, chapter 3 explores the epidemic of spectacular mass killings carried out by white men, paying particular attention to those who have been radicalized while cruising men's rights networks. This chapter examines the digital manifesto of killer Elliot Rodger, a Santa Barbara college student who went on a murderous rampage as retribution for his sexual rejection by women. Rodger was part of growing community of "incels" or involuntary celibates who are unable to find sexual partners. His manifesto offers a dystopian vision of torture and femicide carried out to extinguish sexuality in the name of civilization progress. Rather than viewing this vile text as an aberration, this chapter argues that the network milieu from which the manifesto emerges evinces how white male victimhood so easily attaches itself to fascist principles and fantasies of mass death.

Chapter 4 addresses the body-as-form by examining how white men act out and resist their victimhood by brandishing firearms in public. Legal in all but three states and the District of Columbia, the practice of open carry or open carry rallies are increasingly popular not only among gun's rights advocates but also with members of the alt-right and other antigovernment organizations. In contrast to the ephemeral and often anonymous communication that populates networked media, these paramilitary events deploy the white male body as a metonymic substitute for the law. Open carry is an embodied act that transforms guns into prosthetic extensions of white male power into public space. Corporeal bodies alongside such meaningful objects are capable of performing, enacting, and animating desires.[103] White male bodies in particular are afforded credibility to act on behalf of the law and to exercise sovereignty over public space. In the unification of gun and body, such violent performances figure prominently into the embodied politics of white masculinity in public space.

Chapter 5 explores the incoherent yet powerful script of white masculine victimhood offered by President Donald J. Trump. Trump's unconventional political style is matched by his reliance on unconventional forms of presidential address, namely those that circumvent the professional press and the general public to reach more receptive audiences. As a consequence, the media ecology of Twitter and the reality celebrity spectacle of the political rally are perfect vectors for both Trump's melodramatic style and his rhetoric's perverse lack of empathy.[104] Acclimated to the viewing norms of network media and reality television culture, Trump's reliance on both forms helps normalize a cruel and nihilistic form of white masculinity. Examining a selection of President Trump's political rallies, this chapter argues that Trump's dark portraiture of contemporary American life signals to white men that the apocalypse is nigh: the country has been overrun by nonwhites and foreign enemies, violence and persecution define everyday life, the press and the "deep state" have overthrown legitimate government, language, religion, and culture have become subject to the whims of tyrannical leftists, and America is no longer a beloved superpower. This chapter suggests that his dark ruminations provide an exigence for cruelty and regeneration through violence. Characterizing Trump's rhetoric as *political sadomasochism,* this chapter argues that audience enjoyment is structured both by a perverse desire to be subjugated and a pleasurable anticipation of righteous violence. Finally, the concluding chapter offers some possible ways forward by considering alternative rhetorics and performances of masculinity that could form the basis of coalition politics. This chapter considers how some challenges to Trump-era masculinity, such as call-outs and public emasculations, fail while others that encourage white men to develop emotional intelligence, cultivate intimacy, and express empathy might be the antidote to our cultural melancholia.

CHAPTER 1

Doomsday Preppers

The Man-pocalypse

MARTIN COLVILL considers himself a warrior. In head-to-toe military camouflage, automatic rifle at his side, Martin tells a National Geographic camera crew: "My name Martin means 'warrior' or 'war-like' individual. I try to fight for what's right. I don't like bullies. My greatest fear upon a total economic societal collapse is that I won't be able to protect my wife." Displaced by the 2008 mortgage crisis, Martin and his wife Sarah reside in the cab of an open-road truck. But Martin is of interest to National Geographic not because of his adaptive post-recessionary lifestyle, but rather because he counts himself among the approximately three million Americans who self-identify as "doomsday preppers." Martin is, in his words, "preparing to survive the next great depression caused by economic collapse." Like others who adopt the label, Martin spends his time cultivating food and weapon caches, learning self-defense, and simulating doomsday scenarios. Martin's apocalyptic performances engender the hypermasculine ethos of contemporary doomsday culture (*Doomsday Preppers, Doomsday Castle, Apocalypse Preppers,* and *Meet the Preppers*) in which predominantly white men, such as Martin, perform their feelings of rage and victimhood, deliver diatribes about the collapse of civilization, model their armaments, rehearse paramilitary battles with postapocalyptic marauders, and exhibit their masculine know-how.

One overarching lesson of American doomsday culture is that the future is indefinite but that hegemonic white masculinity—aggression, self-reliance, stoicism, competitiveness—remains necessary. In Martin's grave divinations, the recuperation of traditional manly skill sets will rebuild America after inevitable disaster. Like most doomsday preppers, Martin is enraptured by a regression to the state of nature—a fantasy consummated through repetitive scenario planning and preparation for the apocalypse. Here, the world is made to disappear only to be returned to the viewer with an illusory sense of control and mastery over an uncertain future. *Doomsday Preppers* powerfully illustrates the culture of politics of melancholia at work in the contemporary crisis of masculinity: there was a primal moment to which we will and must return when our survival hinged on the strength and natural ability of men.

Although American television audiences are accustomed to seeing their world eviscerated on screen, outlived by small bands of male-led survivors, the apocalyptic turn in popular culture gives viewers purportedly unmediated access to the masculinized survival rituals performed by ordinary Americans. National Geographic's *Doomsday Preppers* promises to take viewers "into lives of . . . committed preppers who have devised extensive plans, gone to great lengths, and made huge personal sacrifices to guarantee their very survival." Each episode's participants are "ordinary Americans from all walks of life" who are "taking whatever measures necessary to prepare and protect themselves from what they perceive as the fast approaching end of the world as we know it." Unlike spectacular disaster films, *Doomsday Preppers* portrays the manly art of survival as a sensible ritual already practiced by millions of Americans. Drawing from the educational ethos of the Nat Geo, *Doomsday Preppers* invites audiences to emulate "real life" performances of manly survival skills against the background of an uncertain future.

This chapter attends to how the mainstreaming of doomsday prepping figures into the contemporary rhetoric of white male victimhood. As a dominant form of new media, reality television has played a prominent role in modeling white masculinity in precarious political and economic times. Reality television purports to offer unmediated access to everyday-life performances through a valence of authority borrowed from anthropology and educational television. It is a form that affords its subjects an aura of authenticity or realness. Yet, reality television is belabored and produced under conditions of heavy mediation, including the crafting of character types, mise-en-scene, continuity editing, cinematography, and dialogue to name a few. Reality television is also a genre with an agency all its own. Like other forms of media, it is formulaic, but its premises, sets, and concepts can be easily and cheaply copied, recycled, and reused across cable television. For example, the success of *Doomsday Preppers* generated a series of copycat programs on other cable networks, including related programming that features extreme survival trials (*Alone, Dual Survival, Man vs. Wild, Naked and Afraid, Survivor Man, The Alaska Experiment,* and *The Colony*). Hence, reality television is, in part, responsible for the sudden cultural visibility of masculine survivalism. What is novel about reality television is that it imbues extreme everyday-life performances with both authenticity and compelling dramatic structure. This chapter explores how the rhetoric of reality television delivers to the culture a manly sense of apocalyptic excitement.

My central argument is that seemingly "authentic" representations of doomsday prepping have helped reclaim white male sovereignty in the name of survival and resuscitated premodern archetypes of primal masculinity as befitting the laws that govern human nature and, consequently, the postapocalyptic future. Doomsday preppers argue that the feminine attributes that characterize modernity are ultimately unsustainable luxuries that will inevitable collapse into barbarism. Simulating the apocalypse, then, is an opportunity for white men to display masculine traits as a set of survival tools—the antidote for a crumbling and emasculated society. Longing to resuscitate a past that never existed, doomsday preppers seek to domesticate the trauma of white masculinity's displacement by promising a future in which white men are restored to their proper place in both nature and the social order. In short, the apocalypse serves as the ultimately resolution to the so-called crisis of masculinity. Along with a series of other networked platforms, reality television has ushered in the apocalyptic turn in white masculinity.

Once a fringe ritual among survivalists and white supremacists, apocalyptic manhood is now constituted through rhetoric and performances that confirm the necessity of masculine skills as modern society meets its demise. This chapter uses the National Geographic Channel's reality program *Doomsday Preppers* to show how the figure of the doomsday prepper cultivates a militarized version of white manhood capable of reclaiming the future from women and racial Others. Through repeated displays of manly preparedness rituals in machine shops, gun ranges, and wilderness, *Doomsday Preppers* offers a rebuttal to the progressive case for gender and racial equality by testifying to the enduring primacy of white male identity. In a broader context, this chapter also explains how apocalyptic paranoia has contributed to a surge in hypermasculine mass violence in American culture where feelings of white male alienation translate into militaristic preparations for an uncertain future.

REALITY'S MANLY AFFORDANCES

Reality television often involves manly labor: zero-sum competition, shouting matches, gladiatorial sport, cutthroat business dealings, hyperindividualism, survivalism, muscle, sweat, grit, and militarism.[1] But like political melodrama, reality programming also features moral polarities, virtuous suffering, and intractable enemies. It is a genre that relies on conventions associated with femininity, including sentimentality and emotional intimacy. Reality television affords a level of access that cultivates a sense of closeness with the participants, drawing from what Lynn Spigel has noted is the feminine coding of the in-home screen.[2] With soft close-ups of emotional confessions and detailed portraits of domestic life, *Doomsday Preppers* co-opts the so-called feminine intimacy of television to build rapport between participants and viewers. Yet, the program subtly recodes the television as masculine by importing the conventions of action films that hail a male spectator. The introduction to each episode includes action-style zoom-close-ups, a blockbuster soundtrack of loud drums, and dramatic glitch aesthetics wherein the screen flickers and digitizes to simulate the impending failure of technology. The program's action-movie aesthetics maintain the maleness of the big screen as it co-opts the feminine intimacy of the small screen. Of course, as John Corner warns, scholars should mind the distinctions between everyday life and screen performances; however, reality television routinely blurs these performative boundaries, particularly when programs remove the host, interviewer, and other observers from the screen to make interactions feel realistic.[3] This distinction is often too hard to maintain where the subgenre of documentary reality television re-presents staged, self-conscious, and improvised performances as if they were all not-performed. Therefore, there is something about the genre that naturalizes the once-fringe rituals of the white male prepper as a new and repeatable version of manhood.

Staged and belabored as reality television may be, the genre is nonetheless underwritten by a grammar of authenticity and realness. For instance, NatGeo imports the authoritative documentary techniques of ethnographic filmmaking into reality television to provide "realistic" portraits of people as they live.[4] Thus, *Doomsday Preppers* derives its sincerity from a combination of first-person interviews, camera observation of participants' everyday life, authoritative narration, stock footage of natural disasters, and expert assessments. The mixture of formats and techniques offers the audience multiple access points to the subjects' reality, to see not only how they live but also how the world might appear from their viewpoint. Mark Rademacher and I have argued that reality television has evolved into a powerful platform for the display of male labor.[5] This claim builds from Laurie Ouellette and James Hay's observation that reality television emphasizes neoliberal economic values such self-reliance, self-help, and small government.[6] The genre's focus on the labor of ordinary men provides "realistic" models for performing hegemonic masculinity in uncertain circumstances.

Reality television also imparts the illusion that participants are *not* performing, that the camera is documenting organic "everyday life performances."[7] This presumption of authenticity elides the fact that participants are actors in a setting arranged like a theatrical stage. For instance, Ragan Fox observes how "producers use editing to construct tales and characters, and, in the midst of participation, reality TV personalities edit themselves."[8] Similar to Erving Goffman's discussion of everyday-life performances, some reality TV participants' behaviors are constructed as "real" or "authentic," otherwise natural and unselfconscious. Conversely, contrived performances are those that seem transparently constructed wherein the subject is conspicuously acting for the camera. Those who, in Rachael Dubrofsky and Emily Ryalls's terms, "perform not performing" are conferred more legitimacy within the structure of reality television.[9] Reality television scholars contend that the normalization of surveillance through reality television accounts for what kinds of performances count as genuine.[10] While all participants perform, those behaviors that reveal the contrived nature of reality television are constructed as "mere" performances.

This theorization of surveillance explains how masculine performances on *Doomsday Preppers* appear authentic. In particular, scholars who have examined race in reality TV argue that performances of white male identity are often constructed as more authentic than racial minorities because whiteness itself operates with unselfconsciousness. Like the ideal identity of reality TV participants, whiteness and masculinity are enacted through effortless performances from the privileged subject position of being unmarked by identity.[11] Similarly, I suggest that *Doomsday Preppers* builds authenticity by featuring subjects whose white male identity imbues their on-camera performances with the same "realness" afforded to them by virtue of their privileged subject position. In this way, reality TV projects not reality but "an imagined reality" that makes "narrative arguments about socio-cultural ideas."[12] Reality television makes conjectures about what kinds of identity performances are afforded the presumption of authenticity. With its lack of racial and gender diversity, *Doomsday Preppers* frames the performance of "prepping" as an authentic and legitimate expression of white male fear, frustration, and rage in precarious times.

WHITE MASCULINITY AND SURVIVAL CULTURE

In April 2015 thousands (including myself) gathered in Sandy, Utah, for the first annual "PrepperCon," a two-day exhibition of products and services to help conventioneers survive an apocalyptic event. The convention featured displays of underground bunkers, dehydrated foodstuffs, water filtration systems, biohazard suits, ham radios, armored vehicles, gold futures, and military-grade firearms.[13] Some exhibitioners offered seminars on, among other things, hand-to-hand combat, wilderness survival skills, first aid, firearms, and the construction of "bug-out" bags, or emergency survival packs. The convention provides a snapshot of what has become the $500 million *Mad Max* economy of doomsday prepping, an emerging lucrative industry that markets products to Americans who are concerned about everything from natural disasters, pandemics, and terrorist attacks to world-ending scenarios such as a shift in Earth's magnetic poles, the collapse of the global economy, and World War III.[14] The 9/11 terrorist attacks, Hurricanes Katrina and Sandy, the Japanese tsunami, and countless other international disasters have prompted many Americans to invest in emergency preparations that range from the Federal Emergency Management Agency's recommended stockpile of three days of food and water to full-service luxury "doomsday condominiums" constructed in abandoned Atlas missile silos.[15]

The popularity of PrepperCon is one indication that survivalism is no longer reserved for extremists, militias, conspiracy theorists, and survivalists: doomsday prepping is ostensibly for everyone. "Survivalist" is a pejorative term once reserved for paranoid camouflage-clad mountain men like Ted Kaczynski, Timothy McVeigh, and members of the John Birch Society or the sovereign citizen movement who joined militias, stockpiled arms and food, and espoused radical conspiracy theories about nefarious governmental agencies and secret communist plots. Contemporary survivalists, who frequently go by the less disdainful moniker of "preppers," are more economically and geographically diverse.[16] While some estimate that approximately three million Americans can be considered full-fledge preppers, survivalism—its discourses, aesthetic markers, ethical precepts, ritual performances—has become infused into American culture.[17] For instance, one in seven Americans believes that they will experience the end of the world in their lifetime.[18] Another study found that 41 percent of respondents believed that prepping was a smarter investment than saving for retirement.[19]

My attendance at PrepperCon was prompted by my desire to witness firsthand how a generally fragmented, secretive, and clandestine community temporarily self-organized into a public. I was particularly interested in how the image of doomsday prepping figured into the political identity of white men. Moreover, I was struck by the stark contrast between the apocalyptic subject matter of the event and the festive tone conveyed by its organizers and promoters. For instance, the event's website advertises the event as follows:

PrepperCon is the premier event for Preppers of any age or experience. Not only do we showcase the Prepper Lifestyle, but we combine the best of entertainment, emergency preparedness, gun shows, off-grid living and survival into one incredible experience. Come see local and international celebrities in the Prepper World. We bring live demonstrations, survival food cooking contests, fashion shows, disaster simulators, prizes, and a diverse lineup of amazing people. At PrepperCon you'll find incredible entertainment, cutting-edge gadgets, training, and networking opportunities, prepping fundamentals, self-defense and home security, survival gear, food storage, first aid supplies, emergency and disaster response resources, and an unbelievable experience for you, your family, and community.[20]

Yet, promising attendees entertainment and fun seems to be at odds with the community's macabre vision of the future. At the same time, selling the convention as a somber event might conflict with the industry's imperative to put consumers in the buying mood. Anecdotally, I can attest that the organizers delivered on their promise of entertainment. I learned how to forage for medicinal herbs, defend against a knife attack, and start a fire without matches. I talked with exhibitors about the kind of spectacular world-ending scenarios for which they believe we should all be preparing. I was implored by some venders to protect my "wife and kids" from dangerous marauders. At the same time, I was given the opportunity to meet reality television celebrities and 2016 Miss America pageant winner Julie Harman. Admittedly, I was expecting to be surrounded by camo-clad woodsmen and paranoid survivalists—to be sure, there were many—rather than suburban white men with their families in tow. I expected vendors to be distrustful of me as an interloper instead of demonstrating enthusiasm to get the word out about their product to anyone who was willing to listen. While the convention maintained an underlying tone of seriousness, its surprisingly festive atmosphere transformed the apocalypse into an enjoyable if not desirable experience.

Why such a festive tone? In one sense, the convention—much like doomsday prepping itself—staged a game of *fort* and *da,* making the world repetitively disappear and reappear. Upon repetition, subjects might transform themselves from passive to active agent in relationship to world-ending trauma. In short, doomsday prepping is underwritten by enjoyment—taming and retaming the world's end to provide the subject with an illusory sense of self-mastery. In part, the popular image of the doomsday prepper has also reframed the apocalypse as an opportunity to re-envision society and domesticate those anxieties engendered by the simulation of the end of the world. The apocalypse is a blank palette—freed from the psychical strictures and material conditions of possibility in the present—onto which both utopian and dystopian ideals can be projected. It is the fantasy's repetition that matters more than crossing the event horizon. As Matheson suggests, the fantasy of sovereign citizens taking up arms against the government is a powerful source of enjoyment as long it remains at a comfortable distance, since "proximity undermines the conditions for fantasy by revealing the Other's desire as something alien to the subject and outside of its control."[21] Doomsday preppers imagine the horrific possibility that society will implode, food and water will become scarce, and neighbors will turn into bands of hording marauders as much as they imagine themselves happily thriving under such conditions. After all, doomsday preppers imagine themselves as the heirs of the postapocalyptic world. Since the fantasy must satisfy the subject's need for mastery first and foremost, doomsday preppers make conjectures about the iron laws of human nature that will undoubtedly govern the postapocalyptic future. In doing so, they validate their identity in the present and domesticate the trauma of an uncertain future.

But to whom does the future belong? This chapter suggests that what is at stake in the figure of the doomsday prepper is the sovereignty of the white masculine subject itself. Stripped of his autonomy by a feminized, multicultural control society, the virtues of the white male subject are rediscovered when the world returns to the state of nature. Exemplifying the death drive, doomsday prepping pursues not biological equilibrium but a fantastical subject free of tension. There are, of course, racial entailments in the white male vision of self-mastery. Writing about the popularity of zombie apocalypse narratives, Eric King Watts suggests that audience enjoyment is predicated on the evisceration of a blackening biothreat that re-establishes the primacy of the white male.[22] The apocalypse makes what was once fantastical seem plausible, and hence introduces the material prospect of reviving the militia and of "real" Americans taking their country back. The image of the doomsday prepper does cultural work on behalf of beleaguered white men by celebrating a future in which they are both necessary and sovereign. It is not the feminized and blackened male of ornamental culture but the archetypical man of the nation's primal past who rebuilds society in the future: the frontiersman, the gunslinger, the artisan, and the self-made man. The self-sufficient individual, the family, the clan or tribe: for better or worse these are the only units of society that will survive the next great die-off. The dissonant tone of playfulness engendered by the image of the doomsday prepper helps contain white male anxiety about the future while making the archetypes of white masculinity matter in the present.

First appearing in the early 1960s writings of Kurt Saxon, the term *survivalist* described an individualist Übermensch whose self-sufficiency and preparedness for cataclysmic events was crafted through trials in remote wilderness.[23] The survivalist, typically a lone male, was distinguished by a series of lifestyle practices that included, among other things, homesteading, stockpiling food and guns, paramilitary training, hunting, and extended wilderness trials. While survivalists writ large had few if any official umbrella organizations or civic leagues, many populated the ranks of citizen militias, the Minutemen movement, the John Birch Society, the Posse Comitatus movement, and the American Nazi Party.[24] Overall, survivalism emerged as less of an organized political movement than a lifestyle politics of learning to exist "off the grid," so to speak. That is not to say that Saxon's brand of survivalism did not have a political ethos. Survivalism was a reactionary antigovernment ideal adopted primarily by white men bracing for catastrophes induced by post–New Deal government bureaucracy, Leftist protest movements, and international Bolsheviks. Moreover, the looming Soviet threat, the nuclear arms race, and the federal government's push to create an expansive Civil Defense system confirmed the survivalist prophetic narrative of impending doom.[25]

Contemporary survivalism is most commonly associated with an array of white militias, hate groups, and other doomsday cults who gained public attention through high-profile acts of violence (Timothy McVeigh, Ted Kaczynski) or tragic confrontations with law enforcement (Branch Davidians at Waco, Randy Weaver at Ruby Ridge).[26] Militias or cults, however, are but one form of political organizing that arises out of the antistatist paranoid style of survival culture. It is a political form that is attractive to some but is easily dismissed by the public and disavowed by mainstream conservatives. Yet, the emergence of militia movements points to the historical development of an underlying ideology of what James Gibson calls "warriorism," that took root in the early 1980s.[27] A largely masculinist worldview that encompasses survivalism, warriorism is a cauldron of frustration, resentment, and paranoia shared by individuals (white men in particular) who believe that they are embattled by the forces of modernity: secularization, feminism, multiculturalism, globalization, and so-called entitlement culture. Warriorism arises from a perceived loss of power, suspicion of democratic politics, and, most of all, feelings of betrayal. It is a persona enraptured by apocalyptic visions, a steadfast belief that society was a failed experiment. The warrior channels the spirit of the pioneer or the frontiersman to escape modernity, going to war if necessary.[28]

Survivalism has a strong, often underlying appeal because it so easily attaches to the existing constructs of American liberalism: individualism, life, liberty, autonomy, freedom, and self-determination. The logic of survivalism is also rooted in the shared cultural mythology of the American frontier, the lore of white male explorers, gunfighters, pioneers, homesteaders, and other self-sufficient Robinson Crusoes and Swiss Family Robinsons. Survivalism appropriates the philosophical god-terms of American liberalism, even finding support in fragments of the Constitution, the Declaration of Independence, and the writings of Patrick Henry, Thomas Paine, and the early antifederalists. Survivalists even defend their version of radical individualism as the original intent of the American founders. Survivalism is not only a lifestyle but also an appealing belief structure plucked from the heart of American liberalism. Nurtured by alienation, the ideology stretches the philosophical canon to, at its logical limit, reject much of its democratic foundations. Its masculine appeal is in the rejection of feminized society, conveyed by opposition to the "nanny state": a feckless, overbearing, and controlling perversion of government.

The rhetoric of survivalism and doomsday prepping speak directly to white men's perceived victimization by government policies that might be construed to impinge on men's individual liberty and redistribute their wealth to the less fortunate. Prepper discourse addresses white men's perceived powerlessness and offers a revision of the social order made anew. In the face of overwhelming economic and environmental challenges, survival rhetoric offers white men empowerment outside the public sphere, in a retreat to an alternative space outside politics that is both privatized and orderly. Apocalyptic visions are powerful because they allow those who see themselves as oppressed or disenfranchised to imagine the emergence of a new social order. Richard Mitchell argues that survivalists are creative in that they desire social transformation, "not by changing institutions but through discovery and reinterpretation of the cultural assumptions and intrinsic practice that undergird the institutional order."[29] Envisioning the collapse of civilization offers an opportunity to reimagine the individual, the family, and the local community as the new social architecture; a masculine vision precluded by existing feminine modes of governance, and therefore, not achievable by way of reform or collective action.[30]

Apocalyptic discourse appeals to a diverse crowd. From the Puritan theology of Jonathan Edwards and Cotton Mather to the Ghost Dance prophecies of Wovoka and the evangelical divinations of the reverend Billy Graham, most American religious traditions are in some way structured by apocalyptic theology.[31] While its secular appropriations connote the end of existence, "apocalypse" is the Greek word for revelation, meaning the unveiling of previously unknown truth, typically in the end times.[32] In Judeo-Christian theology, during the end of days a heavenly messenger will reveal to all the order of the cosmos. Evil will be destroyed, the righteous will be saved, and human existence will prove to be divinely meaningful. The postmillennial apocalyptic form provides assurances that the end of the world, as we know it, will be followed by a utopian epoch of peace. Both Barry Brummett and Stephen O'Leary argue that the apocalyptic is a genre of discourse that emerges in response to social crisis to assure audiences that there is a cosmic order in which good triumphs over evil.[33] It is no surprise that the genre appeals to white men.

Though men and women alike share in apocalyptic dread, doomsday prepping is largely a masculinist culture. Preppers lambaste the effeminacy of entitlement culture, valorizing in contrast the self-made man of pre/industrial civilization as the only gender modality that guarantees survival. The rhetoric of "feminine dependency" is one of the key ways that conservative men performatively enact their identities. Prepper culture is consummated through masculine performances of self-sufficiency and paramilitary violence, including preparedness simulations, complete with props and costumes such as camouflage and military weapons. Prepper discourse encourages the development of masculine-coded abilities, including mechanical labor, wilderness training, and weapons proficiency. Preppers are animated by calls to remasculinize America, a discourse premised on the assumption that since the 1960s, society has become increasingly feminized and dependent on government. Protest against the feminization of society advances the misconceptions that relative gains in social equality have made the nation "soft," less animated by authority, competition, and aggression. Right-wing movements capitalize on fear of the "nanny state," an overly sentimental and bureaucratic society that personifies weakness.[34] Like their survivalist predecessor, the figure of the doomsday prepper is a composite of premodern masculine archetypes that fashions a heroic self-image for white men. His sudden ubiquity in American popular culture and public life speaks to aggrieved white man's desire to reset the social order to a time when they were whole and necessary.

THE REAL MEN OF *DOOMSDAY PREPPERS*

Doomsday Preppers is an hour-long documentary-style reality television program that chronicles individuals who devote a significant portion of their life to disaster preparedness. Each program is divided between two to four different participants. The program relies on male "voice-of-God narration," or verbal commentary that directly addresses the spectator, and onscreen textual prompts to provide background information on each subject.[35] Though participants address the camera to explain their apocalyptic preparations, the interviewer remains silent and off-screen. Each segment begins by explaining the participant's everyday rituals, followed by discussion and simulations of their particular vision of the apocalypse. Stock footage of mass violence and natural disasters are integrated to help audiences visualize global disasters. Next, episodes document the subjects' "preps," including food pantries, weapons, and security. The camera follows the participants into simulated tests of their preparedness, military training exercises, attacks on the participant's home, and "bug-out" escapes to safe locations. The producers employ Practical Preppers, a disaster preparedness firm, to grade the subject's level of readiness. Finally, each case concludes with a brief expert assessment of the likelihood of each apocalyptic scenario.

Since 2011 *Doomsday Preppers* has become the centerpiece of Nat Geo's apocalyptic rebranding.[36] Although Nat Geo continues to employ the slogan "inspiring people to care about the planet since 1888," the network's most popular programming simulates the planet's destruction (*Apocalypse 101, American Blackout, Doomsday Castle, Forecast: Disaster,* and *How to Survive the End of the World*).[37] *Doomsday Preppers* has emerged as one of Nat Geo's most successful and highly rated series: 1.3 million viewers watched the season 2 premier, the highest-rated premier in the network's history. The show is particularly popular with men (60 percent) with an average age of forty-four.[38] The executive producers contend that 9/11, Hurricane Sandy, and the Japanese tsunami account for the public's fascination with the program.[39] *Doomsday Preppers* also benefits from the historic credibility of the National Geographic Society (NGS), its magazine and television network. The NGS has also long played a role in constructing national manhood. Lisa Bloom argues that the NGS rose to prominence because its rhetoric consummated Theodore Roosevelt's vision of the sporting man/adventurer who promised to recuperate the virile national manhood of preindustrial America.[40] *Doomsday Preppers* returns the network to NGS's roots by simulating the importance of rugged manhood. I analyze masculine performances throughout the first two seasons wherein dominant tropes are established and elaborated. I attend to the interplay between dialogue, narration, simulations, mise-en-scene, and on-camera performances to show how apocalyptic manhood emerges as a sensible ideal. I organize the analysis around how the program constructs the performance of male labor, fatherly know-how, manly rituals, and feminine domesticity. Each of these elements is bolstered by the show's construction of the participants as performing as they would even if the cameras were not present. Authenticity is constructed through "unconscious production of observable trustworthiness and earnestness of character" that develops from reality TV characters "acting" natural while being observed.[41] The presentation of participants "performing not performing" not only invites audience identification with their extreme fantasies but also provides an instructional model for enacting hegemonic masculinity. When participants play out apocalyptical scenarios, the program's realistic veneer gives the male participant's "imagined realities" the presumption of realness.

THE VALUE OF MALE LABOR

Doomsday Preppers responds to the decline in masculine labor by showing images of men putting their skills back to work; putatively "real men" who toil in the real world. If, as Boylorn suggests, "reality television offers a supposed lens into the everyday experiences, thoughts, and actions in the lives of participants," glimpses of participants reclaiming masculine labor in their homes and workplaces provide a convincing portrait of how authentic manliness is performed.[42] In episodes that feature male-headed households, the camera displays male artifice in traditionally masculine spaces: the home garage, machine shop, and primitive wilderness. Male characters show off their working-class skills: welding, automotive repair, mechanical engineering, construction, woodwork, farming, fishing, weapons manufacturing, hunting, among others. The program's male participants show off their homemade gadgets and ingenious methods of cultivating self-sufficiency. After displaying their pre/industrial skills, participants conduct tests that confirm the durability of their "preps." Here, I analyze the various stages for manly performances, illustrating how the program constructs (1) the male-headed household as a model for economic self-sufficiency, (2) the garage as a laboratory of masculinity, and (3) the wilderness as a male proving ground.

First, the show depicts the household of the future as a site of production where men lead and delegate physical tasks. The intimacy of each family home or business is essential to the program's construction of authentic manliness. As Goffman notes, everyday-life performances always take place against a background: "furniture, décor, physical layout, and other background items which supply the scenery and stage props for the spate of human action played out before, with, or upon it."[43] The working home of the postapocalyptic future creates the ideal context for performing manly labor. For instance, Dennis Evers (S1, E2) is introduced to the audience through a montage of gun-shooting, wood-chopping, lathe work, and welding. He tells the camera: "Everyone has a job and an assignment and they know how to do it. My oldest son Tim is in charge of hunting and security, my daughter Jenny and her husband Pat are in charge of fuel, Nate and Betsy deal with communications, Ricky knows how to weld and helps me with the engineering side of things, John is currently training to be an emergency responder. The importance of delegating labor when it hits the fan is no person can do everything, I can only be in one place at one time."

Dennis oversees an efficient system of economic production based on a fantasy of complete self-sufficiency. The Evers family is depicted as an exemplar of a gendered division of labor closely associated with the preindustrial American family. Whereas the women of the family are shown in the pantry and kitchen, or gathering supplies, the men are shown manufacturing weapons, building security systems, and inventing gadgets in the home garage. The camera peers over Dennis's shoulder as he labors in his machine shop, capturing what appears to be the unrehearsed daily routine of the male prepper. The camera closes in on his face to capture his intense concentration and engineering acumen. Dennis's machine shop is a stage, a backdrop against which he performs the valuable role of men in the working household of the future.

Like all other participants, Dennis directly addresses the camera during interview segments only. The remainder of the program documents his everyday activities, as they would supposedly transpire without the camera. Hence, the audience is treated to two distinct performances: the day-in-a-life and the confessional. In the former, Dennis shows the audience what it's like for him to manage the household labor. The camera is attentive to his gestures, movements, and dialogue as he works in the machine shop and assesses the value of his children's work. As Dennis critiques his son's bow-and-arrow design, the audience is invited to vicariously experience what it is like to manage a prepper household. The intimacy of witnessing "organic" family encounters helps convey the relatability of the participant's extreme lifestyle. The latter performance builds sincerity by providing the subjects space to explain their performances. Dennis's interview takes place in the machine shop, his tools the manly props of his one-man act. His workshop stage corroborates his monologue on the importance of delegating family labor. Both performances build audience identification and attest to the subject's sincerity. The episode concludes with scenes of a commonplace, everyday dinner. Like the image of the traditional nuclear family, Dennis heads the table and evaluates the group's daily chores, delegating tasks for the next morning. As the episode concludes, Dennis explains that to survive "we need to come together as a family." This portrait of the laboring household not only sutures working-class labor to the success of the family but also reframes prepping as a natural expression of fatherly duty.

Next, the program portrays suburban garages as laboratories of masculine ingenuity. Here, the program relies on masculine stereotypes about the inherent value of physical labor to render the participant's performances authentic. Tim Ralston (S1, E3) is depicted in his two-car garage happily testing improvised weapons and assembling "bug-out" bags. Pat Brabble's (S1, E3) interviews also take place in his garage, where a display of ammunition, tools, foodstuffs, and the American flag frame the shot. Brabble, too, is routinely depicted modifying weapons and making ammunition. Jim D (S2, E11) is shown pouring sweat over his perfect escape vehicle ("the behemoth"). Jim's garage is arranged as an automotive laboratory where he enacts his road-warrior fantasy. Other participants have converted their businesses into prepping factories. Riley Cook (S1, E6) is introduced through a montage that switches between interactions with his daughters and intense manual labor at his welding business. Riley discloses:

> In most aspects I'm very typical American. I have a full time job. I'm married and have children. We go to work and get our paycheck at the end of the week. We look forward to a vacation. But one of my primary concerns as a father and a husband is will our American Dream be there in the near future for our children, for ourselves?

Folded into American Dream mythology, Riley's monologue reframes male labor as a fatherly responsibility. His fatherly motivations now self-evident, repeated images of Riley welding imply a strong connection between the laboring male body and the survival of the nuclear family. This motif recurs throughout the series. For example, the narrator declares that Glen Rogers (S2, E7) has acquired skills such as making gunpowder because he "hopes this skill will protect his family." Another subject calling himself "Mr. Wayne" (S1, E11) is filmed in his workshop, where he "spends hours tinkering" making bullets and bombs to protect his family from a Chinese invasion. His physical skills are framed as fatherly assets, well suited to the task of family survival. None of these activities appear extraordinary, because they are only extensions of appropriate everyday-life performances for working-class men. What might otherwise seem to be extreme preparations transform into natural extensions of male identity.

Finally, the program's male subjects perform their physical skills in wildlife settings. These episodes use nature as a proving ground for male skills, a vital backdrop for the performance of Nat Geo's frontier manhood. For instance, the narrator praises Christopher Nyerges (S1, E1) for his botanical skills as he is filmed foraging for food among the local flora and fauna of Los Angeles. His performance is made more convincing by his willingness to eat a meal composed of found items. Allen and Franco (S2, E5) are portrayed as caring fathers because they have harmonized with nature to feed their family. Meanwhile, the program's experts compliment John Major (S1, E9) for teaching his children to survive by consuming insects. Doug (S2, E13) proves himself to Practical Preppers by using boulders to protect his doomsday bunker. Michael James Patrick Douglas (S1, E5) demonstrates his fatherly credentials by taking his children on survival retreats into the Maine wilderness. Doug Huffman (S1, E7) teaches children at a survival school, using his collection of camouflage to blend in to the natural environment. Bryan Smith (S2, E8) is commended as the ultimate frontiersman for his display of wilderness ingenuity on his large estate. As Bryan declares: "I've hunted wild boar, I've wrestled alligators, and I've lived in the jungles of Costa Rica. And once I've had to shoot a man in self-defense."

The program's authenticity is belied by the fact that Nat Geo producers sometimes coax participants to perform acts that conform to their extreme impressions of wilderness survival. One participant (Chris Petrovich) refused to appear on the show after the producers asked him to eat an iguana. Craig Compeau (S2, E14), who admitted that he agreed to be on the program to promote his shelter company, complained that the producers staged their Alaskan wilderness hunts to give the impression that he was an extremist. These experiences points to the contrived character of these "authentic" wilderness encounters and how the producers coach subjects to perform. Here, what Goffman calls "frame slippage" reveals how the producers belabor "reality" to fit their preconceived assumptions.[44] Slippages highlight how these performances are crafted to look as if the camera is not present. The program coaches, teases, and edits performances of masculinity to craft a particular narrative. The program's ability to convey that its male participants are "performing not performing" communicates that doomsday prepping is a natural expression contemporary manhood.

FATHER KNOWS BEST

The program provides men the opportunity to perform fatherly knowhow. The concept of personal responsibility unfolds when the subjects address the camera in one-on-one interviews. These interviews give the participants an opportunity to narrate their everyday life, hence corroborating the performances analyzed in the previous section. The participants' direct address of the camera helps confirm that their commitment to prepping as a fatherly duty is sincere. The interview contextualizes their performances as the fulfillment of their paternal responsibility rather than extreme behaviors coaxed by producers. Here, I pay attention to how the program's male participants engage in show-and-tell to communicate fatherly know-how. Fathers both ritualistically simulate tests of their advanced preparations and directly address the camera to explain the importance of fatherhood.

One recurring claim is that prepping represents a primal male instinct to protect the family. Jules Dervaes (S1, E3) explains, "In the years to come I don't want my family to turn around and say 'Dad: why didn't you do something?'" Larry Hall (S1, E4) asserts that "when you become a parent, suddenly you are not the most important thing anymore. It makes me feel responsible to prepare." Snake Blocker (S2, E9) adds, "I need to be a responsible husband . . . I, too, must be strong for the people around me." Paul Haswell (S1, E1) concurs, "I think you need to be responsible for yourself and your family. To do anything less is a criminal act." These examples illustrate how prepping is a portrayed as a sensible commitment when it is performed as parental instinct. These personal confessions often give way to a series of aggressive declarations of paternal rights and direct questioning of the audience's commitment. Pat Brabble asserts: "You should be able to protect your family with your handguns." Similarly, John Major asserts,

"I'd protect my family by all means possible, and I don't feel I need permission from anyone to do that." Mike Mester (S1, E6) takes a more aggressive approach, interrogating the viewer: "Are you going to sit back and wait for the cavalry? They may never come. So, what are you going to do about it? Why don't you start to prepare? Because it's your personal responsibility." Barry (S1, E10), too, addresses the audience: "Who's gonna take care of your family if you can't?" Ron Hubbard (S2, E8) also asks emphatically, "How would YOU protect your family?! Do you have a plan?" The repetition of forceful declarations of the right to self-defense ostensibly berates the male spectator to pursue aggressive measures to protect loved ones. Moreover, these declarations transform the participants into educators whose lives are models of how parental responsibility can be performatively enacted.

Throughout the interview segment, "dependency" on others is considered weakness. Jules contends, "Everyone else seems to be looking to be dependent. Dependent on government, dependent on corporations, dependent on banks, dependent on others. But we are fighting for ourselves." Kevin O'Brien (S1, E4) agrees: "We're all a little too dependent on our government, too dependent on our local grocery store." Bryan Smith brags, "I was raised to not rely on anybody. Don't rely on your government, don't rely on your neighbors, you count on yourself first." Tim Ralston adds, "Anyone who does not take their self-preservation to heart is doomed for failure. I refuse to be a victim." Repeated ad nauseam, dependency develops into a discursive short hand for naiveté, effeminacy, irresponsibility, and childlike vulnerability. These participants use their apocalyptic expectations as a metaphor for what they perceive to be the end of hegemonic masculinity and, consequently, the necessity of its return.

Note how these male subjects attribute the coming collapse of society to the adoption of so-called feminine traits. They describe civilization as "weak" "dependent," and "thin." Jay Blevins calmly asserts, "There is a very thin fabric that holds together a civilized society." Jason Day (S1, E11) also assumes that "every great nation has always come to an end. America is just the same way." John Major presumes that "when law of the jungle reigns, that's when every individual will be responsible for their own security." In each of these comments, the end of the world is taken for granted because civilization (weak, fragile, dependent) cannot contain humanity's primal instincts (aggression, competition, violence). Lindsay (S2, E11) makes this distinction clear when she explains, "back in the day everyone was prepared; they weren't dependent on others. Preppers today are like our ancestors used to be." Her husband, Larry, agrees: "There is so much fragility in our system and it could collapse at any time." These participants anticipate a disastrous end to society's experiment with feminine values. Their certainty in an apocalypse event is hopeful in as much as it means that fathers will return to pre-eminence.

After the interview, the participants are provided space to show how fatherly authority is embodied. The portrait of Jay Blevins is an exemplary case in point. This episode begins with a medium shot of Jay standing in front of his family and suburban home, dressed in a police-issue black uniform, brandishing a menacing AR-15 assault rifle; his costume and props. He declares: "We're preparing for the breakdown of social order following an economic collapse." The episode depicts Jay performing a variety of masculine roles that confirm his fatherly authority. In one scene, Jay performs a priestly role by leading a Bible study in his living room. Next, Jay absconds to the garage, where he adopts a soldier persona—mimicking military-style attacks directly at the camera. This scene is followed by shots of Jay leading a neighborhood prepping organization in strategic home fortifications. He explains in fatherly terms: "I love my kids so much, I love my wife so much, I never want to see them hurt or to go without, so if a crowd were to ever come to my house, I want to defend my family." The "day in the life" portrait of Jay demonstrates a recurring pattern marked by the camera's sole emphasis on the priorities of the male head of household.

While Jay protects the suburban enclave, Brent's (S2, E9) "doomsday castle" consummates a paternal fantasy of feudal domestic life. In the narrator's words, Brent's planning to "get medieval" when the world ends. Brent has begun construction of a fortress in the Carolina mountains that he hopes to bequeath to a male heir contingent upon a series of tests. This particular episode emphasizes intergenerational masculinity, or the imperative to pass male survival skills on to the heirs of postapocalyptic society. Dressed in camouflage, Brent is shown putting his adult children through a series of extreme challenges to prove their loyalty. Embracing the medieval motif, the program positions Brent as a "king" choosing his successor. The episode has a particular lighteartedness, as many of his children possess none of their father's physical skills. He berates his sons for their lack of outdoor skills and weapons training, while chiding his daughters for being "more primpers than preppers." The lesson is that Brent's children must unlearn their civilized femininity and seek tutelage in dark age–era survivalism. As Brent's children endure extreme survival trials, the audience is invited to see archaic masculine virtues as a repository of doomsday ingenuity.

Here, Brent's authenticity is bolstered by how the show portrays the reluctant skepticism and inexperience of his children. Whereas Brent performs his sincerity by dressing in military fatigues, conducting survival tests, and testifying to his certainty in Armageddon, his family's performances appear contrived for the sake of the program. That is, Brent's children express reluctance both about Brent's lifestyle and about taking part in a program that requires them to demonstrate survival skills they clearly do not possess. For instance, Brent pesters his oldest son (Brent Jr.) to prove his proficiency with an assault rifle despite his expressed reticence. After scoffing at his father's demands, he recklessly fires the weapon, almost injuring others. Brent's advanced skills, along with his displays of sincerity, contrast with his son's contrived effort to play along with the show's premise. Meanwhile, his daughters, Ashley, Lindsey, and Dawn-Marie, spend more time attending to their appearance than completing their chores. Yet, their reluctant participation, and sometimes defiance, contributes to Brent's ability to "perform not performing" by showing the difference between committed preppers and naïve skeptics. Through juxtaposition, his children's clumsy and unenthusiastic performances illuminate Brent's more sincere commitment to his postapocalyptic kingdom. The differences in their levels of sincerity create another frame slippage, where acts expose performance as performance. Nonetheless, frame slippage contributes to the authenticity of Brent's performance by providing audiences with a framework for evaluating what reality television constructs as an authentic performance. In the process, Brent's displays of hypercompetitive machismo become conflated with seriousness and hard work.

In other episodes, the program's participants simulate survival rituals to demonstrate the importance of fathers. This is most exemplified by rugged frontiersman Michael James Patrick Douglas. Though

Michael tests his daughter's preparedness in the home, he subjects his youngest son to a series of trials in the surrounding forest. When his son completes the trials, Michael explains to him: "You're entering a new stage of your life. You're no longer a little kid anymore. You're turning into a young man. This is your umbilical cord. It represents your attachment to me and mom. But today you proved that you're a survivor and that you're ready to take the next step." He invites his son to cast his preserved umbilical cord into the fire to confirm his induction into the cult of apocalyptic manhood. Reminiscent of Bly's mythopoetic manhood, Michael and his son perform the ritual behaviors required to locate archaic male archetypes. This portrayal of ritual frames survivalism as the embodiment of the kind of independence that accompanies adulthood. Like Michael's son, the audience is encouraged to "grow up" and develop the manly skills required to survive. To this end, the program also valorizes primitive rites of passage, such as hunting and animal sacrifice. These rituals are premised on many of the participant's insistence that the postcollapse world will return to a hunter-gatherer society. The inference is that men will be charged with the primal task of hunting game. For example, after commanding his son to kill one of the family's goats, Tom Perez boasts to Steven M. Vanasse (S2, E4) that his child is now a man because he has made "his first kill." The kill is ritualistically staged for the camera. Tom's son is compelled to kill and butcher a goat for the camera with little detail spared. Similar to Michael's wilderness trials, Steven and Tom's insistence that their children hunt and kill animals provides visual confirmation that prepping is a primal rite of passage where boys become men.

In summary, these episodes begin with a beleaguered father/ husband's confession of his apocalyptic anxiety, followed by scenes of everyday life where participants move fluidly between masculine archetypes (father, husband, laborer, soldier, and priest), and conclude with a series of staged preparedness rituals. These performances enact the fears expressed in the one-on-one interviews, providing audiences with examples of how to translate apocalyptic fears into productive models of self-made manhood. Lest the audience believe their performances are acted for the camera, the one-on-one interviews provide participants with the opportunity to prove their sincerity.

STAND BY YOUR MAN

Female participants typically move from reluctant to sincere performances of support for men. To this extent, women are relegated to menial tasks. Whereas young men are subjected to specific rites of passage that fortify their skills, young women must be trained to accept their roles. Men are responsible for ensuring that women are prepared to support their fathers and husbands. For instance, Jason Day (S1, E10) is shown routinely forcing his daughters to conduct gas mask drills, John Major enlists his daughters in preparing the house for a terrorist attack, and Braxton Southwick (S2, E1), involves his daughters in regular escape simulations to their rural cabin. In one of the most extreme cases, Johnny O (S2, E2) conditions his wife and sister-in-law to prepare for an attack on their home, calling his efforts "not really tests we run as much as its games we play." Though women are involved in the prepping, the episodes tend to foreground men's need for ritual. Episodes featuring women portray their preparedness training as either fulfillments of wifely duties or manifestations of obsessive-compulsive disorders. Often expressing initial skepticism, wives and daughters are encouraged to recant and acquiesce to the importance of disaster preparedness.

This transformation invites the incredulous female viewer to be more open-minded to the manly arts of preparedness. In these episodes, women often begin by complaining that prepping is a waste of time; however, they conclude with concessions to their husband's wisdom. Tim Ralston observes his wife's initial resistance yet insists that she finally ceded to his wisdom. He explains, "In the beginning my wife was not on the same page as I was," but "the more information I gave to her it opened her eyes to the potential threats that are out there." Mr. Wayne brags, "Because of the popularity of your series, my wife has come around and supports what I do." Although Bob Kay's (S2, E6) wife routinely questions his extreme spending on preparedness, their episode concludes with his insistence that "she does appreciate that being prepared is important." In some cases, the narrator declares their support. For instance, the voice-over declares that Jason Day's wife, Tanya, "supports his passion but it's meant some adjustments." Jason, like Bradford Franks (S1, E7) and Bob Kay, puts his wife through extreme simulations despite her visible discomfort. In other episodes, reluctant wives seem to freely confess their ultimate support of their husband's efforts. Franco's wife admits that she is otherwise helpless; therefore, "I'm glad I have a husband that's doing that for us." After some resistance, Snake Blocker's wife, Sarah, admits, "I've realized the importance of being prepared." Despite some hesitation, Jeremy's (S1, E8) wife, Kelly, divulges that "as long as I've got my son in lap and my husband in the driver seat that's all I need." The series depicts men as natural teachers who must help women understand the importance of preparedness.

To the extent that women are active participants, it is either in fulfillment of traditionally feminine domesticity or as an obsessive extension of motherly instincts. Because women are constructed as the domestic caretakers of the postapocalyptic home, their roles are heavily circumscribed. In a segment featuring Colleen Bishop (S1, E2), the voice-over explains that she is "a Utah housewife who believes a catastrophic economic collapse will cause food shortages and unleash panic across the country. But can she use her passion for cooking and her stockpiles of food to survive doomsday?" Although the episode references a variety of other skills she has developed, a large portion is devoted to her pantry skills. Meanwhile, her husband is depicted performing his fighting skills and elaborate plans for home security. In Kathy Harrison's (S1, E2) case, the narrator observes that "on her picturesque farm you are more likely to find herbs than guns," suggesting that female preppers prioritize feminine care labor over masculine violence. Women are often interviewed in front of pantries and kitchens, whereas men are more likely to be pictured in front of the household gun collection.

In other episodes, female prepping is portrayed as a hysterical manifestation of feminine instincts. Janet Spencer (S1, E9) is shown frantically stockpiling food while her husband is out of the house. Meanwhile, Donna Nash (S1, E4) is shown hoarding medical supplies and obsessively scrubbing her house for germs in preparation for a pandemic. Likewise, Laura Kunzie (S1, E10) is depicted irritating her family with quarantine drills and rants about germs. Other female motivations for prepping extend to the irrational, as only women express supernatural beliefs and prophetic visions. Amanda Bobbin (S2, E11) suggests that she takes direction from a ghost named Greta, and Dianne Rogers (S1, E7) preps because of a recurring apocalyptic nightmare that she believes to be a premonition. Thus, the program ostensibly contrasts male rationality with female hysteria. Men are sensibly concerned with the family's safety; women are obsessive and overbearing. In these segments, *Doomsday Preppers* relies on the archetype of the hysterical woman that is common throughout reality television. Hysteria is a cultural construction that disciplines women who diverge from normative performances of gender identity.[45] As Michaela Meyer, Amy Fallah, and Megan Wood explain, hysterical women in reality TV are constructed as irrational, out of control, and mentally distressed. They argue, "This framing is distinctly gendered, as madness is metaphorically and symbolically represented as feminine, even when experienced by men."[46] Attributing women's transgressive behavior to madness is a way of dismissing and, ultimately, disciplining their behavior. This theorization of hysteria also accounts for why male preppers are constructed as sincere, whereas women have irrational obsessions with cleanliness. The recurring lesson is that "men who surrender to their desires and passions become geniuses; women become subjects of their own self-destruction, eliciting at best pity and sympathy."[47]

Many of *Doomsday Preppers*' female participants are portrayed as obsessive germophobes. The narrator introduces Donna Nash's segment thus: "Like many suburban moms, Donna likes to keep a clean house but it's not because she's expecting company." The camera cuts to scenes of Donna repeatedly disinfecting her kitchen counters and vacuuming her pristine carpet. Ostensibly, Donna should be attending to her normal motherly duties instead of stockpiling disaster kits and forcing her children to endure quarantine drills. Similarly, Laura Kunzie simulates a quarantine in which she forces her visibly reluctant son to shower outside, stay in a barricaded bedroom, and remain home from school. The producer's selection of female germophobes contributes to a portrait of women who prepare as overly concerned, smothering, and compulsive. Though male prepping is portrayed as a natural extension of manly duty, female prepping is a transgressive gender performance.

In other cases, the program reduces women to survival accessories or resourceful accompaniments for the single male survivalist. In Brian Murdoch's case (S2, E3), the narrator tells viewers that "the one prep he needed most of all was a wife" and that "he believes that his new bride Tatania will be the perfect prepper wife." The episode depicts Tatania's arrival in the US from Colombia, followed by her difficult adjustment to prepping. Brian puts Tatania through an apocalyptic simulation to assess her weaknesses. Despite her obvious discomfort, she submits to Brian's wishes. He laments, "Tatiana's got a little learning to do, but soon we'll be married and I know we'll be happier." In Jeff Flaningham's segment (S2, E13), the audience is witness to the prepper's travails in online dating. Jeff brings a date back to his decommissioned missile silo, but is ultimately unsuccessful in securing his ideal prepping partner. Though more lighthearted, Jeff's dates are presented as auditions for a part in his apocalyptic drama more than a genuine search for romance. The quasi-romantic valence of these episodes reduces women to little more than their domestic labor value.

There are exceptions. Three episodes feature single women with varying commitments to prepping. Although a counterpoint to the hypermasculine image of survivalism, these episodes ultimately confirm that the apocalypse will make women's independence extraordinarily difficult. Meagan Hurwitt (S1, E1) is constructed as a "young independent urban woman" who "loves cocktails with friends" but also as someone who must abandon her frivolous lifestyle, including fashion and nightlife, to survive. The episode contrasts carefree images of Meagan swinging on a homemade stripper pole with shots of weapons training and fitness regimens. Meagan's survival as a single woman hinges on her ability to adapt masculine skill sets. But, in the postapocalyptic world, women's independence is a liability. Margaret Ling (S2, E7) corroborates this perspective when she asserts that "women are the most likely to be victimized." These examples could be read as expressions of women's empowerment; however, in the context of the program, where a vast majority of the women acquiesce to their natural roles of the feminine, these participants appear anomalous. Moreover, their independence is presented as much more of a challenge than an asset.

ARE YOU PREPARED?

This chapter suggests that the apocalyptic turn in masculine representations purports to offer the ultimate fortification against threats to hegemonic masculinity. While in one sense the apocalyptic turn is responsive to the decline in traditionally masculine professions, in another it is the by-product of an accumulation of (perceived) white male injuries wherein all challenges to men are framed as assaults on gender entitlement. Apocalyptic manhood constructs imminent disasters as solutions to immanent crisis, or seemingly permanent answers to the recurring crisis of the male self that persist without resolution. Performances of apocalyptic manhood are an illusory attempt to fix the meaning of masculinity against a background of disorientation. *Doomsday Preppers* offers a vision of the future survived by white men who embody rugged national virility. Apocalyptic manhood requires labor, ultimately consummated through ritual performances that visibly demonstrate the male subject's preparedness to return to pre/industrial America. Doomsday culture is underwritten by the notion that the recuperation of manhood will be found in the inevitable demise of civilization. Apocalyptic manhood is the fantasy that beneath modernity exists an essential, timeless, and sustainable version of manhood. The looming threat of the world's end produces not only anxiety but also opportunity.

Previously, as Kimmel writes, men had to "wander through anthropological literature like postmodern tourists" to find premodern archetypes of authentic manhood.[48] But in doomsday culture, old archetypes are "lived" and imbued with the qualities of everyday-life performances. Audiences are invited, temporarily, to welcome the apocalypse as a social vision of masculine necessity. Yet, the vision of the end in doomsday culture is an inadequate and dangerous response to the "masculinity crisis." Seeking relief in imminent destruction does little to ameliorate the anomic crisis of the male self. There is no permanent or sustainable version of manhood that escapes the slippery instability of the subject in late modernity. The salve of a future without women challenging male primacy elides the inherent instability of hegemonic masculinity itself. The myth that there is a pre-performative gender identity found, ironically, in the rituals of the self-made man masks the fluidity of masculinity.

There are also broader political implications that require urgent attention. Unfortunately, men act on the fantasies cultivated in popular media. As examined in later chapters, hypermasculine warriors inevitably come out from behind their screens and enact their identity through aggressive performances, from adopting the paramilitary aesthetics of the open carry movement to the Wild West mentality of the Bundy clan at their armed siege of the Malheur National Wildlife Refuge in Oregon. The proliferation of white men enacting their warrior fantasies through spectacular acts of mass violence points to the real dangers of this millennial turn in masculinity. For instance, on November 30, 2015, Robert Dear killed a police officer and two civilians at a Colorado Springs Planned Parenthood clinic. During his arraignment he declared himself a "warrior for the babies." Sandy Hook shooter Adam Lanza was immersed in survivalist culture, his family stockpiling food and arms in preparation for catastrophe. And Charleston shooter Dylann Roof legitimized his actions as a hypermasculine response to the sexual threat posed by people of color. Roof is a chilling embodiment of apocalyptic manhood. He announced his intention to induce a racialized doomsday event that would restore white men to their proper place in the race/gender hierarchy. This chapter punctuates the argument that the public fascination with the hypermasculine doomsday prepper fans the flames of white masculine victimhood. It is imperative to produce alternative models of masculinity that approach the performative nature of manhood as an opportunity to eradicate racial and gendered violence rather than anathema to the imminent destruction of liberal society.

CHAPTER 2

The Red Pill

The New Men's Rights Rhetoric

LIKE REALITY TELEVISION, networked media also afford new expressions of white masculinity. Amplified by new digital platforms and online social networks, the crisis of white masculinity is no longer relegated to the forgotten silos and distant outposts that once constrained the scope and intensity of men's rights activism. News aggregators, blogs, personal websites, amateur video platforms, social media applications, and digital communities now comprise a network of what were once isolated communities of men's rights proponents, misogynists, white supremacists, and far-right extremists. More importantly, a network provides users with multiple access points and nodes that might plug an individual user into an entire web of harmonized content. Levine reminds us that a network affords connectivity, circulation, and accessibility to ideas and content that were previously unlinked. Each node is a gateway to other nodes, and thus each point in the network is capable of attracting, enabling, and ensnaring a larger demographic of users. It is for this reason that some have suggested that contemporary men's rights activism is often a "gateway drug" to white supremacy.[1] In their recent book on alt-right meme culture, Heather Suzanne Woods and Leslie Hahner observe that the technical infrastructure, design features, and community standards that support sites such as Reddit and

4chan sustain the rapid and unregulated dissemination of racist, sexist, and homophobic content. They note that "Reddit influences public culture via its technological and ideological capacities, namely, the ability to fashion content and disseminate it rapidly across a multitude of sites. One of the affordances of networked publicity on sites such as Reddit and 4chan is that information moves quickly across each sites' nodes—oftentimes more quickly than on other media channels."[2] Reddit provides a central hub for sharing, upvoting/downvoting, and linking content so that stories, videos, and memes can traffic across a wide number of overlapping networks. The ability to rapidly disseminate information and organize collective action enables digital networks to influence public culture in ways that differ from social movements of the past.[3] The loose collection of digital communities that identify as the alt-right have managed to not only organize political rallies IRL ("in real life") but also push their reactionary views into the mainstream.

Hence, this chapter concerns the men's rights networks that have drawn a significant following, converted and radicalized countless followers, and enabled cross-pollination between reactionary communities as well as the social discord they engender. In a network, men's rights rhetorics organizes disconnected ideas into a coherent pattern or, in this case, a kind of metanarrative that governs the rhetoric arising from each node. This metanarrative speaks to men as victim-heroes of their cultural antagonism with feminism and their inevitable triumph over seemingly intractable enemies. The network assimilates new nodes and imposes implicit rules that make each disparate element speak to a larger overall thematic designed to disrupt and supplant competing feminine networks and institutions. Networked men's rights media has crafted a powerful framework through which users and audiences are to make sense of their social reality. The network is compulsively repetitive in that it constantly cajoles its user to think of themselves as dupes of feminist programming but also as burgeoning vanguards of a new masculine consciousness. In other words, the network enlists its users and audiences to think in and through a narrative of victimization and redemption. This is made possible by the cross-pollination of reactionary ideas, from which has emerged a new narrative for men's rights advocates that is underwritten by an amalgam of melancholia, apocalyptic thought, white male victimhood, evolutionary psychology, and revolutionary vanguardism. This chapter seeks to unravel the strands that connect different and sometimes contradictory elements of men's rights activism in networked media and to evince how new rhetorical forms have amplified and woven together a reactionary figure capable of fulfilling a narrative in which white men turn the tables on feminism. This victim-hero transforms their suffering into a political project to quite literally reprogram reality to restore white men to their previous grandeur.

THE MEN WHO SIT AT SCREENS

In a post entitled "Men Who Sit at the Screens," regular *Voice for Men* contributor and men's rights advocate Peter Wright argues that the contemporary men's rights movement is at the forefront of a burgeoning transformation in the mythic and narrative structures that anchor Western civilization.[4] The end of feminine civilization, he wagers, is at hand. Drawing from Joseph Campbell's Jungian-inspired *Masks of God,* Wright argues that men's awakening in networked media—from the frenetic pace of their contributions to the magnitude of their ire— precipitates a monumental shift in the architecture of our collective consciousness. By sheer motion alone, these men are knitting a new social fabric and building a kind of collective organism that veers from feminist mythmaking toward a new narrative structure characterized by masculine techno-rationalism. The "men who sit at screens," Wright explains,

> writers, computer folk, scientists, the intelligence and security services etc [*sic*]—are, in many ways, a certain breed of men—with, loosely speaking, more brain, less muscle, more introvert, less extravert etc. . . . And many of us grow to be this way as we get older! It is men-who-sit-at-screens who will knit together the men's movement. There will be men's activists who will dash hither and thither around cyberspace harassing the enemy and gathering up information to feed to webmasters and authors. There will be webmasters and authors sifting, analysing and re-arranging information to create feeds and ideas to push into the more mainstream media. There will be mainstream media activists who repackage the information for a

much wider audience. There will be computer folk who will help the men's movement to grow inside cyberspace. And there will also be men-who-sit-at-screens in many other walks of life who will do their bit to further the men's movement and its aims.[5]

According to Wright, networked media has birthed a new man, one whose muscles and intellect have been grafted onto the very fibers and networks that control the flow of information in the internet age. Metaphorically speaking, these newly radicalized men operate as the movement's guerrilla warriors—planting booby traps and improvised explosive devices throughout the web, engaging in reconnaissance, and, above all, flanking and sabotaging their enemies. Clandestine and mobile, they tactically traverse networked media, casting doubt on the dominant narratives offered up by feminists and progressives. Although their individual influence may be minimal, their collective voice percolates up and seeps into the culture, now nesting comfortably within the Overton window. Newsfeeds and algorithms amplify their voices while Silicon Valley web designers encode white men's identities into their platforms, thus propelling the movement's ideas into the mainstream for legitimate consideration.

According to Wright, the "men who sit at screens" are powerful because they understand the mythical relationship between storytelling and consciousness. In other words, Wright's theory is grounded in the assumption that social change is the result of paradigmatic shifts in the grand narratives that structure cultural values and beliefs. Echoing the theoretical underpinnings of the narrative paradigm, he claimed that "men and women are after all story creatures, and it's by this mode we can tell ourselves into existence beyond the restrictive stories that currently dominate the discussion on gender."[6] Observing that the secular techno-rationality of internet culture has the capacity to supplant religious doctrine, he explained that "what we need is a New Testament on men's issues, one that will succeed the tired old story of male servitude to a quasi-aristocratic class of women. This process begins by understanding that the persuasiveness of stories will always trump clinical facts—despite their veracity."[7] Here we find a theory of agency that governs the men's rights rhetoric in networked media. As a multitude owing allegiance neither to existing political institutions nor to facts, this nomadic movement swarms internet platforms, redirects flows of web traffic, and plants seeds of doubt in the common sense of a networked public sphere.[8] They will, in his words, "grow into a massive organism" which "no other group will survive its wrath should it engender it."[9] Much like doomsday preppers, this message is apocalyptic—anticipating a cataclysmic reckoning between feminine institutions and male consciousness. Although they tout masculine rationality, they seek not debate on their opponent's terrain but instead to win hegemony by rewriting the narrative paradigms (as well as the computer codes) that govern common sense itself. The idea is to graft their narrative onto networked media so that men might reprogram their consciousness and, thus, reality itself. In one sense, this perspective is not dissimilar from Walter Fisher's approach to the narrative paradigm in which argumentative rationality is consistently outmaneuvered by the probability, coherence, and fidelity of storytelling.[10] Working from this paradigm, they offer a new mythology in which men's triumph over all other social groups is inevitable, philosophically defensible, and of course, necessary.

In another sense, for men's rights advocates the objective is to impose a new form (narrative) onto networked media that is powerful enough to surpass the veracity of other rhetorical forms such as deliberation, debate, and dialogue. Since each user has a role to play in both seeding narratives throughout networked media and playing their part in this cosmic drama, stories afford users agency where they may have previously felt powerlessness. Moreover, men's rights activists are not concerned with simply promulgating any type of narrative. Here, the rhetorical work of genre is also imperative. Men's rights rhetoric in networked media traffics in the conventions of melodrama, evinced by men's preoccupation with moral polarities, pain and suffering, heightened emotionality, innocent victims (men) triumphing over evil (women). The new men's rights rhetoric appropriates the feminine conventions of melodrama to raise the consciousness of men with a compelling agonistic narrative that attempts to turn the tables on women.

Yet, anyone who has perused or studied men's rights in networked media can testify that the seeming continuity offered by such a broad label often belies the factionalism between and sometimes within the various user communities that, at a minimum, nominally identify themselves with the cause. Beyond appeals to victimhood, for the casual observer there is sometimes little that seems to thread these communities together. For instance, Elam's *A Voice for Men* mobilizes around legal and political reform on issues such as false rape accusations, the domestic abuse of men, anti-male bias in the family courts, and various other forms of misandry. By contrast, the next chapter outlines how "incel" websites such as www.loveshy.com, www.PUAHate.com, and r/incel provide a support community for men to vent about women's cruelty and express fatalism in the face of pseudoscientific beliefs concerning the immutable laws of attraction (i.e., "the black pill"). At the other end of the spectrum, male pickup artists on websites such as www.rooshv.com and r/TheRedPill organize male empowerment through the use of evolutionary psychology and cultural mythmaking to manipulate and take advantage of women. Still, other groups such as Men Going Their Own Way (MGTOW) argue that the only pathway to male empowerment is found by separating from women entirely and channeling men's energies into building wealth and making scientific discoveries. Other groups who identify with "Red Pill psychology" see men's rights activism as a somewhat perverse form of consciousness-raising and that through various practices of blogging, creating memes, and trolling they can awaken the "blue pilled" masses to their subjugation by women. As these descriptions demonstrate, men's rights activism in networked media greatly diverges in terms of its assumptions, goals, and tactics.

Yet, networks afford connectivity between nodes, hubs, and spokes that were previously disparate and isolated. Hence the so-called manosphere is diffuse and expansive: a seemingly endless web composed of nodes, links, videos, memes, archived pages, and active threads that ceaselessly direct the user elsewhere to consume (and ideally produce) more content. In this way, the structure of the network tends to harmonize disparate threads of men's rights activism. As Levine contends, a network "provides a way to understand how many other formal elements—including wholes, rhythms, and hierarchies—link up in larger formations."[11] The network allows disparate strands of men's right discourse to function in concert and to circulate, cross-pollinate, and synchronize their symbolic activity. Hence, what unites all these distinct threads of men's rights activism is their alignment and parsimony within the larger overarching structure: a network that intones, repeats, and synthesizes different and sometimes contradictory discourse into a cohesive yet neurotic project in which everything is connected.

Although it is difficult to say where the mansophere begins or ends, because men's rights rhetoric exists within a network, it is possible to provisionally generalize about a common set of principles, forms, and genres of discourse that seem to govern it. If we widen our view, Wright's archetype of the "men who sit at screens" offers some perspective on what ultimately unites these disparate fragments of men's rights rhetoric in cyberspace. Wright concludes his essay by noting that factionalism is in no way a liability to the overall goals of men's empowerment. From his perspective, mere participation in any discussion of men's empowerment throughout networked media necessarily embeds them within the networks, algorithms, and codes that underwrite the changing mythology. He explains that

> it does not matter whether they are on the left or on the right, and if they are fighting like dogs. The truth of the matter is this—whether they like it or not. If they are "men," and they also sit at screens and they also keep reading about the same kind of stuff, then they really, and truly, and very deeply have a great deal in common—far more so than they usually recognise. And the reason that they usually do not recognise this commonality is largely due to the fact that they do not see themselves as "men"! But, one day, they will! And, at some point in the future, the psychological force that they create will dwarf all others. And so, all in all, the future seems quite rosy for men-who-sit-at-screens.[12]

Wright sees a larger picture in which men's rights activism inevitably brings participants to the same end point; that is, the structure of consciousness referenced by advocates of taking the *Red Pill*. Regardless of their boutique complaints, as the story goes, these innocent men will inevitably awaken to the reality of their oppression, find their place in the epic struggle between good and evil, and, based on their new consciousness, organize against women based on their shared interests as "men." This narrative represents a hybrid between melodrama and the feminist rhetoric of consciousness-raising (which consisted of small, leaderless groups who mutually encouraged individuals to share their personal feelings, experiences, and problems that are unique to their status as women).[13] By mapping the commonalities in form and genre— as well as their ad nauseam repetition within an expansive network—

the chapter illustrates how men's rights activism in networked media draws its style from the appropriation of feminine forms.

Of course, Wright's theory of bottom-up consciousness is rooted in a fairly naïve if not magical reading of social and psychological theories of social change. However, I believe that he is correct that there are overarching forms and genres within the men's rights network that unite, tame, and organize such wildly divergent content. While the substance somewhat varies, many of the most visited men's rights websites make space for discussions of men's innocence and personal suffering and, then, connect that suffering to larger structural forces at work to keep men subjugated by women and separated from one another. Communities are connected by a kind of rhythmic repetition of the same narrative form. Virtual democracy creates the networks that afford connectivity between different nodes that are preoccupied with white masculine victimhood, including men's rights activists, militia movements, survivalists, white nationalists, and other groups. They not only recruit new adherents but coordinate individual threads into patterned responses to public controversies, in some cases even augmenting the national discourse.[14] This claim is based not simply on the demographics of usage but rather on the assumption that new modes of civic participation are frequently reinvented to replicate old modes of domination.[15] Hence, the democratizing function of networked media is often occluded by those in positions of power and privilege. Recent work by digital scholars such as Safiya Umoja Noble on the racism and sexism of algorithms illustrates the degree to which structural oppressions are literally encoded into virtual platforms.[16] In this case, men's rights advocates speak with such an amplified voice because the individual nodes with the network harmonize their message with the same general narrative pattern.

The existence of white men within networks—or their desire to see themselves as embedded in networks—evinces an ancillary effect of new media technologies: paranoia. As Tung-Hui Hu suggests, we can understand virtual networks as paranoid structures because they invite users to envision all information and activity as somehow connected. The resultant network fever represents that "desire to connect *all* networks, indeed, the desire to connect every piece of information to another piece. And to construct a system of knowledge where everything is connected is, as psychoanalysis tells us, the sign of paranoia."[17]

It is for this reason that men's rights networks are structurally predisposed to understand the basic practices of socialization as a kind of grand conspiratorial design that ultimately disguises an intentional and well-coordinated campaign of ideological indoctrination. As users circulate across networks, the information and experiences they encounter invite them to interpret disparate grievances as experiences with a diffuse yet well-orchestrated and totalizing system of oppression. White men who produce and consume networked media might circulate across various channels or linger at particular nodes; yet, their embeddedness within networked logics organizes content so as to fit a particular paranoid pattern that makes possible unseen and even outrageous connections between individual nodes.

The metanarrative that structures adherence within this network is composed of four major components: (1) the innocent (white male) masses have been narcotized and live under an illusory, simulated reality characterized by the unthinking acceptance of progressive narratives (i.e., "the blue pill"); (2) under the canopy of this false reality, men are incapable of perceiving the ways in which they are victimized by women and kept a part from one another; (3) participation in the manosphere shocks (and raises) the conscience of the user, thereby unveiling to them the "desert of the Real" or the "true" and bleak material conditions that constitute their existence ("the red pill"); and, finally, (4) the subject who once accepted society's programming is reborn in cyberspace, where they can join a mythical multitude or collective body of liberated men who will overthrow the evil autocratic rule of feminism. The narrative promises men that in the new world they will be invulnerable to women and capable of channeling their energies into achieving new civilizational heights. Women will return to their subservient roles in the kitchen and the bedroom. Only men who embrace the Red Pill will be the beneficiaries of this new order. Similar to the rhetorical style of the Second Wave feminists, this type of story provides "affirmation of the affective, or the validity of personal experience, of the necessity for self-exposure and self-criticism, and the goal of autonomous, individual decision-making."[18] That this form would come to predominate the style of men's rights activism is not entirely surprising given the movement's early cooperation with feminist organizations. Male liberation retained some of the stylistic elements of consciousness-raising yet began placing such a premium on the male mystique that it became a tool for preserving men's structural advantages. So although there is a clear homology between these two forms of discourse, the men's rights movement's appropriation of a feminist style ultimately transforms rhetoric about men's suffering into a mythology of reverse discrimination and innocent victimhood.

This common narrative praises the death of the "blue pilled" male and the rebirth of a new mythic male consciousness that is ready to enlist in the struggle against victimhood and emasculation. Yet, the achievements of men's liberation come at a significant cost—for men in particular. While men's subjugation seems to be a given, this narrative portrait of the new male is also invested in his own self-subjugation in line with the imperatives of late capitalism. The male self becomes a project of constant self-improvement. Freed from women's control—and in some cases women entirely—this new man will be free to invest his productive energies in generating wealth and advancing civilizational progress. It is here that we see the concept of men's liberation captured by the death drive and made to generate surplus repression in the name of capital. In Kellner and Pierce's words, this liberated subject is "free" to sublimate his erotic energies "toward greed, violence, aggression, and emotional satiation that re-produces the repressive social order."[19] In other words, the Red Pill narrative ultimately asks its audience to invest in the very mechanisms of the social repression that keep men alienated from one another and preoccupied with trauma. While it stokes fantasies of independence, wealth, and sexual gratification on demand, networked masculinity is also dehumanizing, deeply cynical, and devoid of all emotional bonds.

FORM AND GENRE IN THE MANOSPHERE

As discussed in the introductory chapter, form predicates not only the kind of content that populates men's networked media but also the kinds of thoughts, behaviors, and emotions that users are expected to mimic. Like form, genres also emerge as recognizable patterns of discourse in the public imaginary whose recurring commonalities condition audience expectations. Hence, I am concerned with the shared internal dynamic that structures men's rights rhetoric even where the content seems to be in tension. In this sense, the narrative form of networked men's rights rhetoric courts particular audience expectations and investments through patterned repetitions of an overarching drama. The narrative structure of men's rights rhetoric foregrounds how individual men's participation in networked media is tied to the fulfillment of a larger paradigm shift that will agitate and unsettle men to resist their oppression by women. This narrative pivots on whether adherents can successfully shock the conscience of their ideal audience. On a more granular level, men's rights rhetoric privileges personal melodrama wherein one awakens to the reality of their suffering and finds their place in an epic struggle between good and evil.

To understand the narrative structure of networked men's rights rhetoric, the remainder of this chapter will address each of the four elements that compose the melodrama of the Red Pill awakening. This story begins with an illusory reality imposed by women that structures male adherence to a false consciousness. Next, the narrative transitions to rising action when subjugated men are availed of the Real and concludes with liberated men assimilating into a collective resistance that will restore the traditional gender order. Like political melodrama, the Red Pill features men, in Anker's words, "as both the feminized, virginal victim and the aggressive, masculinized hero in the story of freedom."[20] To embrace the Red Pill is also to turn one's self into a project: learning and practicing the art and science of "gaming" women for sex, recoding one's mind to be invulnerable to women, and expelling women's power and influence from one's life. Patterning one's life after this narrative purports to channel desire into a lifestyle politics that is devoid of Eros and preoccupied with the will-to-power. Although there are hundreds if not thousands of men's rights blogs, websites, and subreddits, I select representative examples from popular portals such as A Voice for Men, Men Going Their Own Way, Return of Kings, and The Rational Male as well as subreddits such as r/TheRedPill and r/MensRights to substantiate my claims about the structure and function of the movement's narrative. To be sure, there are a variety of other websites, platforms, portals, and digital practices (meming, shitposting, trolling) that one could examine to explain the internal dynamics of men's rights rhetoric in networked media. For heuristic reasons, I confine my examination to the recursive narrative elements that are expressed and enacted on the most widely accessible and trafficked nodes of the manosphere.

Networked men's rights rhetoric begins with the premise that there exists something that resembles the Lacanian concept of the Real: a material reality that is external to discourse and independent of our perceptions. While Lacan argued that our access to the Real is never unmediated even though it influences reality (hence, we necessarily fail to represent the Real within the Symbolic), Red Pill advocates opt for a more theatrical and pseudoscientific impression of the concept in which it is possible—though exceedingly difficult—to pierce the veil between the simulation of reality and the Real. To build this aspect of their narrative, they borrow their theory of consciousness from the 1999 film *The Matrix*. In that film, the protagonist (Neo) is forced to make a choice between living in a reality simulated by artificial intelligence (represented by a Blue Pill) or the actual conditions that exist outside the simulation—an apocalyptic hellscape where machines harvest human beings for energy (the Red Pill). For men's rights advocates, the Blue Pill signifies the illusory reality of both men and women who are unaware that their perceptions of the world are mediated by a cruel feminist ideology. For instance, the r/TheRedPill welcome page for newcomers argues that "men who are still growing up—from the 80s, 90s, and even the last decade, they're starting to realize that what their parents taught them, what television and chick flicks taught them, what church and sunday [*sic*] school taught them . . . it's all wrong."[21] A similar post on www.marriedmansexlife.com argues, "You've been fed the Blue Pill from birth and you've never had a proper chance to win at love because you've been told the lie about how the game is played."[22] In other words, the Blue Pill signifies the narcotized state of contemporary men, their unthinking adherence to feminine dominance—not merely in dating and relationships, but in all aspects of personal, social, and political life. "Grasping the truth about women and sex is one thing," as one Reddit user suggests; "there are many, many Blue Pills in life, and nobody's going to make a discussion group for each and every one."[23] Blue Pill men, as it were, go along with their social conditioning and capitulate to the rules of an invisible infrastructure that is exploitative of men's courtesy, worshipfulness, and backbreaking labor.

Red Pill theory also suggests that women's biological programming has been overridden by feminism and that its emphasis on empowerment actually conceals its underlying motive to exploit men. The theory suggests that women ultimately desire to be dominated and confined to their traditionally assigned role as wives and mothers. Leaning heavily on evolutionary psychology, Red Pill forums and websites offer advice and tips on male sexual strategy in society organized around men catering to women. Some Red Pill proponents advocate pursuing women from foreign countries in regions such as Southeast Asia and Eastern Europe because they believe that such women are more submissive, sexually available, and adherent to traditional gender norms.[24] At the same time, the Red Pill offers a cynical social philosophy in which feminism is toxic, rape and sexual discrimination are myths, and men's victimization is to women's advantage. The Red Pill represents more than just an opportunity for men to improve their sex lives; it is a misogynist political worldview that offers women no quarter.

A vast majority of men remain indoctrinated by the Blue Pill; yet, like Neo, the men who make their way to the Red Pill narrative do so because they harbor suspicions that the system is rigged against them; that the norms of courtship implicitly favor women; that women do not have to work as hard as men for the same privileges; that feminism is not about equality but domination; and that society is indifferent to men's suffering. Part of what might attract and awaken a potential adherent is a traumatic experience, typically humiliating encounters with women. A commentator on *The Rational Male* blog surmised that "the most common way men find the Red Pill community is via an experience like this. Unfortunately, it often requires a significant life trauma to shake the sleeping awake, but having your outlook on intersexual dynamics challenged is the only way most men will ever be open to anything contradictory."[25] For the Red Pill community, the traumatic encounter represents a glitch in the Matrix, so to speak, a crack in the seams in which the system avails exploited men of its totality. They argue that the shock of seeing the system at work opens Blue-Pilled or so-called beta males to a previously unperceived reality.[26] As one Reddit user puts it, "part of the reason we enjoy the *Jerry Springer Show* type posts where we see the naked behavior of women exposed for all to view it [sic] that it SHOCKS our system in such a way as to become enlightened . . . What is needed to wake up the beta is some 'glitch' in the Blue Pill Matrix where the mythology that says '*Women can do no wrong*' is exposed as pure brainwashing, a pure mythology."[27] Later in the same thread, another user argues that rational argument is pointless because it neither shocks nor uplifts the audience. Defending the use of extremes and hyperbole, the user writes that "whenever we tried to exercise the moderate position, men never got the message. It didn't stick, because it failed to vindicate and uplift. It only demanded more mental resources that our visitors had to spare. Remember, we are emotional creatures first and rational creatures second. We cannot think effectively when we are wounded. The men that we have the potential to help come here because they are hurting."[28] Here we see how moderation is cast as a co-optive tactic that works within the framework of the Blue Pill, a perspective that largely negates men's pain and suffering. The Red Pill, however, retains a powerful charge because it vindicates men's feelings while explicitly alienating its opponents. Although Red Pill advocates offer a therapeutic response to loss, its imagined subject would nonetheless retain its melancholic attachment to his wounds as an engine for the constant remaking and improvement of the self.

By shocking its audience, the Red Pill both consummates male identity and intentionally repulses skeptics, casual observers, and half-hearted supporters (what adherents dismissively call the "Purple Pill"). One contributor concludes by explaining how they have built a networked community in which "the Red Pill [is] too toxic for the uninitiated to inhabit."[29] Moreover, the user's comments suggest that men cannot see themselves as being capable of exercising agency outside of their Blue Pill programming until their feelings are vindicated and their wounds are tended. Unfortunately, Red Pill theory posits that betas ostensibly suffer from *false consciousness*: they identify with an oppressor class with whom they have no interest in common. Absent some form of shock or trauma, dissonant assault on their senses, or tough love, betas will remain incapable of perceiving and naming their exploitation. The so-called toxic climate of the manosphere is, by design, directed at affirming the in-group's experience and expelling their tormentors from their networks. This part of the narrative gives concrete form to the audience's inchoate sense of alienation. They suffer because they have been conditioned to accept their programming; and while that suffering may be personal, it is connected to a set of broader sociopolitical arrangements. Suffering, however, is an opportunity for self-improvement. The narrative acknowledges that men are emotional and, consequently, require personal affirmation to see that their suffering is at once productive and not their fault. There are much bigger forces at work.

At the same time, the narrative also acknowledges that men must be willing to swallow some hard truths before they are availed of the true state of the human condition. Taking the Red Pill is presented as a journey from which there is no return. As one men's website puts it, "The Red Pill is the truth . . . you can't unlearn the truth. Some of it is going to sting . . . Your life will change forever as you see the true nature of how men and women interact and everything will look almost scripted. The good news is that once you know the tune, the dance is easy to do."[30] Using a metaphor from *Alice in Wonderland,* a blogger on the *Return of Kings* suggests that "Taking the red pill often leads us to realizations we'd rather not have to face as awakened men continuing our journey *down the rabbit hole* of reality. Rather than running away from those unpleasant truths about women and the world, we face them. This is the essence of science and masculinity— openness to new ideas and ruthless scrutiny of old ideas, leaving emotional considerations aside."[31] The Red Pill is also characterized as a form of debunking that "shows us that The System is ruthless, it will do anything to keep the wheel spinning."[32] Taking the Red Pill signifies an individual willingness to be awakened to this bleak reality—a kind of arresting shock to the conscience that precedes men's enlistment in collective resistance.

But to what truth are men to awaken? *A Voice for Men*'s Tom Givens explains the harsh reality of men's existence under feminism:

> How did feminism become the vehicle for this destructive principle, and was it always so? The answer is yes, it was always so, since female supremacy and social "deconstruction" is at the very heart of feminism. In point of fact, Feminist writers openly stated their plan to "deconstruct" (Orwellian doublespeak for "destroy") society in the 60's and 70's. They also openly advocated for Gendercide (some feminist musicians still do), the internment of men for purposes of slavery and breeding, and other means of "smashing the Patriarchy" and installing women in the seats of power.[33]

Across the manosphere, the ubiquity of this kind of bombastic claim helps suture threads about "game," dating, and seduction to the broader sociopolitical agenda of the men's rights movement. In short, the Red Pill politicizes men's personal woes. Advocates suggest that the Red Pill is merely a counterpoint to feminism that offers men a pathway to both personal self-improvement and political affirmation. Proponents assert the necessity of Red Pill theory because it is the only unabashedly male-affirming discourse in a culture without positive representations of men. And though the Red Pill may be difficult to swallow, it putatively avails men of the lie of their own social conditioning and prepares them to turn the tables on women. Although difficult to accept, proponents argue that men who choose the Red Pill have little to lose in the prevailing climate of misandry. For instance, the website *Illitable Men* characterizes the Red Pill as "cutting through all the bullshit fed to men to keep them docile," and "fill[ing] that void" where "boys and men alike are led astray."[34] It is here that we can observe how the Red Pill narrative becomes patterned after the rhetoric of contemporary feminism. However, the narrative borrows the language of feminism without drawing equivalences because, after all, men's rights putatively asks for equality where feminism seeks domination.

Once one is thoroughly enmeshed in the Red Pill network, there a variety of pathways they can follow—all of which, in one way or another, contribute to the burgeoning transformation in cultural mythology. For men on sites such *Voice for Men* and r/MenRights, taking the Red Pill channels the user's rage into concrete political action.[35] For example, Elam compares the new men's rights activism to the 1960s civil rights movement:

> Social change doesn't happen because a majority wants it. Social change happens because a minority of people recognize an injustice and make noise until it starts getting fixed, if they have the truth on their side. This was true with the civil rights movement, it certainly wasn't every African American in the United States that was hitting the streets and protesting in the '60s. It was enough to burn Watts and Detroit and there was enough to get on cameras and get people's attention and refuse to back down from water cannons and police dogs and all other manner of brutality and oppression to get them to shut up. But they got the message through and things have begun to change quite a bit.[36]

Again, this statement illustrates how men's rights activists seek to craft an image of their struggle as consonant with other historic movements for gender and racial justice. This line of argument suggests that white men too have faced brutal oppression, and, consequently, that violent resistance is not only a likely outcome but a reasonable one at that. In accordance with the conventions of melodrama, men are both feminized victims and masculinized heroes. He portrays men as a valorous minority group, heroically standing up for truth and justice even in the face of harsh retribution from the state. The narrative puts men's misplaced anger to good use, rising to a crescendo of justified rebellion.

Elam's version of the Red Pill speaks to some very specific social harms and policies at which his followers may direct their animus. *A Voice for Men* is less interested in the politics of dating than in other nodal points in the men's rights network, dedicating significantly more space to topics such as male suicide, inequality in family courts, and false rape accusations. While the site advances its own form of cultural mythology, *A Voice for Men* completes the Red Pill's narrative with a concrete message of radical social reform, "to provide education and encouragement to men and boys; to lift them above the din of misandry, to reject the unhealthy demands of gynocentrism in all its forms, and to promote their mental, physical and financial well-being without compromise or apology."[37] Elam's version of the Red Pill is structured less around mythology—though that does play a role—than around creating social change and overcoming victimization through petitioning, direct action protests, education, and civil disobedience.

For those drawn to the Red Pill by their frustration with dating and relationships, the narrative ends with men re-establishing the rules of the "game" and recapturing sexual and relational dominance from women. The Red Pill subreddit introduces newly conscious devotees to a tactical war against a competing sexual strategy: feminism. The site reads, "it [feminism] puts women into the best position they can find, to select mates, to determine when they want to switch mates, to locate the best dna [sic] possible, and to garner the most resources they can individually achieve. The Red Pill is men's sexual strategy."[38] The discussion threads largely direct their user's rage into personal rather than political transformation. Here, the anger and toxicity woven throughout the site is designed to repel the uninitiated and to create the conditions for users to unlearn feminist doctrine and come to accept the immutable laws of sexual attraction. Drawing an analogy to the five stages of grief (denial, anger, bargaining, depression, and acceptance), one moderator explains, "If we really want to understand what gets written here, in its proper context, we need to understand that most 'Red Pill Theory' posts will belong to one of these five stages. *Each stage has value,* because to reach a later one, you must go through the earlier ones. And, as in grieving, the progress through is seldom linear, smooth, uniform, and one-directional."[39] One of the discussion rules prohibits "concern trolling," or user responses that try to moderate anger or express trepidation about a conversation's tone. In part, this rule is designed to allow users to experience each stage in the process, no matter how painful or misguided. The suffering of overwhelmed victims is required to inevitably reach the final stage of acceptance. The Red Pill narrative posits that anger is a necessary part of the process of personal empowerment. As one user summarizes, "anger isn't just expected, it's encouraged—not because we want this to be the final stage in waking up, but because there's simply no other place that men are welcome with this rage. The anger will subside, and out of it: hopefully a constructive philosophy towards a better us and a better future."[40]

Ultimately, this version of the Red Pill narrative is more therapeutic than political. Through self-care, self-improvement, consciousness-raising, and taking responsibility for one's own happiness, adherents can find, in one user's words, "unbridled power & [*sic*] enlightenment."[41] This version sees the self rather than society as a project—though certainly proponents would argue that society would be better off as well. Exchanging the putatively self-serving feminist myths of romantic love for the cold reality of evolutionary psychology, the objective of the Red Pill is for men to rebuild their psyches and bodies in accordance with the rules of the game. The community considers "game" to be amoral or a neutral tool of pursuing happiness based not on ideology but on empirical observations of human nature. The community's construction of the instincts seems to privilege the id's drive for immediate gratification. That is to say that in the name of putting men in touch with their baser instincts, the Red Pill plays its part in the capitalist project of repressive desublimation. "Game" does not represent the liberation of Eros but instead a conduit to a better and more productive version of the self. Sex desacralized can be thought of as simply another consumable—a form of gratification pursued with speed and in quantity. At the stage of acceptance, followers have learned how to be emotionally detached with women, to approach sex and relationships as practices governed by instincts, and to act only in their enlightened self-interest. As such, the Red Pill narrative stokes fantasies of total self-mastery, power, wealth, and invulnerability to women.

A more exemplary vision of surplus repression can be found in the uptake of the Red Pill offered by Men Going Their Own Way. MGTOW is a separatist offshoot of the larger Red Pill community that focuses on achieving emotional, physical, and financial independence from women. Those who identify with this label seek to extract themselves from all relationships with women as a strategy for living "in nations dominated by feminist laws and institutions."[42] For this community, consciousness-raising entails a radical embrace of personal self-interests over the needs and interests of women. Using hashtags such as #icethemout and #walkaway, MGTOW forums are populated with the personal narratives of men attempting to sever their relationships with women. While there are some overlapping themes shared in common with incel groups, MGTOW do not ascribe to the fatalistic notion that success or failure is predetermined by genetic advantages and disadvantages. In their version of the narrative, men's purpose is to conquer the instincts by channeling their libidinal energies into self-improvement and technological discoveries. They also prompt their audience to dispense with feminist doctrines that keep men distracted from their ultimate purpose. Their version of the Red Pill narrative, then, concludes with men "walking away" from women altogether and channeling their energies into productive pursuits of historical consequence. Sex is to be pursued only as a release or for the purpose of reproduction, not as an end in and of itself.

The group places a premium of "male sovereignty," or the complete ownership of the self. According to their central hub, MGTOW is "a statement of self-ownership, where the modern man preserves and protects his own sovereignty above all else."[43] They claim a noble ancestry of great men who had forsaken women for the common good of civilizational advancement. They assert that the movement reaches "way back to Schopenhauer, Tesla, Beethoven, Galileo, or even Jesus Christ—if you're up to arguing that. MGTOW is not as old as fire, but it's as old as a man's first discovery of it."[44] The group not only attempts to redefine success away from sex, marriage, and children, but also suggests that the pursuit of these goals is antithetical to scientific progress.

The site argues that "marriage and children are not the highest pin-
nacle of success for Men . . . For millennia, men have accomplished
and contributed far greater miracles of science, discovery and human
endeavor."[45] The MGTOW history page is populated with antimar-
riage quotes from famous male scientists and inventors, such as Nikola
Tesla, Wilbur Wright, Isaac Newton, and Galileo. They contend that
women take for granted, and therefore should not be entitled to, the
great inventions, scientific discoveries, and risks ventured by men. For
example, the site explains that "Men are no longer revered or respected
on a most basic level for their contributions and past sacrifices, and
are now reduced to 'idiots' for that. The recent cultural explosion of
MGTOW should have long been expected in the face of this kind of
nonsense which is force-fed to the sheeple [*sic*] who will buy it by the
trough. *Men Going Their Own Way* have now learned and adapted."[46]
The sovereign man, then, refuses to alienate himself from his labor by
sharing its benefits with women. In other words, "he shows his value by
removing himself entirely."[47]

Although some nodes in the Red Pill network explain MGTOW
as simply a phase in the process of unlearning feminist coding, many
MGTOW advocates see abandoning the pursuit and accommodation of
women as the final step. Like many other Red Pill communities, they
ascribe to the theory that women are evolutionarily programmed to
engage in "hypergamy," meaning that they are always looking for ways
to mate with a man of higher status than their current relationship.[48]
While users on r/TheRedPill seek to use this theory to their advantage
in sexual strategy, MGTOW contend that any encounter with women
puts a man's earning potential, self-worth, and sovereignty at risk. For
some, even sex without commitment or a relationship might undermine men's ability to nurture their careers, improve their happiness,
and build their personal wealth. This conclusion to the Red Pill narrative invites the audience to invest their libidinal energies in productive pursuits that are necessary for personal success and fulfillment in
capitalist society. MGTOW rhetoric implicitly endorses a form of social
organization that is premised on sublimating the pleasure principle
into the *performance principle* by repressing erotic energies and channeling them into alienated labor. In Marcuse's words, the performance
principle is "the violent and exploitative productivity which made
man into an instrument of labor."[49] While they promise authenticity

and happiness, neither outcome exists independently of capitalism. In this regard, MGTOW imagines a future in which men can be *hyper*productive precisely because they are the sole instrument of civilizational progress. Ironically, liberated men are then "free" to pursue constant self-improvement in the name of happiness and independence. This is not to deny that men who ascribe to MGTOW express feelings of empowerment, but instead to argue that the community's definition of empowerment is nonetheless invested in the alienated labor that sustains advanced industrial capitalism and the compulsive repetition that underwrites the death drive. In other words, MGTOW seek an escape from women's domination by investing in the illusory liberatory promise of the Protestant work ethic.

RED PILL MEN, BLUE PILL WORLD

Ultimately, what unites all these various strands of the Red Pill narrative is a formal structure that moves unidirectionally from false consciousness to enlightenment; from victimhood to empowerment. All agree that most men live in an illusory reality that disadvantages them in everything from their pursuit of sex and relationships to how they navigating structurally biased political institutions. Moreover, they argue that Blue-Pilled men are incapable of seeing that they share no interest in common with their oppressor. Introduction to Red Pill theory avails men of the brutal condition of their existence, which in turn engenders rage and indignation. The narrative concludes with promises of wholeness: a sexual strategy that guarantees power and invulnerability, a political platform that returns us to a time in which men were valued, or a collective project of technological innovation and personal prosperity. As a network composed of diverse content, the Red Pill is elastic enough to capture and aggregate the felt intensities of a wide demographic of men. As such, a white male subject looking for a place, purpose, or affirmation of their identity can choose which specific iteration of the same narrative speaks directly to their experience. In this way, the manosphere unites men of diverse ages and political affiliations in a millennial project of remaking society. At the same time, the underlying appeal of these sites cannot be read outside of the politics of white male victimhood. While the Red Pill makes few race-specific appeals, the narrative does speak to an imagined audience that feels marginalized despite their entitlements, desires a collective identity that privileges masculinity over all other categories, and ascribes to political beliefs that skew toward the conservative and/or libertarian side of the spectrum.

This chapter demonstrates that audience enjoyment of the Red Pill narrative is predicated on a network that repeats one metanarrative that translates victimhood into a both a sense of mastery and a legible political platform. Put another way, both the form and narrative structure of the manosphere mirrors itself after the emotional and cognitive states ideally experienced by the converted: powerlessness, sadness, and rage followed by confidence, conviction, and self-possession. Audiences are invited to traverse the stages of consciousness and, in doing so, to enact their agency in such a way as to make the narrative a self-fulfilling prophecy. The narrative leads its audience through a cathartic experience of consciousness-raising that validates their personal experience and connects like-minded men in a collective project of empowerment. The Red Pill retains a powerful charge because it invites individuals to write themselves into the story, to consummate their identity by joining the collective organism of the movement—the "men who sit at screen." In doing so, masculinity is reborn when it enters networked media. Yet, however therapeutic the message may seem, the Red Pill expresses a melancholic attachment to trauma as the underlying engine of personal and political transformation.

In sum, the Red Pill appropriates consciousness-raising, victimhood, and melodrama as instruments of male power. Despite the Red Pill's promise of enlightenment and redemption, adherents may not end up any better off. In the context of late capitalism, self-improvement projects align with the broader social and economic forces that invite us to invest in being more productive subjects. Even our personal tragedies are fodder for continual self-improvement. Like other "ideological manipulation(s) of human suffering," the Red Pill externalizes the suffering and loss that constitute the melancholic subject.[50] The Red Pill is no different from other projects that capitalize on human suffering and loneliness with magical promises of power and enlightenment. Its various iterations invite men to view sex as a commodity, to pursue lost objects with futility, to channel libidinal energies into wealth creation and scientific innovation, and to return to the archetypes of the self-made man. All these iterations of masculinity reduce intimate relationships to transactions that are subject to the ruthless laws of both nature and the marketplace. Red Pill masculinity promises something that it cannot deliver: *to make the subject whole.* Its fantasies of invulnerability and sovereignty merely underwrite a compulsive return to an imagined period in the past in which men's biological superiority was not usurped by feminine programming. In this cross-section of the manosphere, sex and intimacy are folded into the imperatives of late capitalism to turn the self into a project of constant self-improvement, to divest from relationships and interpersonal solidarity, and to worship power and dominance. Unfortunately, the Red Pill has little to say about this bleak reality.

CHAPTER 3

Incel Rebellion

Fascism and Male Autarky

ON MAY 23, 2014, Santa Barbara college student Elliot Rodger murdered seven and injured fourteen people before taking his own life in Isla Vista, California. Before his murderous rampage, Rodger uploaded a video to YouTube entitled "Elliot Rodger's Retribution," in which he sketched his plan to punish women who spurned his sexual advances and so-called alpha males he despised for their ability to readily find sexual partners. Rodger also emailed an autobiographical manifesto to friends and family titled "My Twisted World: The Elliot Rodger Story," in which he expressed his sexual frustration and violent hatred of women and racial minorities. Rodger's account of his life mirrors that of a growing online community of involuntary celibates ("incels"), composed largely of white men who express difficulty finding sexual partners and blame women and people of color for a state of national degeneracy. To some who populate incel websites, Rodger is considered a martyr for crafting a template for paramilitary resistance to women's sexual liberation and racial cuckolding. In response to Rodger's violent rampage, a blogger for the incel website www.loveshy.com wrote:

What happened is punishment for evil and violence of feminists and liberals. Any of you supporting atrocities like women's suffrage, immodest clothing, child support/alimony, no ban on adultery, ban on prostitution and a lack of female premarital chastity, all the things that drove this young man to be unable to find a girlfriend, are disgusting, horrible people and you created a culture where this is possible.[1]

Rodger's "retribution" resonated with some white men's indignation that progressive movements toward gender equality have tilted the scales against men in every arena of public life.

In light of the previous chapter's examination of the Red Pill, it is perhaps not surprising that supporters echoed Rodger's claim that he was not culpable for his actions because feminism and sexual liberation struck the first blow. For instance, a poster on the r/TheRedPill responded to the attack: "Even without fixing modern women, legalized prostitution could easily prevent at least some of these killing sprees. The people of modern culture are stupid beyond help: they refuse to understand that if you kick a nice dog enough times, it will become a mean dog. No dog is entitled to even one bone, they say."[2] Other Reddit users praised Rodger's manifesto as a "good read" and "a Greek tragedy for the 21st century" that proved that "all women look for in a man in his face, is he hot or not."[3] Another contributor to a thread on r/unpopularopinion casually sympathized that "ER [Rodger] was an intelligent guy and his way of expressing himself was quite interesting. It is even evident in his YT [YouTube] video—the way his [sic] speaks." Other users went further by blaming the victims, writing that "females dont [sic] seek out intelligence as then he would not have went [sic] on a killing spree." While such toxic discourse could easily be dismissed as the idle words of anonymous internet trolls or bitter sexless men blowing off steam, the harsh invectives emanating from online incel communities have been cited by some as justifications for real-life violence. In April 2018, Alek Minassian killed ten and injured fourteen (mostly women) with a rental car in Toronto.[4] In a Facebook post prior to his murderous rampage, Minassian cited Rodger as a source of inspiration: "The Incel Rebellion has already begun! We will overthrow all the Chads and Stacys! All hail the Supreme Gentleman Elliot Rodger!"[5] In January 2019, Christopher Cleary was arrested for posting on his Facebook page that he was "planning on shooting up a public place soon and being the next mass shooter cause I'm ready to die and all the girls [that] turned me down is going to make it right by killing as many girls as I see."[6] Such fantasies of spectacular mass violence characterize the once-obscure "incel" as they begin to garner public attention, bringing with him an amalgam of perverse doctrines that circulate throughout men's networked media.

Rodger and his predecessors are the by-product of network circuitries that seamlessly shuttle users through subreddit threads, news aggregators, blogs, and social media sites that on the whole paint a bleak portrait of reality for distressed young men. The men's rights network connects young men's personal travails to larger structural and natural forces—culminating in a perverse mixture of evolutionary psychology, scientific racism and sexism, and nihilism. Rodger himself was a contributor to numerous incel conversations on sites such as PUAHate.com, ForeverAlone.com, and miscellaneous forums on BodyBuilding.com.[7] For instance, in April 2013, Rodger posted on PUAHate that "feminism must be destroyed. Humanity is devolving into primitive animals."[8] Elsewhere he posted, "that's the problem with women. They are attracted to the worst kinds of men. They all have some sort of mental illness."[9] In the threads in which he participated, users exchanged ill-informed and pseudoscientific viewpoints on physical attraction and women's psychology. The participants blamed feminism for their sexual frustration and loneliness—waxing nostalgic for a time in the past in which "beta males" were guaranteed marriage and, consequently, a stake in society. Users even expressed violent fantasies of enslavement and mass murder of women. Here we see that same themes that populate "My Twisted World": inborn dignity, male entitlement to sexually available women, fascistic fantasies of control and invulnerability.

Rodger's manifesto, and the violent misogyny that he put into practice, reflect how networked men's rights discourse seduces and recruits aggrieved men. "My Twisted World" offers yet another fantasy of power and invulnerability that rehearses the loss that is central to the melancholic subject. The impossibility of Rodger's preposterous fantasies speaks to some other investments and sense of enjoyment at work in his chilling vision of his "perfect" society. Incels argue that women should not be allowed to make choices concerning their bodies, love, sex, careers, and reproduction. According to incel websites, feminism disrupted natural laws governing courtship, the family, and sexual reproduction by giving women the power to make decisions about who to date, when (if at all) to marry and have children, and whether to pursue a career or other personal aspirations. As a consequence, this so-called unnatural order reserves sex and relationships for a privileged few (alphas) and an unfulfilling life of sexual rejection for most (incels). Adopting this tragic frame, Rodger and his supporters contend that white men's so-called persecution legitimizes spectacular acts of violent resistance against the evils of feminism. Incels are animated by narratives of white masculine victimhood and share a strong affinity with other men's rights organizations and members of the alt-right movement. As expected, then, they express virulent misogyny, decry the violation of their birthright entitlements, and fantasize about torture and mass murder.[10]

To be sure, Rodger's manifesto is a nauseating rumination on white male persecution. His 100,000-word poisonous diatribe sutures birthright nationalism and white male victimhood to what I will characterize as an implicitly fascistic ideology that entails a large-scale industrial project of sexual repression, and ultimately, femicide. Like other incels, Rodger extrapolates from his experience of sexual rejection an ill-informed theory of human nature underwritten by primal cruelty and a lay political ideology that seems vaguely informed by hypermasculine interpretations of Frederick Nietzsche's will-to-power as well as fascism's affinity for male autarky. This text emphasizes chaos and disorder alongside a deployment of tropes such as antimodernism and regeneration through violence. Perhaps not surprisingly, the manifesto is incoherent—vacillating between affection for women and fantasies of torture and femicide; self-pity and self-aggrandizement; fatalism and magical agentalism. Of course, contemporary white masculinity is strategically incoherent, and therefore able to disavow its hegemony via unintelligible claims of marginalization. Thus, while Rodger enjoyed a life of opulence and material privilege in the affluent community of Santa Barbara, he represented himself as a victim of both women and men whom he deemed inferior. Upon the eve of his violent rampage, Rodger wrote, "I am the true victim in all of this. I am the good guy. Humanity struck at me first by condemning me to experience so much

suffering. I didn't ask for this. I didn't want this. I didn't start this war
. . . I wasn't the one who struck first . . . But I will finish it by striking
back. I will punish everyone. And it will be beautiful. Finally, at long
last, I can show the world my true worth."[11]

Although there are an unfortunate number of mass shooters and
other white terrorists whom one could examine to understand the
interplay of masculinity, violence, and victimhood, Rodger's manifesto
perhaps best illustrates the relationship between white male victimhood and the compulsive repetition of the death drive. At its heart, the
manifesto expresses a fantasy of control that is predicated on recover-
ing a lost object. Rodger's toxic manifesto adds new layers to the public fantasy of male persecution by, quite ironically, appropriating from
Second Wave feminism the framework of the "personal as political."[12]
Rodger's intimate though prosaic confessions of a powerless life—
composed of recollections of perceived slights and petty injustices—
reframes white men's quotidian experiences of human vulnerability as
systemic structural oppression. "My Twisted World" proscribes spectacular, even unprecedented acts of gender violence, to return men to a
position of unquestioned authority and privilege. The text constructs a
dystopian society founded upon the uniform industrially orchestrated
mass subjugation of women and the eradication of the life instinct. The
text wallows in sadism to counteract women's sexual agency and writes
women out of the arc of progressive human equality.

Rodger's manifesto demands our attention not because it provides
insights into the psychology of misogynist mass murder, but because
it spells out conclusions that one can draw from their encounter with
the manosphere. The text is inseparable from the network circuitries
that cross-pollinate men's rights with white supremacy, scientific racism and sexism, fascism, homophobia, and other violent ideologies.
"My Twisted World" also remains enmeshed, analyzed, praised, and
rebuked within the same networks from which its content was, in part,
derived. Thus, the manifesto is evidence of how networked thought
processes have made possible new and dangerous forms of white male
subjectivity. The logics of the manifesto both reflect and concretize the
toxic miasma of networked ideas that attempt to constitute a unified
and invulnerable white cisgender heterosexual male subject. It is both
the product of networked men's rights rhetoric and a notable fragment
that remains entangled in those very networks.

Despite his preposterous demands for women's enslavement, racial eugenics, and autocratic omnipotence, I do not wish to gawk at what one could suggest is an extreme aberration of contemporary white masculinity. The text is remarkable not as a result of its incredible divergence from but because of its terrifying alignment with the broader corpus of men's rights rhetoric. Certainly, the ever-growing number of white male terrorists—Alek Minassian, Adam Lanza, James Holmes, Dylann Roof, Robert Lewis Dear, and Nikolas Cruz to name a few—suggests that manifestos such as Rodger's evince a rhetorical pattern of white masculine self-radicalization that constitutes the logical limit, perhaps even the event horizon of the politics of white male victimhood. Drawing from Kenneth Burke's approach to Adolf Hitler's *Mein Kampf* in Burke's essay "The Rhetoric of Hitler's Battle," I am not inclined to deprive such a ghoulish text of its necessary critical judgment. In other words, to dismiss this text is to deny us crucial insights concerning the rhetorical appeal of its dystopian vision. As Burke writes, "There are other ways of burning books than on the pyre—and the favorite method of the hasty reviewer is to deprive [themselves] and [their] readers by inattention."[13] It was Burke's hope that we might better understand "what kind of 'medicine' this medicine-man has concocted" if we are to "forestall the concocting of similar medicine in America."[14] We are at a point in which fascism, demagoguery, and radical populism continue to gain traction—and of which the rhetoric of white male victimhood has become a defining feature.[15] The ideals that can be extrapolated from Rodger's somewhat mundane life story can be characterized as fascistic, particularly his fantasies of eugenics, autocratic male rule, and biopolitical control of women and racial minorities in the name of civilizational progress.

In this chapter, I identify the patterned fascistic discourse that underlies white male victimhood.[16] This pattern begins with a fantasy of persecution brought on by an unnatural political and social order—frequently underwritten by a toxic feminism—that denies white men's "inborn dignity" and birthright entitlement to cultural and material capital, including access to social status, wealth, and sex.[17] Second, having been unjustly displaced, the white male victim disavows that hegemonic masculinity nonetheless structures the existing social and political order and calls for its restoration on a civilizational scale.

Even personal slights and the mundane struggles of everyday life can be interpreted as a form of systemic structural oppression—as if the vulnerability of human existence itself were somehow an experience of white male precarity. Third, any positive differential in enjoyment, privilege, or cultural capital that is experienced individually by women or people of color becomes evidence of a generalized deformed state of the human condition. This enables white men to politicize personal travails and scapegoat women and people of color for any perceived slight, however inconsequential. Finally, in rejecting the modernist notion that powers and privileges should be shared throughout the polity, white male victims align themselves with a fascistic politics that denies the humanity of those who have violated their inborn dignity. Confronted with the demands of historically marginalized groups to be afforded their humanity by universalizing democratic principles, fragile white masculinity turns toward apocalyptic fantasies of death and omnipotence to extinguish their cries.

Examining Rodger's digital manifesto, this chapter offers two primary insights into the relationship between white masculine victimhood and an underlying fascistic imperative that structures the new men's rights activism. First, Rodger's manifesto illustrates that white masculinity is organized around a fantasy of regeneration through violence; of male virility restored through a fascist doctrine of militarism and permanent revolution. Second, the manifesto reveals how white masculinity and fascistic ideologies are sutured together through evocative imagery of death, the macabre and the apocalyptic to negate the demands politics of women, queers, and people of color to be recognized as human. In short, theorizations of masculinity and contemporary fascism would benefit from an account of the sex/gender investments it engenders; namely, in a politics animated by domination, control, and death.

FASCISM AND MASCULINITY

A fascist politic is underwritten by a defense of a traditional concept of virile masculinity and staunch antimodernism. For instance, as Sandro Bellassai argues of Italian fascism, adherents emphasized the hierarchal relationship between the sexes and the natural imperative of women's subjugation.[18] German and Italian fascists' campaigns against urbanization were, in essence, directed at negating modernity's liberation of women's sexuality. Fascism in the West promulgates an exaggerated and even repellant vision of masculinity that liberates the bourgeois man from prohibitions against violence and grotesque idealizations of virility while aestheticizing the white male body as the reproductive engine of the race-nation.[19] In fascist discourse, the white male body is identified with order and progress. The "European species" is exalted as physically beautiful and morally superior to the feminine (which here references both the immutable inferiority of women and the sexual and racial inferiority of men of color).

Fascism is also organized around fantasies of control, domination, militarism, and the will-to-power. Daniel Woodley argues that "fascist propaganda is replete with references to virility, fertility, male invulnerability and superhuman power, suggesting an asymmetric differentiation between a masculine 'totality' and a feminine 'lack.'"[20] In as much as femininity represents a loss of power similar to the threat of castration, the fascist man is caught in a queer and uncanny relationship to the feminine. That is to say that while fascism idealizes women's fertility as a political imperative, it also identifies itself with the homosocial fantasy of male autarky in which men are both invulnerable to and independent of women. According to Barbara Spackman, fascism is largely a male event whose homoerotic charge promotes a "cognitive and ideological apartheid around homosexuality."[21] Yet, while fascism implicitly advances a dark, even gothic sense of queer world-making, homosexual desire must be sublimated in the interest of a virtuous masculinity capable of biological reproduction (and we see in Nazi Germany and fascist Italy the brutal repression and extermination of GLBTQ individuals). All desire, for that matter, must be sublimated to the will of the national good; a task which, according to Marcuse, is made easier by both the atomization of industrial production and the surplus repression generated under late capitalism.[22] One only need observe the chiseled male sculptures commissioned by Mussolini to understand the perversely queer futurity of male autarky.[23]

Fascism shares a strong affinity with feelings of victimhood and powerlessness.[24] Hence, as Kimmel argues, the "forgotten man" is frequently evoked as a warrant for a more expansive and reactionary political agenda that seeks to "restore, to retrieve, to reclaim something that is perceived to have been lost."[25] This political agenda is structured around profound felt intensities, that the "system" is somehow rigged against men and, thus, they have been denied the jobs, opportunities, enfranchisement, family tranquility, freedom, status, and sexual satisfaction to which they are entitled. In short, the *forgotten man* is angry, or at least he is told to feel that way. Of grave concern, anger is an emotion easily attached to reactionary political commitments. Underwritten by narratives of victimization, American neofascists direct much of their bile toward feminism and the liberal values and institutions that support gender equality.[26]

In this chapter, I focus on incels as a growing male community underwritten by fascist principles as well as a community where the sexual mandate of fascism is most clearly articulated. Last year Reddit removed the r/incel portal (which had approximately 40,000 users) because its content violated the site's updated policy against posts advocating or expressing support for violence.[27] Of course, there are many others including loveshy.com, incel.me, and PUAHate.com. As evidenced from Rodger's manifesto, incel communities trade in fantasies of domination, control, and sexual violence.[28] While some of the community's discourse is sometimes therapeutic and at other times pitiful, it is, by and large, saturated with sadism, nihilism, and cruelty. Fantasies run the gamut from banning public displays of affection, to killing women and sexually active alpha males (whom they refer to as "Chads"), to interning women in camps for procreative purposes and abolishing sex altogether. The message is: if *they* cannot have sex *no one can*. These fantasies implicitly take up Marcuse's concept of surplus repression as if it were a dystopian blueprint for establishing a sexual dictatorship—seeking to extinguish Eros and conquer the pleasure principle in the name of civilizational progress. And even as it negates homosexual desires, incel discourse cruises a queerly apocalyptic dystopia of male homosociality that is devoid of pleasure, of sexuality, and of course, women. Incel rhetoric intensifies the death drive of late capitalism by investing energy in toil, domination, and subjugation as an ironic form of liberation from sexual repression.

READING RODGER'S MANIFESTO

Rodger's manifesto is an excruciatingly detailed autobiographical account of his life, beginning with his earliest childhood memories. The text is subdivided into years; each a more ominous account of the factors that he believed contributed to his victimization, including details about his parent's divorce, bullying at school, rejection by girls, and alienation from his friends and family. Perhaps the most important meridian in the text is between a period of his life he classifies as "childhood innocence" and the onset of puberty and sexual development. He writes wistfully about pre-adolescence as "a time of discovery, excitement, and fun. I had just entered this new world, and I knew nothing of the pain it would bring me later on. I enjoyed life with innocent bliss." He continues, "I was enjoying life in a world that I loved. I was happy, and completely oblivious of the fact that my future on this world would only turn to darkness and misery because of girls."[29] The text's somewhat Christian division between grace and Fall identifies women with a secular form of original sin and Rodger with piety and Edenic innocence. While Rodger ruminates on the development of sexual urges and their lack of satisfaction, he frames sexuality (and women for that matter) as a flaw in human development that negates both pleasure and civilizational progress. In this traumatic narrative, it is this imagined period of presexual childhood innocence to which he would ultimately have us return. That is, in his dystopian vision of a future without sexuality—dispensing with the pleasure principle altogether—humanity would be free to channel their energies into discovery and progress. Perhaps the more important purpose for Rodger is to identify himself with innocence and progress in order to cast himself as either blameless or righteous in exacting revenge against his external tormentors. And while it might seem quite contradictory, his innocence is also corroborated by his appeals to an inborn dignity or birthright privilege to material and cultural capital.

Although the manifesto is extreme, it nonetheless carries out a familiar pattern of victimization, disavowal, purification, and re-established order. While much of the manifesto might remind readers of Burke's observations about guilt, victimage, and scapegoating, this chapter narrows the focus to the unique contours of white male victimhood; its recursive attachment to trauma and its related need to project death and repression onto others.[30] First, the manifesto evinces a specific pattern of white male self-radicalization that begins with recasting one's personal suffering as a structural manifestation of a corrupt and unnatural political order. Here, the subject ambivalently desires his own persecution, as it is the rationale for a return to the imagined moment when he was whole. Second, personal suffering becomes *political* suffering, and therefore serves as a diagnostic of a larger failure in the existing social order. This perhaps explains why the manuscript is extraordinarily tedious in documenting even the most trivial of slights and challenges. Rodger's account for each petty insult, confrontation, and dispute in his life mobilizes tedium as evidence of systematic pattern of victimization. As such, the manuscript is a ledger of petty personal slights reframed as political persecution. Yet, Rodger expressed an ambivalent desire for his own victimization, as its existence served as a warrant for regeneration through violence. Note the enthusiasm he expresses in his recounting of the most egregious of violations. In his recounting of rejection, he recalls, "I was giddy with ecstatic, hate-fueled excitement. I wished I could spray boiling oil at the foul beasts. They deserved to die horrible, painful deaths just for the crime of enjoying a better life than me."[31] The text expresses a perverse desire for meaningful suffering; the greater the ego is bruised, the greater enjoyment of retribution.

In politicizing personal suffering, the manuscript introduces a vile political order that wages war on men like himself. He begins his manifesto by stating:

Humanity . . . All of my suffering on this world has been at the hands of humanity, particularly women. It has made me realize just how brutal and twisted humanity is as a species. All I ever wanted was to fit in and live a happy life amongst humanity, but I was cast out and rejected, forced to endure an existence of loneliness and insignificance, all because the females of the human species were incapable of seeing the value in me. This is the story of how I, Elliot Rodger, came to be. This is the story of my entire life. It is a dark story of sadness, anger, and hatred. It is a story of a war against cruel injustice.[32]

Note that the context for his suffering is extraordinarily broad. For Rodger, these are species-level forces at work. As his suffering is "at the hands of humanity, women in particular"—as opposed to specific actors (family, friends, acquaintances)—the drama of his life can be cast as tragic and fatalistic. His use of the passive voice to explain how he "came to be" cedes agency to mysterious forces much larger than himself, thus exonerating his actions. It is an introduction to a melodrama in which the righteous suffering of innocent victims transforms them into avenging heroes.

Moreover, as the argument unfolds, his suffering evinces a kind of biological determinism to explain his actions as responses to forces outside his control. That is to say that Rodger's melodrama takes place within the brutal scene of the Hobbesian state of nature that is cruel, competitive, and chaotic. Oddly, Rodger constructs his identity in opposition to humanity, which, as discussed below, transforms into an expression of megalomania. To the point made here, this separation between humanity and his "war against cruel injustice" is grounded in his sense of inborn dignity. While he claims to be the victim of humanity, he also argues that he is vastly superior to the rest of the human race. After establishing this fact, he is able to name all small and seemingly unconnected assaults on his ego as part of the systematic war against him. Hence, he claims that "in this magnificent story, I will disclose every single detail about my life, every single significant experience that I have pulled from my superior memory, as well as how those experiences have shaped my views of the world. This tragedy did not have to happen."[33] Hence, his account of the rather boring details of his childhood and adolescence are supposed to reveal something more significant about the supposed nature of women and the unique quality of Rodger's character. Rodger's reference to his "superior memory" suggests that the manifesto is told by the omniscient and objective voice of a neutral outside observer. This reference authorizes him to connect unrelated events so that they might tell a coherent and linear story in which an objective voice gives greater meaning to personal struggles. And although the notion that this tragedy could have been avoided contradicts his assertions about human nature, this contention directs the audience's attention to the actions of others who supposedly *provoked* his violent rampage.

Rodger's inborn dignity would not be of such significance were there not enemies who had systematically denied Rodger his birthright: women and alpha males (particularly men of color). Thus, the next step in his narrative was to disavow that white masculinity affords men such as himself extraordinary social and material privileges. Instead, he contends that society is governed by the whims of cruel women and the select few alpha males whom they allow to experience sexual intimacy. For Rodger, women's cruelty is owed to women's connectedness to the natural world. Drawing from the long-standing cultural association between femininity and nature, Rodger constructs his feminized enemy as animalistic, primal, elemental, chaotic, and instinctual.[34] As he explains, "The world truly is a brutal place, where a man must fight a bitter struggle against all other men to reach the top. Humans are nothing but vicious beasts in the jungle."[35] Rodger, however, considered himself above the fray of primal instinct as a consequence of his superior European ancestry. Hence, his status as a refined "gentlemen" provides a stark contrast to the unrepressed expression of primal desires exemplified by women, alpha males, and racialized Others. In countering women's cruelty, Rodger described himself as not only a victim but a cultured man of civilization, noting, "I am the perfect, magnificent gentleman, worthy of having a beautiful girlfriend, making the world see how unreasonable it is that I've had to struggle all my life to get a girlfriend."[36]

However, much like the cultural mythology of the frontiersman, it is the burden of the Euro-American gentleman to subdue nature and contend with the chaotic forces of the natural world.[37] Thus, despite his Asian ancestry, Rodger identifies with what he characterizes as his royal European blood in contradistinction to hypersexualized men of color. He contends:

How could an inferior, ugly black boy be able to get a white girl and not me? I am beautiful, and I half white myself. I am descended from British aristocracy. He is descended from slaves. I deserve it more. I tried not to believe his foul words, but they were already said, and it was hard to erase from my mind. If this is actually true, if this ugly black filth was able to have sex with a blonde white girl at the age of thirteen while I've had to suffer virginity all my life, then this just proves how ridiculous the female.[38]

For Rodger, women, being of nature, gravitate toward the savage and inferior masculinity of men of color and so-called alphas. He writes, "That is why they are attracted to barbaric, wild, beast-like men. They are beasts themselves. Beasts should not be able to have any rights in a civilized society. If their wickedness is not contained, the whole of humanity will be held back from advancement to a more civilized state."[39] The stakes of his struggle are no less than the advancement of humanity, achievable by the repression of the instincts and the subjugation of femininity. For Rodger, it is the duty of "gentlemen" such as himself to lead the return to civilized virtue, by violence if necessary.

By positioning himself as a gentleman, Rodger recalls a Victorian-era masculinity characterized by restraint of the passions, self-mastery and self-denial.[40] Moreover, he recasts the hypersexuality of the alpha male as a sign of effeminacy, much in the way that the Euro-America legitimized violence against American Indians and Black slaves.[41] At the same time, women and people of color are also strong, cunning, and physically threatening. It should come as no surprise, then, that Rodger later goes on to both defend racial eugenics and rail against miscegenation and the threat of Black and Latino sexuality. The manifesto contends that it is the gentleman's imperative to subdue the brutal forces of the natural world, even if that requires that they temporarily lift their prohibition against violence. The text thus contrasts Rodger's purported attainment of civilized virtue against the degeneracy of women and people of color. Rodger also inverts existing social hierarchies to characterize women and people of color as the perpetrators of violence against incels.

Building from this inversion, the manifesto illustrates a third feature of white male victimhood in which recognizing the humanity of women and people of color necessarily comes at the expense of white men's dignity. In the rhetoric of white male victimhood, all social gains are portrayed as zero-sum. Yet Rodger contends that liberalism pretends that this is not the case and, therefore, ignores the boundary conditions of the state of nature. In other words, the notion that women are rights-bearing subjects with bodily autonomy contravenes higher natural and divine principles that mandate their subjugation in the name of the family and civilizational progress. Although such a vile text makes no claim to ideological consistency, Rodger's defense of repression and women's subjugation in the name of civilization is quite contradictory. On the one hand, he seems to believe that men such as himself are entitled to sex by virtue of the natural order. He routinely pauses in his personal accounts to ask questions like "Why do they give their love and sex to other men, but not me, even though I deserve them more?"[42] and "Other men are able to have such a life . . . so why not me? I deserve it!"[43] Rodger freely admits his desires. On the other hand, the same natural order that underwrites Rodger's entitlement also grounds the cruelty of women and the degeneracy of inferior men. For instance, he writes that "if women had the freedom to choose which men to mate with, like they do today, they would breed with stupid, degenerate men, which would only produce stupid, degenerate offspring. This in turn would hinder the advancement of humanity."[44] To work through this contradiction, albeit unsuccessfully, Rodger ostensibly charges modernity with abandoning its pursuit of repression and, therefore, allowing nature to conquer culture. As an extension of modern individualism, women's sexual freedom precludes the masculine imperative to make nature conform to order. While nature anoints men rulers of their dominion, it does so under the condition that nature also be subdued in the name of civilization. Hence, Rodger reads women's sexual freedom as a chaotic harbinger of death and oppression or, in his words, "a plague that must be quarantined."[45]

But Rodger's claim to inborn dignity is rooted in neither nature nor modernity but in the dark spiritual recesses of the fascist imagination. That is to say that Rodger imagines the existence of a parallel natural order that has to date been precluded by the corrupt rise of liberalism, an ideology which holds the possibility that women should be seen as rights-bearing subjects. Here, modernity has veered away from the virtues of order and hierarchy, to which Rodger owes the totality of civilizational progress. Thus, toward the end his manuscript, Rodger sketches a dystopian fantasy of totalitarian control and the rigid subjugation of the natural instincts. Here he expresses devotion to a divinely ordained natural order, though his beliefs cannot be characterized as Judeo-Christian. Instead, Rodger's devotion is directed toward a spiritual sense of the will-to-power in which the civilized Übermensch embodies the characteristics of a god. He claims "I am like a god, and my purpose is to exact ultimate Retribution on all of the impurities I see in the world."[46] His references to transcendence and purification legitimize and give divine mandate to violence in the process of perfecting the natural order. Modernity is constructed as the enemy of civilizational progress, as it grants license to women and people of color to love and have sex with whomever they wish. Thus, hierarchy and order must be imposed to correct for the unnatural order conjured by the defenders of liberalism.

In searching for these hidden divine laws, Rodger's expressions of megalomania help reframe his impotence as omnipotence. Put differently, Rodger imagines a new social order that turns the tables in recognition that the rights of others are an affront to the spirit of white masculinity. The fantasy is apocalyptic and entails the punishment of the wicked with extraordinary cruelty in order to consummate a new millennial order. His victimization is thus not a consequence of his inferiority or weakness, but instead the failure of a cruel and hedonistic world to recognize his likeness to God. He suggests that his victimization proves his superiority. In one passage I wish to quote at length, Rodger observes that his rejection from society legitimizes his megalomania:

> I am not part of the human race. Humanity has rejected me. The females of the human species have never wanted to mate with me, so how could I possibly consider myself part of humanity? Humanity has never accepted me among them, and now I know why. I am more than human. I am superior to them all. I am Elliot Rodger . . . Magnificent, glorious, supreme, eminent . . . Divine! I am the closest thing there is to a living god. Humanity is a disgusting, depraved, and evil species. It is my purpose to punish them all. I will purify the world of everything that is wrong with it. On the Day of Retribution, I will truly be a powerful god, punishing everyone I deem to be impure and depraved.[47]

As this passage conveys, the manifesto is saturated with delusions of grandeur and expressions of entitlement, mythic superiority, destiny, and greatness. More importantly, violence against those who would deny his pre-eminence served as a necessary and inevitable correction to an unjust social order. Imagining himself as God positions women and alpha males as wicked and thus deserved of punishment. He frames his retribution as an act of purification. As such, the text implicitly adopts features of the jeremiad, composed as a bitter invective against society's morals followed by a prophecy of impending doom.[48] As shown here, the more apocalyptic features of the text offers men such as Rodger a fantasy in which victimized white men are returned to their proper place atop the social hierarchy. At the same time, his fantasies of omnipotence and predestination also free Rodger from responsibility, ethics, and morality.

Rodger also couches his omnipotence in secular fantasies of wealth and social status. The manifesto goes on to argue that riches, fame, and sex were owed to him by virtue of birth. Throughout his life, Rodger claimed to have been draw to books and movies about people who rose to power after being treated unfairly. He recalled spending thousands of dollars playing the lottery in the hope that winning would transform him into an alpha male. He was drawn to the magical thinking of self-help books such as *The Secret* and played the lottery obsessively in order to fulfill his supposed destiny to be rich and powerful. He believed that a collection of cars and mansions would solve his problems.[49] Hence, his manifesto is latent with regal fantasies of control and power over those subjects who denied him that to which was entitled. He wrote that "I would use my powers to rule the world and set everything right" and "I deserve it, I am magnificent, no matter how much the world treated me otherwise." He continued, "I am the image of beauty and supremacy. I kept saying it over and over again, as if it was a mantra."[50] Moreover, he suggests, "I wanted to believe that I had the POWER to invoke this into my reality. I have craved power and significance all my life, and I will stop at nothing to find ways of attaining it."[51] Rodger understood wealth and power as birthrights; therefore, he possessed an inalienable right to attain them. Moreover, wealth and power are constructed as spiritual forces rewarded to the deserving.

But, if we take his account of life at his word, Rodger did little of anything to achieve that which he felt was his birthright. He wanted the attention of young women yet only expressed contempt, misogyny, and disrespect. Throughout the text he shows neither empathy nor emotional reciprocity, let alone feelings of friendship and comradery with women. He expressed a desire to be rich and powerful but communicated nothing but disdain for his studies and hard work—both of which he felt were beneath his station. In short, he did little to make himself attractive other than make superficial investments in illusions of success: cars, clothing, and get-rich-quick schemes.

It is curious that Rodger frames his revenge in such grandiose terms. Why imagine himself as God? Revisiting past traumas, this time as a god, undoubtedly helped domesticate the pain associated with remembrance. In narrative form, his traumatic memories are recast as meaningful suffering. Aside from the enjoyment of total control, this fantasy constitutes an attempt to reclaim the power he believed had been unfairly wielded against him by his tormentors. In planning his "Day of Retribution" he explains that "the tables will indeed turn . . . I will be a god, and they will all be animals that I can slaughter. They are animals . . . They behave like animals, and I will slaughter them like the animals they are."[52] The metaphor of "turning the tables" to describe such profane acts of violence belies the fact that white men not only continue to benefit from accrued structural advantages but also are the predominant perpetrators of sexual violence against women. Here we see how the mixture of inborn dignity, victimization, and scapegoating foments gendered fantasies of destruction and retribution. His writing ennobled the suffering and violence of white men as part of his metamorphosis.

Finally, the manifesto concludes with a dystopian vision of the future governed by eugenics and the industrially organized repression of the instincts. The incel community is fond of popular misinterpretations of evolutionary psychology to explain women's sexual behavior. Before the thread was deactivated, participants in r/incel devoted significant attention to genetic and evolutionary predispositions, including an obsession with chin size as the distinction between "Chads" (alphas) and "incels" among a number of other pseudoscientific laws of attraction.[53] While some theories are more outlandish than others, all seem to agree that genetics, and more importantly race, explain their sexual woes. Hence, the real injustice for Rodger was that he believed himself to be morally and genetically superior to nonwhite men who seemed to have no trouble finding love. In one of his many tirades against miscegenation, Rodger directs specific rage at dark-skinned men dating blonde white women. Despite his own racial lineage, Rodger recounts a moment in which he was humiliated by African American teenager. He goes on to make similar remarks about Latino and Asian men as well. Rodger summons the myth of the Black rapist and the deep culture ambivalence about Black male sexuality to legitimize his righteous indignation. For Rodger, Black and

Latino sexuality are animalistic and primal; far less refined than that of a white gentleman such as himself. Rodger suggests that white men have been cuckolded; emasculated and sexually humiliated by Black men sleeping with white women. Naturally, eugenic racism, a touchstone of European fascism, provided Rodger with additional warrants for his turn to violence. More importantly, his thoughts on eugenics, race, and sexuality led him toward a chilling vision of a repressive white male autocracy.

The manifesto concludes with elaborate torture fantasies—both concrete plans for this "day of retribution" as well as abstractions of a society governed by extraordinary cruelty toward women. His fantasies involved mass organized violence against so-called hedonistic scum, concentration camps populated with female chattel, and the abolition of sex.[54] I do not wish to wade through the details of how he believed such a "perfect civilization" could be enacted. Suffice it to say that the dissonance between his gleeful tone and his portrait of women's enslavement is a pre-eminent example of the kind of misogyny that underwrites sexual violence against women. Of greater rhetorical significance, however, are the reasons he provides for his dystopian investments. One characteristic of apocalyptic manhood is the impulse to destroy even the most beloved institutions, organizations, and social goods or conventions in response to the demands that other groups be permitted to also partake in their enjoyment. This impulse can be summarized by the colloquial phrase "burn it all down!" White masculinity is underwritten by a desire to save a beloved object from being tainted by the presence of women, queers, and people of color. In other words, if I cannot have an object of desire (or, more specifically, I cannot have it all to myself), then no one shall. It is fitting, then, that Rodger would conclude his manifesto with just such a demand: that the pleasure principle be abolished. Although Rodger admits his desire for sex, he nonetheless explains, "Sex is by far the most evil concept in existence. The fact that life itself exists through sex just proves that life is flawed. The act of sex gives human beings a tremendous amount of pleasure. Pleasure they don't deserve. No one deserves to experience so much pleasure, especially since some humans get to experience it while some are denied it."[55] In short, he concludes, "If I cannot have it, I will do everything I can to DESTROY IT."[56] Characteristic of the death drive, Rodger takes enjoyment in the destruction of both the very object of his desire and the death of the life instinct. The text exemplifies white masculinity's perverse fascination with death and chaos. Here, death offers the absence of tension within the subject, a relief in finality, and the ironic inversion "kill to save."

Rodger's fascination with death and omnipotence ultimately consummates the fascist dream of male autarky. After women's enslavement, Rodger speculates that "future generations of men would be oblivious to these remaining women's existence, and that is for the best. If a man grows up without knowing of the existence of women, there will be no desire for sex. Sexuality will completely cease to exist. Love will cease to exist."[57] Rodger imagines fascism as a pathway to perfect and total repression of the drives. Both men's and women's bodies are recast in terms of their pure use-value—husks or envelopes for the advancement of civilization. This is a world devoid of any social affinity that might bind together the body politic; a dark world without intimacy and a singular allegiance to progress; a world without art, creativity, and personal expression. The subject of this fascist imaginary has fully conquered their nature only to be freed to invest in their own toil and domination. If we return to Marcuse's insights about the slow eradication of Eros that is demanded in the name of civilization, we find that Rodger merely takes the repressive hypothesis to its logical conclusion in totalitarianism.

Fascism's response to expressions of the drives is to glorify the total conquest of those libidinal energies that cannot be harnessed by the repressive apparatus. For Rodger, such a task would be nothing short of historic. He concludes, "In such a pure world, the man's mind can develop to greater heights than ever before. Future generations will live their lives free of having to worry about the barbarity of sex and women, which will enable them to expand their intelligence and advance the human race to a state of perfect civilization."[58] While the scenario he presents is preposterous and superlatively violent, it exemplifies how white masculine victimhood so easily attaches itself to fascist principles. Once one accepts the premise that they are entitled to privileges by virtue of birth, and that they have been ordained by God and nature to rule, and further, that the advancement of inferior social classes unfairly threatens their privilege, talk of hierarchy, order, and retribution are not far behind. Elliot Rodger's manifesto is not an aberration but the politics of white male victimhood extended to its logical conclusion.

THE MALE DEATH CULT

Margaret Atwood, author of *The Handmaid's Tale,* surmises that "men are afraid that women will laugh at them. Women are afraid that men will kill them."[59] While spectacular and fantastical, Rodger's manifesto is far less of an outlier than it might be comforting to believe. Expressions of victimhood and the demand for compensation for injustices, however slight, resonate with a misogynistic culture in which violence against women is prevalent. Rodger concludes his story with a frightening vision of something resembling Atwood's *Handmaid's Tale* in which women are enslaved for reproduction and all nonprocreative sex is abolished. In what Rodger calls his "perfect ideology," women's bodies would be reduced to husks, envelopes, and mere vessels for men's procreative needs. But this quite far from science fiction when you consider that, as Luce Irigaray suggests, women's bodies in a patriarchal culture do not belong to themselves.[60] There is only one sex, she writes, and that is male. Woman is ceaselessly reduced to an exchange commodity, an object trafficked between men, but never a subject in and of itself. To that extent, Rodger's vision builds a futuristic totalitarian infrastructure organized around ideas and ambitions that exist in the now. He describes women as a "plague" that must be eradicated or as "animals" that need to be slaughtered for the common good. Dispensing with sexuality, the ultimate act of repression, he fantasizes about a world of unending progress predicated on women's suffering.

Rodger's fantasy, then, is of endless toil and domination—a fantasy in which advanced industrial society has conquered the pleasure principle and rendered all nonproductive human capacities and instincts obsolete. This utopia is more George Orwell's *1984* than Aldous Huxley's *Brave New World.* Like the totalitarian dreams that precede him, Rodger's fantasy is of civilizational perfection achieved by means of industrial mass murder. Female sexuality is the only impediment to the perfection of Rodger's fascist Übermensch: a hyperproductive male body fully dedicated to the repression of the drives. Yet, this is a politics animated by the drives. As Marcuse writes, "The education for consent to death introduces an element of surrender into life from the beginning—surrender and submission. It stifles 'utopian' efforts. The powers that be have a deep affinity to death, death is a token of unfreedom, of defeat."[61] In this tortured manuscript, death is the animating force of a productive society—even reproduction falls under its purview. Here the dictates are merely explicit: the life of men is to be underwritten by the death of women.

CHAPTER 4

Sun's Out, Guns Out

Open Carry and the White Male Body

THE FACEBOOK PAGE for Open Carry Virginia features a banner photograph of founder Ed Levine in the midst of running daily errands at his local Lowe's Home Improvement store. Levine is smiling while giving the camera an enthusiastic "thumbs up."[1] A holstered handgun rests on his right hip in plain sight of the camera. His blue and yellow T-shirt reads "Sun's Out, Guns Out." The photo conveys a fairly lighthearted sentiment toward guns while indexing a kind of perverse enjoyment of introducing a deadly weapon into a peaceful civilian context. And while brandishing a handgun in public is not against Virginia law, the gleeful image with its accompanying tongue-in-cheek slogan suggests that firearms should be not only a routine feature of public life but a source of pleasure for those who choose to carry them. To be sure, this is not beyond the pale of contemporary gun advocacy. While the epidemic of mass shootings might compel some gun activists to adopt a more somber tone, Levine's bravado is the preferred style of the open carry movement. A loose collective of gun owners who are committed to an unbridled interpretation of the Second Amendment, the open carry movement seeks to normalize the public display of guns, including both handguns and assault rifles, in the name of public safety, personal protection, and above all, liberty.[2] Recently, members of the open carry movement have staged protests by carrying assault rifles while shopping at Starbucks, Chipotle, Target, among other businesses that express opposition to the public display of firearms. Some groups have protested at the site of mass shootings to counteract calls for gun reform.[3] A group in Kentucky even protested a children's lemonade stand raising money for Moms Demand Action for Gun Sense.[4] Central to their case is the mythology of "the good guy with a gun"—a figure not unlike the minuteman fighting British tyranny or the Wild West cowboy protecting homesteaders from American Indians—who dispenses with criminals and terrorists that wish to do others harm. Although they generally express support for law enforcement, open carriers see themselves as a necessary supplement to the directives of law and order. They generally oppose any gun control measures and believe that gun ownership, particularly gun visibility, is an essential bulwark against the tyranny of "big government."

"Sun's out, guns out" is hardly the official slogan of the open carry movement; yet, this playful rhyme provides an interesting summation of the movement's underlying cultural politics and its connection to new forms of men's rights activism. In one sense, the phrase illustrates the movement's emphasis on illumination and visibility—that guns must be seen in the right kind of (sun)light to serve their purpose. In another sense, the phrase highlights the long-standing and interchangeable relationship between guns and white masculinity. Typically printed on summer beachwear, the slogan playfully refers to displaying one's arms ("guns") in public. That "guns" could just as easily refer to large biceps as it could a revolver or semiautomatic rifle suggests that firearms are woven into the fabric of masculinity. Hence, this chapter shifts focus away from the affordances of new media and virtual men's rights networks to those of the white male body itself and the weapons that extend its power. Here I am concerned with how white men come to embody the virulent arguments and angry dispositions that also populate men's rights networks—virtual or otherwise. Unlike the protest movements of marginalized communities, open carry concerns the deployment not of unruly bodies but of law-engendering bodies.[5] Gun protests represent condensations of themes that circulate throughout contemporary men's rights rhetoric, primarily the notion that white men have been displaced and subjugated by an oppressive feminine state apparatus. The gun is a technology of the body that reinvests the white male subject with the efficacy, sovereignty, and able-bodiedness that was allegedly confiscated by the oppressive state. The gun also affords that white male body to enjoy its own subjectivity—to rehearse loss and subjugation but this time as an active rather than passive agent. Open carry imports the disposition of men's rights activism into public space—casting a shroud of death over anyone who wishes to challenge white male authority.

Guns are virtually synonymous with the white male body. There is no shortage of gun metaphors one can draw from to index sex acts that privilege the male anatomy.[6] Consider lurid masculinist metaphors such as "banging" to refer to sexual intercourse, "blowing" for oral sex, "shooting a load" for ejaculation, and "firing blanks" to refer to male infertility. Guns are also symbolically interchangeable with body parts ("fire*arms,*" "*hand*gun") or help operationalize the anatomy ("trigger *finger,*" "dead *eye*"). "Sun's out, guns out," then, implores gun owners to flex their muscles in public and to show off their physical prowess to criminals and law-abiders alike. The phrase gestures at the phallocentrism that underwrites American gun culture and that conveys male dominance, power, and sexual primacy. As C. Richard King argues, "guns provide a language for talking about sex, offering a set of culture metaphors, similar to those made available by other symbolic domains, such as sports or animals, the inscribe power and conscribe pleasure. For several hundred years, firearms have provided a fecund sexual vocabulary, noteworthy for its flexibility and productivity, which describes bodies, acts, and relationships."[7] Hence, it is no coincidence that white masculine archetypes tend to be virile gunslingers: cowboys, frontier lawmen, militia men, hunters, and soldiers, to name a few. The phallocentrism of gun culture is not premised on the demographics of gun ownership alone but instead on the symbolic and substitution logics that render guns co-extensive of white male power. As surrogates, the display of guns in public helps organize worshipfulness, adherence, and obedience to white male authority. This chapter argues that guns are a technology of the white male body, a prosthetic that affords its user the ability to project power over others.

In another sense, the gun itself is a conduit to the fantasy of white masculine redemption. Gun are not only prosthetics, then, but *mediums* for traversing the fantasy of redemptive violence. The unification of gun and body constitutes an embodied rhetoric that engenders the unification of incorporeal signifiers, symbols, and ideas in a concrete material form.[8]

Although women and people of color also engage in open carry, guns and gun aesthetics in American culture are as much raced as they are gendered. In addition to phallocentrism, here we might also consider how the racist association between Blackness and criminality renders African American participation in open carry inherently violent and threatening to white communities. The history of gun ownership in America demonstrates that the Second Amendment is intertwined with the history of white supremacy. In part, the Second Amendment was conceived in the interests of the slave-owning class who sought to enlist voluntary militias to disarm and return escaped slaves.[9] Throughout Reconstruction and the Jim Crow era, the Ku Klux Klan terrorized and confiscated weapons from freed slaves, creating a virtual white monopoly on gun ownership throughout the South. For the many Black communities terrorized by the KKK and the police, gun ownership was a life or death imperative. It is for this reason that Bobby Seale, Huey Newton, and the Black Panther Party would later embrace open carry as a militant symbol of community self-defense.[10] At any rate, within the rhetoric of firearms, advocacy of the "good guy with a gun" is implicitly white.

Nowhere is this racial disparity more transparent than in how law enforcement responds to legal gun possession in public. In 2014 a Black man named John Crawford was shot and killed in an Ohio Walmart for carrying a toy rifle that he was about to purchase. In that same year, twelve-year-old Tamir Rice was shot and killed for brandishing a toy gun that police say they mistook for a pistol. In 2016 Philando Castile was shot by police on a routine traffic stop after disclosing that he was in possession of a legally concealed firearm. In all these cases, the officers were not charged with a crime. By contrast, in 2017 two white men (Jason Craig Baker and Brandon Vreeland) staged an open carry protest in the lobby of the Dearborn, Michigan, Police Department, masked with balaclavas and armed with body armor and assault rifles. The two were subdued without a shot fired. At the 2016 open carry protests in Dallas and at the Republican National Convention in Cleveland, the police showed remarkable patience and deference to groups of white men dressed in paramilitary gear and brandishing deadly assault rifles. These contrasting anecdotes suggest not only that white gun owners assume less risk when carrying firearms in public but that for white communities "the bad guy with a gun" is implicitly Black. This assumption is remarkable given that since 1982 an overwhelming majority of mass shooters have been white and male.[11] Yet, carrying guns in public is predominantly the prerogative of white men, who occupy a privileged position in relation to the law. White men are not only permitted exception from the rule of law but are ostensibly delegated the sovereign power to make decisions about who lives and dies in the name of both liberty and public safety.

With the gendered and racial politics in clear view, this chapter explores how the public display of guns figures into the rhetoric of white male victimhood and recuperative logics of white male power. I argue that the open carry movement extends the argument of men's rights networks and reasserts white male sovereignty over public space by manufacturing shocking image events that prompt spectators to respect and fear white men's phallic power.[12] Rather than focus on the verbal arguments offered in favor of open carry, this chapter is concerned with the gendered and racialized embodiments of gun culture. Thus, I attend to guns in public as signifiers of white male power. Through an exploration of the embodied dimensions of American gun culture, I identify three ways in which the open carry movement enacts a men's rights politic and courts manly investment in victimhood. First, the public display of guns consummates the fantasy of an oppressive state and therefore manufactures the conditions that call forth aggrieved white men to reclaim the polity. The result is a hypermilitarized public that favors the de facto authority of white men. Second, the phallic symbolism of guns offers proof that white masculinity retains its potency and, therefore, compensates for white men's symbolic castration by the "nanny state." Finally, displaying guns recovers the symbolic efficiency of white masculine archetypes (cowboy, solider, militia)—all of which conflate white masculine authority with law and order. Ultimately, gun displays threaten those who might challenge white masculinity by restructuring public space to keep white men safe while making public life precarious for women and people of color. Moreover, guns constitute part of a persecution fantasy wherein civil norms, progressivism, and big government have collapsed and therefore necessitate the building of a new social order organized around the resurrection of white masculine sovereignty.

GUNS AND EMBODIMENT

Despite the recent wave of gun reform protests, open carry is only prohibited in three states (California, Florida, and Illinois) and the District of Columbia. Two states (New York and South Carolina) narrow the right to long guns, while three states (Massachusetts, Minnesota, and New Jersey) permit only handguns. There are no federal laws that prohibit the open carry of firearms, and while there are some permit- and place-based exemptions (schools, public transportation, state-owned businesses, and places that serve alcohol), in most cases the right to open carry is generally not infringed.[13] Moreover, the lobbying efforts of the National Rifle Association ostensibly preclude the passage of state or national gun reform despite popular support for policies such as universal background checks.[14] With the general trend toward gun law liberalization, it is remarkable that gun advocacy has become more aggressive and vitriolic over the past decade. In part, the NRA has manufactured a narrative in which any form of gun control can be construed as a surreptitious effort to disarm the public and pave the pathway to tyranny. This narrative was particularly salient during the Obama administration, particularly within the radical fringes of the Tea Party movement.[15] Some extreme gun advocates took up conspiracy theories that explained mass shootings as pseudo-events manufactured by the Obama administration and the liberal media to justify disarming the public. Following the massacre at Marjory Stoneman Douglas High School on February 18, 2018, trending pro-gun posts on Reddit and YouTube suggested that vocal student support for gun reform was the work of paid crisis actors—an elaborate hoax orchestrated by the left.[16] While gun advocates remain convinced that gun confiscation is just around the corner, the evidence seems to suggest otherwise.

If it is true that Second Amendment rights are not in jeopardy, it is worth asking what needs *are* addressed or, more specifically, what fantasy is consummated by the narrative of an oppressive state hell-bent on gun confiscation? What new configurations of white masculinity are made possible by an investment in both gun possession and gun confiscation?

Linda Collins answers this question by illustrating how supporters of an unbridled Second Amendment organize around a demand politics that cannot and must not be fulfilled if the subject is to purchase a marginalized subject position.[17] It is the demand itself (and hence, its denial) that is foundational to the group's identity. Using Lundberg's theorization of the demand, Collins argues that gun advocates need a narrative of victimization in order to enjoy their subjectivity.[18] Much like a hypochondriac, the enjoyment in Second Amendment rhetoric is in the lodging of the complaint.[19] Open carry is a way to revisit loss but this time change one's disposition from passive to active.

Unbridled Second Amendment defenders also see gun ownership as an immutable identity category (much like race), and hence view any restrictions as an affront to an aggrieved class. Some gun owners believe they are more vulnerable than other marginalized groups because anti-discrimination law offers them no special protections or civil remedies, unlike racial and sexual minorities. Collins illustrates how, underwritten by the compulsive repetition of the death drive, open carry advocates take a stake in their own marginalization, for it offers them the ability to procure their subjectivity as an aggrieved class. Their portrait of an oppressive government that is brutally indifferent to liberty and the cause of the gun owner is necessary to prolong the enjoyment entailed in displaying firearms in public. At the same time, the oppressive state must also be feckless and weak (feminine) if the well-armed citizenry is to succeed. Ultimately, however, open carry constitutes an identity movement that, while open to almost anyone, has particular resonance with white men because it offers them an antistatist identity politic without reference to whiteness. The gun functions metonymically, and thus can be read as a stand-in for white identity without ever having to reference whiteness or maleness as the key identity categories that are actually at stake. As guns are already synonymous with white male power and white male history, a politics organized around gun possession becomes an easy route to an aggrieved identity without having to utter "white power" or "men's rights."

While the myth of a well-armed public fighting a tyrannical government discloses the affective investments in gun ownership as an identity category, much of the rhetorical work of American gun culture is visual and embodied. As Barry Brummett writes, "It is the style and the mass of people *displaying* or *performing* that style who make up the gun culture. The style and mass provides a core of signification, a set of signs and practices with symbolic gravity that draws toward the core of an imaginary community and certain subject positions."[20] While the technical features (caliber, firepower, accuracy, magazine capacity) and utilitarian attributes (fighting tyranny, hunting, self-protection) of guns matter a great deal to those who carry them, open carry is primarily concerned with how the aesthetic quality of guns and gun culture convey the gravity of their cause. In other words, public gun displays provide proof that "the people" called into being by the Declaration of Independence and the Preamble to the US Constitution—not government—are sovereign. The publicly brandished firearm begs an oppressive state to show its ugliness and, thus, creates the very conditions that necessitate gun ownership in the first place.[21] For example, consider the provocative slogan adopted by the Texas open carry movement: "Come and Take It."[22]

Guns embody the argument and disposition of the new men's rights rhetoric. In other words, carrying guns transforms the body into a synecdoche for the aggrieved white male subject. By embodiment, then, I mean the way by which expressions take material form and give concrete presence to abstract principles, many of which are hard to articulate because they exceed the capacity of language. As Sonja Modesti writes, embodiment is "the radically material condition of humanity that necessarily entails both the body and consciousness, objectivity, and subjectivity."[23] Thus, we find in the materiality of guns the potential not only to open up the capacities of the body to assert control over others but also to symbolically convey the demand politics of the white male subject. The gun, in assemblage with the white male body, overflows with the iconicity of justified violence. In popular mythology, guns won the nation's independence, defeated tyranny abroad, and "civilized" the continent.[24] At the same time, gun advocates often portray guns as innocent, or at the very least, neutral (i.e., "guns don't kill people, people kill people"). In the hands of white men, guns are virtually synonymous with power and authority, law and order, freedom and liberty. The gun *transforms* the white male body into an instrument or extension of the law.

Yet, this performance is delicate and contingent. Although the open carriers wish to convey to the public the more heroic virtues of guns, the sight of firearms also cites a history of terror and mass death. Since 1968 more Americans have died in gun-related incidents than all

American soldiers lost in combat since 1776.[25] Even as some open carriers seek to resignify guns outside the context of crime and mass shootings, where the supporter might read virtue, the skeptic may only see the threatening capacity to render a death sentence. My task here is not to evaluate the relative safety or efficacy of guns but instead to illustrate how the visibility of guns organizes public life around the imperatives of the white male body. To unpack how the public display of guns figures into the politics of white masculine victimhood, I attend to the embodied entailments of guns and gun culture that privilege white men's authority to make decisions about who lives and who dies. Gun visibility operates as a series of signs that reference both white men's aggrievements and their virtually monopoly on institutional power. Hence, the remainder of this chapter unfolds by attending to visual enactments of white male power embodied in the practice of open carry. Each set of images and image events reveals the racialized and gendered entanglements of displaying guns in public. Seeking deference to their authority, open carry shows spectators what society *looks like* when it is structured according to the prerogatives of white male sovereignty. Here I draw from Kevin DeLuca and Jennifer Peeples's concept of the *image event,* a visually stunning occurrence staged for popular consumption in a culture of screens. Image events are those moments that interrupt, disrupt, or otherwise stand out among a media ecology that is saturated in images. As such, open carry shocks and visually commands the spectator's attention, particularly where the intent of the carrier is unclear. Guns cast a silhouette of death over public life by prioritizing violence as the precondition of a civil existence.[26] Given the gun's metonymic relationship with white male identity, open carry functions as a theater for white men's concerns, priorities, and grievances. Using the aforementioned three propositions about the relationship between gun culture and white masculinity, I engage a series of images from open carry rallies to unpack the embodied capacities of the armed white male body.

THE OPPRESSIVE STATE

The open carry movement is underwritten by tension between two conflicting impulses. On the one hand, the movement organizes against a tyrannical government that is determined to disarm the citizenry. It is under these conditions that gun owners forge an oppositional and marginalized identity. On the other hand, the movement is fervently patriotic and expresses reverence for the military and law enforcement—the very instruments of the oppressive state against which they have mobilized. Thus, open carriers must confront the oppressive state without overtly usurping white male authority. One way in which the movement addresses this tension is to cast the state as emasculated by women and cuckolded by inferior men. Even the masculinity of the NRA is not immune from scrutiny. For instance, a post on the Nevada open carry blog suggests that "All you [the NRA] know is compromise and loss. So like a cuckold husband who feels 'empowered' watching another man sleep with his wife, the NRA is a willing accomplice to the gun control agenda."[27] The movement then separates itself from this compromised masculinity by reclaiming American men's revolutionary roots in the form of the voluntary militia.[28]

Visually, this tensions plays out through the movement's well-choreographed interactions with law enforcement. While open carriers often show deference to law enforcement, they also supplant their authority by showing off superior firepower and preparation for violent contingencies. Some open carriers coordinate their activities as a unit, dressing in similar paramilitary gear (including camouflage and body armor), and carry loaded AR-15s AK-47s, and G3s. In many cases their armaments and equipment far surpass that of local police.[29] While open carriers often interact amicably with police, going out of their way to shake hands and converse about weapons, they also upstage law enforcement with a disproportionate display of firepower. As representatives of the state working under its constraints and regulations, the police are made to look meek, fat, and powerless when contrasted with their virile and heavily armed counterparts. I contend that open carry distinguishes itself from the compromised and constrained masculinity of the state without getting too proximate to the fantasy of insurrectional violence. Rather than confront the state with open warfare, open carry relies on the menacing aesthetics of assault rifles and paramilitary uniforms to embarrass and humiliate the state, suggesting that it is incapable of adequately protecting its own citizens. In doing so, they also lay claim to a seemingly more authentic version of white masculinity, consummated through the visual threat of armed insurrection.

Here, I want to pause on two images of the West Ohio Minutemen engaging with police at the 2016 Republican National Convention in Cleveland. According to the group, the purpose of their gathering was unrelated to Donald Trump or the Republican platform, but instead was motivated by the imperatives of community protection.[30] Citing shootings of police officers in Baton Rouge and Dallas, the Cleveland police union unsuccessfully petitioned Governor John Kasich to temporarily suspend open carry leading up to the RNC.[31] The police's public opposition to open carry provided an ideal context for the Minutemen to align themselves against an oppressive yet feckless state apparatus. As such, the optics of the event featured an ineffectual, fearful, and emasculated police force upstaged by a hypermasculine patriotic militia. In the first image (figure 1), six Minutemen surround a lone officer standing next to a police cruiser. Each man carries a military-style assault rifle slung over his shoulder and resting on his chest. The men cast a stern gaze at the police officer. The man at the center of the frame and closest to the police offer appears to tilt his right shoulder slightly forward, his right hand covering the trigger of his rifle, so as to give the officer a clear view. His left hand freely lingers near his holstered side arm, and his eyes remain fixed on the officer's face, observing his reaction. By contrast, the officer appears to be smiling. His eyes are downcast, and his sun glasses are pulled back to provide an unencumbered view of the rifle. While his posture seems relaxed, his right hand rests on his holstered sidearm. His left arm rests on something obscured by a man in the foreground. The officer is noticeably less physically fit than the Minutemen, with extra weight around his stomach and waist. His official black police uniform sharply contrasts with the group's paramilitary aesthetic.

This image captures a power reversal at work between the state and the people. Within the frame, the officer is outnumbered and outgunned by the Minutemen. His authority and capability to keep public order is called into question by the presence of a self-deputized armed citizenry. The men embody an alternative to civilian law enforcement that is more capable of keeping the public safe. The Minutemen appear to be more unconstrained, militaristic and tribal. Their overwhelming numbers suggest that distrust of government and civilian law enforcement is warranted. That is to say that the Minutemen present themselves to be more serious and vigilant than the police when it comes to

FIGURE 1. Ohio Minutemen gathering at the 2016 RNC. Photo courtesy of Peter Larson.

the task of maintaining public safety. Yet, these intimidating men also threaten the existing institutions charged with maintaining law and order. With the officer encircled, the group commands his gaze toward their powerful armaments. Likewise, the event invites the spectator to observe the contrast between each weapon at the center of the image. The Minuteman boastfully presents his large, high-caliber automatic rifle for the officer's closer inspection. In response, the officer reaches for his small sidearm all the while seeming to admire his counterpart's superior firepower. The two are sizing each other up.

While making an embodied argument in favor of an armed citizenry over a feckless civilian government, the protestor's actions also emasculate the state. As an emissary of an oppressive government, the officer cannot help but admire and express deference to a superior and more intimidating form of masculine power. Emboldened by their phallic weapons, the militia are able to visually impose their will on the officer. Rather than draw his weapon, the officer's keeps it holstered and smiles. This image invites a comparison between different forms of white masculinity: one constrained by the rules of civilian government, the other unbridled and primal. Confronted by hypermasculine challengers, the officer's admiring gaze admits the inadequacy and inefficacy of civilian authority. Here the sovereign power of the militia man supplants the authority of the state to govern the public. The protestor's actions force a series of contrasts between hard and soft bodies; long and small guns; authentic and phony authority. As an image event that embodies the movement's core principles, such an interaction between open carriers and the police calls into question the state's monopoly on masculine authority—but not masculine authority writ large. The compromised masculinity of the state is subverted by the primal masculinity of the tribe or militia. These image events humiliate police, as they are not permitted to carry such overwhelming firepower. Such interactions visually illustrate the impotence of the state against the portrait of the self-sufficient and well-armed individualist. In short, the protestors' gun displays exclaim "ours is bigger than yours!" In this moment, it is the state that should fear the militia, not the other way around.

In other instances, open carriers go out of their way to show respect for law enforcement. In one sense, shaking hands with police officers communicates the group's peaceful intentions—that they, too, are "good guys with guns." While the open carrier visually upstages the police, he also keeps himself at a safe proximity from the fantasy of armed insurrection. In other words, visual armed insurrection is enacted as an ersatz substitute for the visceral pleasure of violence.

In another sense, politely greeting police while heavily armed concretizes the connection between the law and white male authority. As stated earlier, there is a pronounced racial disparity in police treatment of guns in public. Moreover, the same conservative news outlets that praise open carry when it is conducted by predominantly white citizens also express fear and outrage at the sight of Black liberation organizations doing so in the name of civil rights and self-defense.[32] Although the state must be cast as oppressive for gun owners to lay claim to their victimhood status, images of handshakes neither undermine such claims nor are a sign of capitulation to the state. Instead, the performance of amity between white police officers and white open carriers codifies white sovereignty over public space. In these exchanges, it is the prerogative of white men to police the public, regardless of state sanction. Moreover, the authority of the police is provisionally granted by the (white male) citizenry rather than by the state.

Another striking performance (figure 2) at the 2016 RNC illustrates how open carriers visually enact white authority over public space.

In this image, a Minuteman halts as he crosses the street to shake the hand of a police officer. The Minuteman is accompanied by several of his compatriots, all of them dressed in camouflage with rifles strapped to their chests. One man leans his right arm forward, where it is met by the police officer's embrace. The Minuteman appears to be directly addressing the officer—his facial expressions conveying solemnity and earnestness. Although his back is to the camera, the officer's arm extends his body forward to meet the Minuteman's gesture of respect. Two of the Minuteman's companions watch the officer closely and tentatively, seeming to gauge his reception of the greeting. Another officer, partially visible in the left foreground on the photograph, is smiling as he appears to engage in conversation with one of the Minutemen bringing up the rear of the group. A lone flag flies at half-mast in the background, completing a portrait of reverence for the sacrifices of the police and the military.

One interpretation is that the Minutemen are performing deference to the authority of the law. This interpretation might privilege a strategic narrative in which the Minutemen must convey their respect for police in order to demonstrate that they are not a threat to public safety. Another interpretation, the one I wish to argue for here, is that the act conveys only the provisional authority of the police granted by the people rather than the state. The authority that remains static in this image is that of the larger identity category that subsumes and accounts for the character of each party: whiteness. Here, the white male citizen and the white police officer—both armed yet representing different visions of the polity—find common ground in the public streets. The handshake demonstrates precisely the operation of whiteness in public—a series of informal though structural advantages accorded to white people that un-races and normalizes white identity.[33] As a result, white people are unburdened of having to consider whether their identity—particularly when carrying a deadly weapon—will be a factor in how others treat them. As this image illustrates, the ability to approach and make physical contact with a police officer while being heavily armed with a militia in tow is a superlative embodiment of white privilege. That such a gesture would be read by police as an expression of respect rather than a threat of bodily harm speaks to how whiteness and white privilege are implicitly aligned with law and order. Here, two groups of white authorities share in the privilege of policing

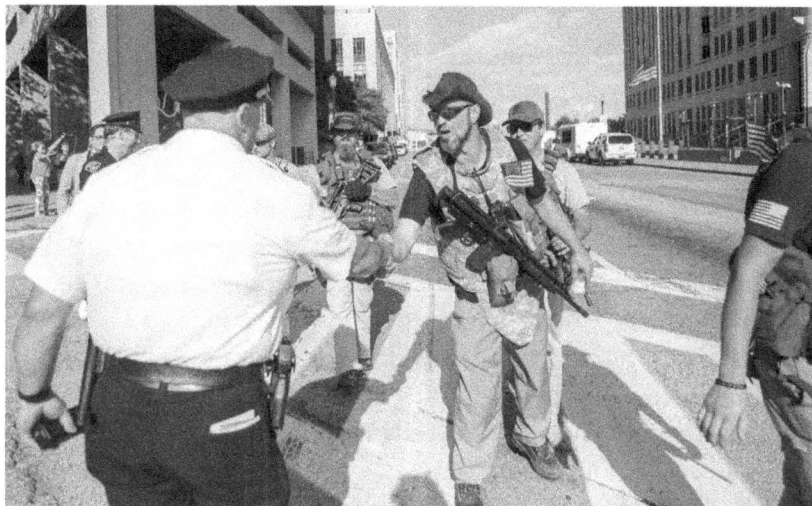

FIGURE 2. Ohio Minutemen greeting police at the 2016 RNC. Photo courtesy of Kyle Grillot.

the public. Their amity quite literally halts traffic and invites others to take notice. The Minutemen's ability to carry assault rifles with the tacit support of law enforcement and without being considered a threat to public safety suggests that whiteness and the law are virtually synonymous. Their handshake extends and entrusts the official capacity of law enforcement to the white armed citizenry. By returning the gesture of respect, the police symbolically devolve the tacit power of the law to an extralegal, unbridled, and unregulated militia.

Ultimately, friendly encounters with police are a necessary counterpart to direct confrontation. That is, open carriers must remind the police that they serve the people without subverting authority in general and white authority in particular. They must generate an optics of an oppressive state without ceding the agency of the armed militia. Either way, these image events constitute a spectacle of white male authority in which the compromised masculinity of the state is supplanted by the authentic manhood of the rugged individual. Ultimately, these choreographed interactions between the police and gun owners function as a form of ritual purification of white masculinity. In other words, the protests symbolically purge the emasculating force of the liberal "nanny state" from public life. In forming a revolutionary militia to fight the tyranny, open carriers revive the imagined masculinity of the nation's founders. In seizing the public eye, they renew and concretize the imagined relationship between white masculinity and the law. The movement presents the public with a hegemonic portrait of "a good guy with a gun": a self-deputized white man.

PHALLIC PANIC

It is perhaps painfully obvious to observe that guns and gun culture are phallocentric; however, connecting this observation to white men's attachment to trauma evinces how displaying guns in public procures for white men a sense of order in what otherwise seems to be a chaotic social and economic context. Hence, brandishing big guns might be read as a response to castration anxiety. The threat of castration ceaselessly returns trauma to the male subject, operating as an exigence for the continual restaging of male subjectivity. Castration compels men to disavow their oedipal desires and assimilate into the law of the figural father. What is at stake, Silverman surmises, "is a *psychic* disintegration—the disintegration, that is, of a bound and armored ego, predicated upon the illusion of coherence and control."[34] Phallocentrism, then, is a form of symbolic prosthesis that both staves off the threat of castration and extends male power, domination, and control. Displaying guns, then, demands that spectators attend to the power of phallus and, in doing so, observe that white masculinity—though wounded—has not lost its potency. Put differently, guns are white male power by another name. Their naked display of male toughness and aggression reorganizes public life in ways that privilege white male needs—psychic or otherwise. In King's words, guns "center on men: pursuit, predation, precision, dominance, aggression, toughness, conquest, and immediacy."[35] Thus, guns in public normalize a social order underwritten by the tacit threat of white masculine violence. Open carry is a practice that (re)masculinizes the public sphere.

Here I focus attention on the symbolic entailment of open carry in mundane commercial spaces. While public rallies are politically organized spectacles that confront the state, open carriers also seek to normalize guns by introducing them into everyday situations, often targeting restaurants, groceries, sporting goods and department stores who have expressed opposition to customers brandishing firearms in their establishment. Although open carriers argue that people's fear of guns (hoplophobia) should not negate their right to carry, police are often flooded with 911 calls from customers and employees who have no way of distinguishing a "good guy with a gun" from a mass shooter.[36] Aside from terrifying citizens as they eat or shop, the displaying of guns symbolically extends white male power into everyday spaces. Perhaps because of its informality, this is perhaps a more shocking display of guns than the coordinated public performances that are characteristic of open carry rallies.

The movement's choice of commercial spaces as a staging ground is not solely premised on business opposition to open carry, but instead can be read as an anxious response to the transformations in the gendered division of labor within the commercial sphere—a primary concern for men's rights activists. The so-called he-cession describes a conservative media phenomenon that promoted the notion that white men have been the most disproportionately affected by the lingering effects of the 2008 recession.[37] As the narrative is told, white men's dislocation in the marketplace was amplified by both more women entering the workforce and affirmative action programs that put men at a significant disadvantage. Meanwhile, workplace sexual harassment policies have men wondering whether that innocent joke they told to their female co-worker will get them fired. Kimmel's interviews with "angry white men" reveal the extent to which many feel emasculated by their dead-end, unskilled service industry jobs.[38] While white men's pain and frustration are real, given the overwhelming data that white men are still objectively well-off in the workforce compared with others, the narrative of masculine precarity is suspect. But, there are seemingly other emasculating forces at work. The increase in dual-career households has men sharing in domestic duties once coded as feminine, including child care, cooking, and shopping. I have argued elsewhere that as men have taken on a greater share of feminine home care labor, popular culture has helped ease their transition by recoding some aspects of women's work as manly.[39] For example, men have been authorized to think of shopping as hunting, competition, gamesmanship, and/or an expression of shrewd masculine know-how.[40] As a source of economic and gender anxiety, the consumer marketplace is where white men are most vocal about their feelings of vulnerability. Thus, the militarization and masculinization of commercial space enables white men to reassert power over forces that feel beyond their control. I read this form of open carry as an expression of phallocentrism that addresses white men's vulnerability by reasserting the primacy of men's power (the phallus) in spaces coded as feminine.

For instance, Figure 3 features Texas open carry activist Kory Watkins shopping at his local Kroger grocery store. Watkins was a libertarian candidate for the Texas governorship and the leader of Open Carry Tarrant County, a splinter group of the Texas open carry movement that is opposed to gun licenses and background checks. Watkins is known for carrying rifles and handguns into local businesses and chain department stores as a form of gun advocacy. This image was featured on Watkins's Facebook page and circulated online after Moms Demand Gun Action started a petition for Kroger to prohibit firearms in their stores.[41] In this image, the gun takes the scene hostage by introducing an implicit threat of violence. Much like those of his militia counterparts, Watkins's large weapon recasts the relative peace and securing of commercial life as a tentatively thin veneer under which lurks the constant threat of criminal violence. Yet, Watkins presents himself not as part of voluntary militia but as an ordinary civilian conducting his daily errands. He is dressed casually in khaki shorts, a blue polo shirt, and a white fedora. With the exception of his rifle, the image is fairly ordinary and would otherwise attract little attention. Watkins merely pushes his cart of groceries through the aisles of his local grocery store. The introduction of the gun is discordant and thus renders the mundane and everyday as spectacular and menacing. The feminine realm of shopping and consumer culture is reframed as a masculine theater of justified violence—a space that could not peacefully exist on its own without the civilizing influence of the gun.[42]

It is perhaps unlikely that any individual will need an assault rifle at the grocery store; however, the efficacy of guns is beside the point. Instead, the image politics exemplified in this photo illustrate how the brandishing of guns both genders public space and organizes men's relationship to feminized space. An important aspect of the "good guy with a gun" myth is that when presented with danger, ordinary men might transform into masculine superheroes. This myth particularly resonates in spaces where white men lack primacy and agency. The fantasies stoked by gun culture suggest that the low-skilled service industry worker and the emasculated organizational man alike can be redeemed through the judicious use of violence. To enter the putatively

FIGURE 3. Kory Watkins open carrying at Kroger grocery store. Facebook.

feminine realm of shopping armed with a long gun reasserts the primacy of the phallus in all aspects of public and commercial life. Moreover, the presence of guns demonstrates how men may be permitted to enter feminized spaces without losing their claim to manhood. Here, the gun functions as a proxy for physical endowment that corroborates the subject's virility and power. The gun penetrates and rules over a space whose purveyors wrongly assumed that male violence would no longer be necessary to enforce civility among the populous. The act implies that, one way or another, the commercial sphere will be subjected to masculine control—the only question is whether his intentions are benign or not. By suggesting that guns are appropriate in the context of even the most mundane of daily chores, this discordant performance confirms that there is no space or place beyond white men's rule.

What is more, the act addresses white men's intense feelings of insecurity in the commercial sphere by projecting a fantasy of invulnerability. His rifle casually slung over his shoulder, hand gently resting on the trigger, Watkins's confident gaze back toward the camera communicates a sense of calm self-assuredness. This image is a stark contrast to the anxiety expressed by white men concerning outsourcing, diversity, immigrant labor, and the like. Where economic precarity might displace some men from the workforce or relegate them to feminine care labor, the gun reminds the spectator that men's power and strength remain necessary for peace and security. To accomplish this objective, the publicly exposed gun violates and coerces the spectator into a relationship of involuntary voyeurism, wherein they are expected to admire and respect the signifiers of men's power. The gun's interchangeable and metonymic relationship with white masculinity makes an emphatic statement about the irreplaceability of white men in any context in which the gun is presented. Men need not feel castrated or emasculates by economic forces that have somewhat minimized white male primacy in the market. Open carry domesticates those fears by offering white men an illusory portrait of control and self-mastery.

Finally, Watkins's actions expand the parameters of white masculinity's police function beyond the official security apparatus. Unlike the Ohio Minutemen, Watkins is dressed as a civilian performing daily routines. He is not, by contrast, acting in the capacity of a soldier, police officer, or voluntary militia. But the presence of guns elevates those daily routines to civic duties. Thus, Watkins's portrayal of gun ownership is less formal but nonetheless important. This iteration of open carry expands the definition of civic duty to include securitization in the absence of formal institutions. It is the individual (the sovereign citizen) who must take up the roles once ceded by the people to government authority. Read in this context, open carry invites spectators to think of the relative security of civic and commercial life as dependent on the threat of judicious white male violence. The provisional freedom and security of civilian spaces seems to only thinly veil the more chaotic and violent aspects of human nature. Moreover, if the state security apparatus represents tyranny, policing the public falls squarely on the shoulders of the individual. Put simply, this iteration of open carry asks the viewer to think of public and commercial life as inherently dangerous. There is no aspect of daily life that men with guns cannot make more secure. Watkins presents himself as fulfilling white men's unique civic duty.

In sum, this civilian portrait of open carry normalizes the threat of white masculine violence. Displaying guns in peaceful civilian contexts coerces spectators to accept the inevitability of white male rule and extorts respect or fear of white men's power. For white men, the phallic symbolic economy of gun culture domesticates those threats and challenges that might otherwise invalidate their primacy in all aspects of social and commercial life. In short, the embodied argument presented to the viewer is that the tentative peace we enjoy as civilians is always already underwritten by the phallus. The "good guy with a gun" myth suggests that participation in gun culture is also an escape from the emasculating forces of service work and mindless consumerism. Open carry transforms mundane care labor such as shopping into an occasion for emasculated men to become action heroes. As a substitute for lack, the gun offers white men a sense of mastery against disorienting social and economic changes.

PLAYING COWBOY

During the Republican primary campaign leading up to the 2017 special election, Trump-backed senatorial candidate Luther Strange ran a series of campaign ads that accused his opponent Roy Moore of being "soft" in his support of the Second Amendment.[43] Not to be outdone, Moore responded to this thinly veiled attack on his manhood by exposing his .32 revolver at a September 25, 2017, campaign rally. Rebuking his opponent's claims, Moore held up his handgun and declared "I believe in the Second Amendment."[44] Lest his constituents believe him to be flaccid, Moore bolstered his masculine authority by dressing as a cowboy, complete with a white cowboy hat, leather vest, and American flag lapel pin. Later, Moore arrived on horseback to cast his ballot on Election Day. Although Moore was unsuccessful in his bid for the Senate (narrowly defeated by Democrat Doug Jones), his campaign stunt attracted national attention by challenging de facto taboos against displaying firearms in public. This event is notable, as Moore extended the open carry cause beyond the practices I outlined earlier, including normalization, militarization, and reverent memorialization of the volunteer militia. Instead, Moore made open carry a test of fitness for public office. Rapidly circulating throughout American media culture, this moment was a spectacular demonstration of virility and white male authority, an asymmetrical escalation in a masculine power struggle over the levers of institutional power. Moore crafted an image of himself as a cowboy—a good guy with a gun—whose right to rule is aligned with a triumphant history of civilizing the American frontier.

Despite his loss, Moore's arresting public display illustrates a third and final aspect of white masculine gun culture: guns allow men to recover the symbolic efficiency of white masculine archetypes. It was not enough that Moore dressed in Western gear, rode horses, and expressed his love for the Second Amendment. These are merely affectations that on their own, at best, constitute a costume rather than embody a way of life. Similarly, Western lore suggests that the cowboy is less defined by ranching and cattle drives than he is by the ability to bring law and order to a wild, rugged frontier. In frontier mythology, it was the gun that allowed them to dispense justice, keep the peace, and clear the land of hostile Indians.[45] Much like the militia man, the cowboy archetype is defined by proficiency in the use of firearms. From the early accounts of cowboy adventures in dime novels to John Ford's American westerns, it is the cowboy's gun that symbolized his status as the keeper of the law.[46] In short, the archetype lacks veracity without its relation to the aesthetics of gun culture. As such, Moore's status as the "law and order" candidate was not consummated until he presented his gun to his constituents. Escaping its modern trappings, the aesthetics of guns visually reroutes white masculinity through its nostalgic past, giving some men access to a period of time in which masculinity's hegemonic attributes were virtually unassailable. This version of white masculinity is seemingly heroic, lawful, and beyond question. As such, Moore's loss fits the narrative of white masculine victimhood wherein the progressive modern world no longer values the vital and enduring contributions of white men. At the same time, Moore's cowboy revival cultivated reverence for a time in which America was "great." When asked by reporters about what period in American history he believed the nation was great, Moore replied, "I think it was great at the time when families were united—even though we had slavery—they cared for one another . . . Our families were strong, our country had a direction."[47] Moore also made this argument by adopting the gunfighter aesthetics of nineteenth-century gun culture mythology. For Moore, America was great when families were headed by strong patriarchs and the nation's success was underwritten by slavery and imperial conquest.

Moore does not present the weapon in a threatening manner; he merely holds up the gun and presents it to the crowd. In part, the whiteness of American gun culture makes it possible for Moore to brandish a pistol during a stump speech and not be viewed as a risk to public safety. The gun, then, serves as a condensed form of visual testimony that speaks not merely to his commitment to gun ownership but rather to his fitness for public office. It is the gun that links Moore to a history of "law and order" discourse and resurrects the values and ideals of an age in which America was "great." More pointedly, the gun operates as a sign that cites the historical power of white men as a warrant for white male sovereignty in the present. The gun accomplishes this by tracing a pathway through American collective memory to those imagined moments in which gun violence seemed justified and necessary for national progress. Of course, these memories are largely drawn from the American western, a genre that romanticizes the settlement of the frontier and exonerates white men of their culpability for the genocide of American Indians.[48] As a part of a cowboy performance, the gun references only those historical moments at which frontier violence was justified, or, more likely, those moments of historical violence that the dominant culture *imagined to be* justified. The image thus summons those selective and/or contrived memories of western expansion that authorize the use of power in the present.[49] The gun is a form of proof that testifies to Moore's likeness to this simulacrum of American frontier heroism.

Although the gun is the primary signifier in this staged performance, the cowboy hat and vest also do important rhetorical work. For a public figure from the Deep South, Moore's likeness is to that of a generic frontier lawman from the American West. It is significant that Moore was not dressed as the white vigilante of the Deep South: the antebellum voluntary militiamen who hunted escaped slaves or the Jim Crow era's hooded KKK lynch mob that terrorized free Black communities. In that context, the gun would necessarily reference a different history of systemic racial violence. While he romanticized slavery, his campaign rhetoric did not explicitly resemble that of racial demagogues such as George Wallace or David Duke. Moore's racism can be characterized as much more of an insidious "dog whistle," implicit, subtle, and read between the lines.[50] As such, his self-presentation as a cowboy of the Wild West references a generic history of justified violence that, while implicitly white, does not need to explicitly reference race. In other words, the western gunslinger offers its emulators a kind of plausible deniability where race and violence are concerned. Performing as a cowboy enabled Moore to forge an oppositional identity without referencing whiteness or masculinity. The nostalgia and patriotic mythology surrounding the cowboy myth allowed Moore to draw from the past without owning the traumatic violence and military conquest that accompanied nineteenth-century nation-building.

Though opening a new front in the open carry movement, this performance ultimately failed to get Moore elected to public office. But the failure has less to do with the symbolic efficiency of the cowboy or the rhetorical power of dog whistle politics than with his ability to persuasively embody the cowboy archetype. During the campaign, nine women came forward with allegations of sexual misconduct from his time as an assistant district attorney. One allegation involved the sexual assault of a fourteen-year-old.[51] Although the allegations in their own right likely dampened Republican turnout and mobilized democratic voters (Black women in particular), his history of sexual misconduct contradicted his Western lawman persona. As moral exemplars, frontier heroes are supposed to protect women and children from the so-called savage masculinity of American Indians and frontier outlaws.[52] But the women who came forward offered lurid descriptions of Moore's harassment, assaults, unwanted sexual advances, and stalking. They described how Moore abused his authority as a district attorney to extort silence from his victims. Such behaviors are at odds with the moral virtue and chivalry that American cultural mythology attributes to the frontier lawman. Moore was nearly elected to the Senate despite credible evidence of his gross sexual misconduct. This event illustrates how the display of guns by white men automatically confers moral legitimacy. It is only when overwhelming evidence to the contrary is presented that white men might be denuded of their metonymic relationship to the law.

DEADLY ENACTMENTS

This chapter illustrates how displaying deadly firearms in public embodies a white male identity politics that is responsive to expressed feelings of powerlessness. Extending the work of networked men's rights media, open carry represents a concerted effort on the part of white men to domesticate the trauma of their supposed displacement in public and commercial life. Open carry consummates a number of persecution fantasies that circulate throughout the manosphere and conservative media outlets, including that of an oppressive state deposed

by armed sovereign citizens, feminized commercial spaces re-mascu-
linized by self-deputized white men, and the reins of political leader-
ship returned to gun-slinging lawman of frontier mythology. In each of
these fantasies we see how guns are phallic implements that operate as
symbolic substitutes for white men's misguided feelings of powerlessness. As such, guns are part of an economy of signs that reorganizes
public space according to the imperatives and priorities of white men,
including individualism, competition, self-reliance, strength, and violence. Gun culture offers white men an identity of empowered marginality that need not explicitly reference race or gender—though it can
certainly be read between the lines.

The case studies presented herein illustrate how the culture of guns
coerces spectators to both respect white male power and attend to its
expressions of fragility. Speaking to the former, open carry demands
that audiences recognize white men's power. The threat of force supplants the authority of a feckless state with the seemingly inherent sovereignty of the armed male citizen. As for the latter, the threatening
presence of guns in public demands not only that white men be heard
but that their fears and anxieties be prioritized over others. White
men's safety and security is predicated on the precarity of those most
likely to be the victims of white masculine violence. Open carry is yet
another case in which white masculinity is organized around images
of death; a culture in which embattled white men must be ready to use
force in the absence of a just and effective state apparatus. The public
display of firearms militarizes public space and normalizes the threat
of violence as a substitute for civic norms, all to procure for white men
an illusory sense of self-mastery and coherence.

CHAPTER 5

Midnight in America

Donald J. Trump and Political Sadomasochism

IN HIS nomination acceptance speech at the 2016 Republican National Convention, then candidate Donald Trump painted a dark portrait of American life. Defying the narrative conventions of uplift and hope that typify the genre, Trump presented a vision of America as a postindustrial landscape strewn with the wreckage of abandoned factories and failed dreams; a country whose citizens had been sold into bondage by their own government; entire communities held hostage by foreign enemies; an entire nation humiliated and victimized by globalist schemes to transfer America's wealth to its unfit and unworthy adversaries. Dispensing with such frivolity as inspirational candidate biographies and encomiums to the American Dream, Trump boldly declared,

> Our Convention occurs at a moment of crisis for our nation. The attacks on our police, and the terrorism in our cities, threaten our very way of life. Any politician who does not grasp this danger is not fit to lead our country. Americans watching this address tonight have seen the recent images of violence in our streets and the chaos in our communities. Many have witnessed this violence personally; some have even been its victims.[1]

In Trump's unconventional address, he portrayed himself as a great emancipator; the only one capable of restoring law, order, and safety to our overrun and decimated communities. Struck by his arresting vision of the republic, political commentator Paul Begala observed the vast chasm between Trump's rhetoric of doom and the unbridled optimism of President's Ronald Reagan's portraiture of "morning in America." For Trump, he averred, it was "midnight in America." He elaborated, "Donald Trump's America is fearful. Afraid of crime, afraid of terrorism, afraid of immigrants. His America is angry. Angry about political correctness. Angry about international trade. Angry with President Obama. And very, very angry about Hillary Clinton's candidacy."[2] While Begala rightly observes Trump's attunement with the fear, anxiety, and rage percolating among his followers, he overlooks the veiled messages of deliverance that mingle between the lines of oblivion. After declaring himself the voice of the forgotten people, Trump goes on to lay out his platform for national redemption, in which his "new Administration will be to liberate our citizens from the crime and terrorism and lawlessness that threatens their communities."[3] For his supporters, the message might appear as a response to a distress call, a rare acknowledgment from a politician of a crisis hiding in plain sight. In his address, the nation's foreign enemies are expelled and its birthright entitlements to wealth and prestige are restored. The people are virtuous because they suffer, and their humiliation will be revisited upon their tormentors. Darkness is a matter of perspective.

At the same time, Trump's rhetorical vision of America pivots on a sense of vulnerability experienced as structural oppression and the promise of revenge of behalf of his forgotten electorate. Expressions of victimization are the price of entry into Trump's project of national redemption; yet, for his white supporters there is no need to demonstrate the veracity of one's claim of marginalization beyond that of feeling that it is the case—be they an unemployed coal worker in West Virginia or a wealthy corporate CEO in California. Victimization, in turn, underwrites a vague theory of retributive justice wherein one feels entitled to count coup on their enemies and take delight in seeing their supposed cruelty revisited upon them. His harsh invectives against international trade agreements, Islamic extremism, gangs, and Mexican immigrants are matched by the counterweight of enthusiasm for the brutality entailed in avenging America's humiliation. Paul

Johnson's erudite observations about Trump's fixation with humiliation suggests that his repeated use of collective pronouns such as "we" and "our" reference not Americans in general but instead those who consider themselves weak and victimized by the nation's foreign enemies. America's strength is defined not by its commitment to democratic values but instead by "its capacity to repel foreign penetration and deport threats to the nation's purity."[4] Trump calls forth an American subject who understands themselves in opposition to the acceptance of the kind of cultural pluralism and racial equality that democracy nominally entails. To this point, Robert Terrill points out how Trump, unburdened of having to acknowledge race, authorizes his white audience to reject any sense of shared civil obligations to build racial trust or strive for civil virtue. Instead, his rhetoric "invites us to dig ourselves in, and then to defend our positions, so that our presumptions and prejudices are not questioned but calcified."[5] In expecting nothing except unflinching loyalty, Trump's subject is owed something that was taken from them by racial Others: jobs, respect, prosperity, safety, freedom, and community without the threat of difference.[6] And while his speeches are often untruthful, incoherent, and even perverse, they nonetheless validate his audience's feelings of marginalization, fear of difference, and entitlement to something greater.[7] The revenge they are promised will be sweet.

This chapter seeks to situate Donald Trump's rhetoric within white masculinity's broader turn to the macabre. I suggest that his dark portraiture of American life, under siege by treacherous enemies, provides an exigence for cruelty and national regeneration through violence. And although one might hope it would be otherwise, there are no shortage of recurring discursive forms that already modulate the public's enjoyment of cruelty—even if it comes at their own expense. Trump's sadism is attuned to a public saturated in reverence for hypermasculine blood sports such as football, boxing, and mixed-martial arts. His masculine revenge fantasies are not unlike those commonly played out in blockbuster action adventures and horror films.[8] His apocalyptic and prophetic visions share a great deal in common with the eschatology taught in contemporary Christian churches. His competitiveness, bluster, insults, and callousness toward others reflect the values of reality television.[9] His naked embrace of cruelty and glibness are at home in the Twittersphere. His melancholia for a bygone era without safe spaces and political correctness fits well with the selective public memories of the 1950s that once filled our television screens. In many ways the popular enjoyment of contemporary media culture as a whole, through its compulsive repetition of form, has courted in his devout electorate an investment in this structural perversity. Through a combination of reality television, social media, and rock-concert-like rallies, Trump stokes fantasies of opulence and success all the while cultivating resentment toward those enemies that would deny their entitlement.

These unconventional forms of public address afford Trump opportunities to both maneuver around traditional public intermediaries and speak in such a brash manner as to dispense with pesky conventions like civic virtue and empathy. Kendall Phillips argues that Trump's political style is attuned to what he characterizes as the changing affective structures of public life. He writes that "the public feelings circulating within American culture in the years preceding the 2016 election resonated with a particular shift in American cinematic myths about the state, the notion of cruelty, and the role of violence."[10] This insight builds from the recognition that American media culture throughout the War on Terrorism has been fixated on survival and extreme suffering—preoccupied with subjecting bodies to "brutal, anonymizing death."[11] Mary Stuckey suggests that Trump's hyperboles and disavowals are effective because they speak directly to this highly charged "affective environment" in which political rhetoric is "unmoored from its institutional routines."[12] Trump's rhetoric is "aimed at the viscera," meaning that institutionalized conventions and common virtues have lost their symbolic efficiency.[13] In many ways, Trump does not merely use networked media to access his electorate; his behaviors are a reflection of the norms that those networks manifest. His political address, then, patterns itself after the transgression and perversity of networked media—its cruelty, lack of empathy, paranoia, narcissism, and negative emotions. While seemingly repellant to his opponents, Gunn recently observed, Trump's rhetoric is structured around routinized enjoyment of civil and psychic transgressions such as those routinely found in networked media.[14] Trump's address demonstrates a simultaneous awareness and denial of social conventions—cruelty delivered with a menacing yet ambiguous smirk of irony. That is to say that Trump's patterned disavowals, his use of ad hominem attacks, his liberal use of *occultatio* and *paralipsis,* his delight in cruelty, and his indifference to civil norms all constitute a style, genre, and statement of political perversity.

I would suggest that this perversity is a reflection of rhetorical conventions nurtured elsewhere—networked media and reality television—that have cultivated an appetite for Trump's unconventional style. I wish to draw from these insights to consider how Trump's expressions of cruelty and doom operate as an extension of the modalities of spectatorship and the culture of networked media that condition our relationship to pain—lived and simulated.[15] It is not simply that Trump's rhetoric is indifferent to the pain of others—that would hardly differentiate him from his predecessors—but that his political perversity aligns with affective attachments, cultivated elsewhere, to a cultural form of sadomasochism that fetishizes both the delivery and the receipt of pain and suffering—particularly that of white men. My interest here is not to rehearse the many ill-advised and unsolicited public psychological diagnosis of the flesh-and-blood Trump but instead to make sense of the figure or persona who manifests the rhetorical perversities that repeat across the culture.[16] Here, we find a figure who draws on our collective sadistic compulsions and directs our psychical investment toward outcomes that hurt or humiliate "our" (and his) enemies: the press, immigrants, gangs, Islamic extremists, China, Democrats, celebrities who speak ill of Trump, and the list goes on.

But it does not stop there. The Trump spectator is also enjoined in a *masochistic* relationship—that is to say, one typically characterized by a request for the infliction of pain and humiliation, and from which the supplicant derives pleasure. Note that Trump does not merely validate the pain of his supporters by addressing them as aggrieved subjects but also delivers to them a painful and humiliating portrait of their own existence. Although Trump offers to take away their pain with utopian promises to "Make American Great Again," Trump's speeches also wallow in the audience's misery and humiliation—all under the veil of him "telling it like it is." It is not uncommon for an attendee at one of his rallies to hear that the American Dream is dead, they have been "raped" by multilateral trade agreements, and laughed at by criminals and foreign adversaries.[17] Trump keeps his audience's wounds fresh and, thus, always in need of tending. Yet, his rallies are often festive, if not carnivalesque events that convey a celebratory tone even as supporters are joyfully berated with painful news of their latest defeat. At the same time, his opponents are also caught in a masochistic relationship when they consume a ceaseless flow of articles, comedy routines, late-night news segments, and videos that capture his latest obnoxious stunt. In sum, this chapter seeks to disentangle the sadomasochistic entailments of Trump's rhetoric and how his abject vision of America invites his supporters, white men in particular, to invest in both their own suffering and the suffering of others. Trump is a president who reflects the enjoyment of casual cruelty encoded into the ecology of new media—the vindictiveness routine portrayed on reality television and the dissolution of empathy cultivated in social networks.

Trump supporters' motives are the subject of constant debate and scrutiny by the press.[18] Confounded by his transgressive behavior, media pundits compulsively decry the seemingly unwavering support of his base. Their incredulous response to his perversity remains "this is not normal!" They ask: Is there no offensive statement or odious behavior that they will not tolerate? Are there no lies or contradictions so beyond the pale that they will refuse to accept? Is there no humiliation or debasement of their own self-interests that they will not endure? Addressing the media's incredulity, Trump's short answer was "no." During an Iowa campaign event, Trump himself confidently declared "I could stand in the middle of 5th Avenue and shoot somebody and I wouldn't lose any voters."[19] Expressing nostalgia for a time when a misplaced sigh or an overzealous yelp was enough to disqualify a candidate for the presidency, the press remains astonished with Trump's ability to evade rebuke from his loyal electorate. Gunn rightfully points out that Trump's detractors seem to neglect the enjoyment of transgression, the affective charge of Trump's refusal to obey civic conventions, and the fantasy that one might enact similar transgression in their daily life (i.e., imitating his rejection of "political correctness" concerning issues of race, gender, and sexuality). Although it is not possible to speak here about the psychology of Trump supporters, it is feasible to account for the psychical structures of enjoyment that organize his rhetorical appeal. In this light, I want to situate the enjoyment of Trump's rhetoric within the categories of *sadomasochism* to make sense of what perverse investments he generates in his electorate. In other words, why might an individual enjoy vacillating between being subjected to humiliation and suffering at one moment and, in the next moment, doling it out to others? The answer to this question returns to the subject of cultural trauma and the death drive introduced at the outset of this book to explain how white masculine victimhood has come to be defined by both self-abasement and violence toward others.

MORAL MASOCHISM AND THE TRUMP AUDIENCE

Despite its incoherence, Donald Trump's style and content does not tend to vary. He is inclined to cover the same subjects with various levels of cogency and formality depending on the context. Although his rallies are more transgressive (or unhinged) than his formal speeches, the content often vacillates between declarations of victimhood and promises of revenge against the nation's enemies. His more formal speeches contrast apocalyptic imagery of America overrun by rapists, murders, drug dealers, ISIS, MS-13, and Mexicans against a virtuous public forgotten by special interests and career politicians. And, of course, his speaking style is hypermasculine: he brags and embellishes his personal accomplishments, portrays life as competition with winners and losers, emphasizes radical individualism, fantasizes about violence and revenge, insults and humiliates women who challenge him, valorizes domination and control, and speaks assuredly without expertise. At the same time, he also devotes significant attention to bemoaning even the slightest criticism, noting how poorly he has been treated by the media, foreign leaders, Democrats, Republican detractors, and even celebrities on Twitter. Across a vast majority of his publicly available speeches, suffering and humiliation are the dominant themes.

Here, I would like to consider the entailments of masochism in Trump's rhetoric; namely, the repetitive listing of grievances and humiliations that he and his supporters have been continually forced to endure. More specifically, I consider the submissive position of the audience in Trump's rhetoric—a persona invested in its own subjugation.[20] At his rallies, he subjects his audience to news of the latest usurpation by their enemies, inducing a call-and-response expectation for the audience to "boo" or chant "lock her up," "USA," or "build the wall" at appropriate moments.[21] At times he summons his audience's rage to support policies that will unlikely benefit his working-class supporters. But masochism is more nuanced than simply the receipt of sexual gratification as the result of a partner's cruelty. Recall that Freud observed three forms of masochism: erotogenic, female, and moral. The first he argued was sadism—the residue of the death drive—introjected back toward the subject and registered as the physiological experience of pain as pleasure. The second—problematized in the introduction—he classifies as feminine passivity, which he equates with the child's fantasy of being beaten by their father.[22] It is the third category, moral masochism, that makes sense of Trump's overtures to suffering. Moral masochism is detached from an external object (as well as sexuality) and is characterized by unconscious guilt that must be assuaged through punishment. Freud observes that "the suffering itself is what matters; whether it is decreed by someone who is loved or by someone who is indifferent is of no importance. It may even be caused by impersonal powers or by circumstances; the true masochist always turns his cheek whenever he has a chance of receiving a blow."[23] Moral masochism of the ego requires a cruel superego to enact self-punishment for unconscious guilt. It is for this reason that Savran argues that Marcuse's concept of surplus repression is virtually synonymous with moral masochism, as in both cases the ego learns to enforce its own repression through guilt, and, consequently, the masochistic subject takes pleasure in their own subjugation.[24]

The masochism that organizes Trump's relation to his audience manifests in two forms: (1) continual references to the nobility of enduring the torment of one's enemies, and (2) an expressed desire for impenetrable obstacles.[25] As with melancholia, the first compels the subject to repeat and endure traumatic experiences that render them passive and thus capable of deriving pleasure from subjugation. The second addresses the subject's disillusion and displeasure with defeating their rival. In short, upon achieving their object of desire, one shrugs: "is that it?" These expressions of masochism are related by their investment in subjugation but differ in how they manifest. For instance, René Girard explained that in the latter form a masochist requires a rival to play a triumphant role so that they can be the object/victim of their violence. He writes, "The only type of model that can still generate excitement is the one who cannot be defeated, the one who will always defeat his disciple."[26] In this case, only the creation of an impenetrable obstacle can generate excitement (i.e., "a big fat beautiful wall"). As I illustrate below, Trump's rhetoric focuses on abstract policy goals where it is difficult to discern their attainment as well as rivals who, even with all his political power, can never be vanquished. The moral masochist is not one who finds pleasure in pain per se but one who positions themselves to never be satisfied.

Sharply departing from his predecessors, Trump devotes significant attention to America's passivity and humiliation by sexually aggressive enemies and predatory states. Unbound by "political correctness," Trump routinely subjects his audience to the harsh "truth" of their victimhood. For instance, in his RNC acceptance address, before listing America's failures, he explained that "here, at our convention, there will be no lies. We will honor the American people with the truth, and nothing else."[27] This theme was established early when he announced his candidacy. At that time, he decried how America was being "beaten" by their foreign adversaries:

> We used to have victories, but we don't have them. When was the last time anybody saw us beating, let's say, China in a trade deal? They kill us. I beat China all the time. All the time. When do we beat Mexico at the border? They're laughing at us, at our stupidity.[28]

Here, America has been debased and forced into submission, not because of the strength of other nations but because of the nation's own willingness to accept such treatment. He goes on to sexualize the nation's victimhood by reminding his audience that their border has been penetrated by Mexico, who are "bringing drugs, they're bringing crime. They're rapists."[29] Drawing from racist lore of dark-skinned predators who prey on the innocent, Trump positions America as prone—ostensibly inviting tormentors into their communities and even their bodies. As our enemies get stronger, he reminds us, America has lost its phallic potency: "Even our nuclear arsenal doesn't work."[30] Thus, he constructs the nation as a womanly object of sadistic violence. The implication here is that the nation has lost its desire to make other countries submit to its will. It is not that our nation is incapable of asserting its power; it is that we have collectively agreed to submit to others: "We have losers. We have losers. We have people that don't have it. We have people that are morally corrupt. We have people that are selling this country down the drain." In Trump's estimation, "the American dream is dead."[31] While he also presents a sadistic fantasy that I discuss later, note here that Trump says nothing of the strength and resilience of the national character, and avoids talk of America overcoming obstacles or any subject that might illustrate the agency of his audience.

Instead, Trump positions his audience as weak, submissive, naïve, and subject to the whims of sadists. As a nation, we have expressed a desire to be dominated; that is to say, we used to enjoy beating our competitors but now we have collectively chosen to let them play the triumphant role in our economic and diplomatic relationships. If we take him at his word, his bid for the presidency was not premised on empowering the American people. Instead, this address extends to his audience an offer to be dominated by an autocratic strongman. He promises that "if I get elected president I will bring it [the American Dream] back bigger and better and stronger than ever before, and we will make America great again."[32] As he goes on to note in his RNC acceptance speech, "I alone can fix it."[33] While America seems unable to beat its competitors, Trump brags: "I beat China every time."[34] The lack of a collective vision in this address reflects an image of a passive audience that must cede their agency to a powerful leader who can singularly make the nation strong again. The imagined audience here is invited to exchange one relationship of dominance and submission for another—to forsake foreign adversaries for a domestic paternal figure.

Elsewhere, Trump routinely characterizes his public as agentless victims: forgotten and abandoned by weak and ineffective leaders. In his inaugural address he refers to his electorate as a "forgotten people" who will be "forgotten no longer."[35] His vision of their reality is quite bleak: "Mothers and children trapped in poverty in our inner cities; rusted-out factories scattered like tombstones across the landscape of our nation; an education system, flush with cash, but which leaves our young and beautiful students deprived of knowledge; and the crime and gangs and drugs that have stolen too many lives and robbed our country of so much unrealized potential."[36] At the RNC he claimed, "Not only have our citizens endured domestic disaster, but they have lived through one international humiliation after another. We all remember the images of our sailors being forced to their knees by their Iranian captors at gunpoint."[37] As Johnson rightfully observes of this passage, imagery of Americans forced to their knees bespeaks an implicitly sexualized humiliation of being coerced into submission by a rapist.[38] I would add that his choice of verbs associated with criminal violence reinforces this point. Note that Americans have been "trapped," have been "robbed," have "endured"—all of which bespeak a fundamental lack of audience agency. Government regulations in particular operate as signs of coercion. Describing anonymous supporters who Trump claimed approached him with "tears in their eyes," he recounts their lament at being "forced to pay not to have health care. Very unfair."[39] When speaking about international trade agreements, he compares the nation's adherence to global norms and domestic regulations as doglike obedience. At an August 22, 2017, rally in Phoenix, he claimed that we "were like the lap dog. Great for other countries. Our country was so behind."[40] Later he extends the dog obedience metaphor by suggesting that abolishing regulations is "*unleashing* our economy," a phrase he continually invokes.[41]

Based on such ruminations, his ideal audience seems to be one that recognizes themselves as victims—who in finding their way to Trump's vision of America are implored to attach meaning and identity to their suffering. They are invited to find themselves to be a historically oppressed people who share a serial relationship to ruthless persecution manifest in everything from environmental regulations to taxes. Ironically, Trump's valorization of the "forgotten people" renders suffering and exile as the preconditions for political subjectivity. The problem, however, is that suffering must continue for this subject to claim their place in the polity. This exemplifies the perverse structures of enjoyment that Trump's speeches offer to his adherents. Recall that the masochist is incapable of gratification when their rival is absent. Moreover, Lundberg and Collins remind us that the politics of the demand locates enjoyment in lodging the complaint. This is an imagined audience constituted via cultivated investments in its own victimization. Though he never explicitly references their gender or race, Trump's strongest appeal is to a subject looking for an identity politics but seemingly lacking access to symbolically efficient categories such as race, gender, and sexuality. This ideal auditor would feel shut out of national dialogues about suffering and attacked by the visibility of identity movements that seem to out-compete them for national attention. Although Trump acknowledges their suffering and claims to be above the fray of insider politics, his rhetorical challenge is to find new ways for his adherents to coalesce around suffering and stay on the margins while also taking back their country. In short, he must invent new ways in which his audience suffers even as they "Make America Great Again."

Trump's solution, then, is to identify new enemies—and resurrect old ones—to both signal his attunement to his audience's grievances and continue their political exile. This task was not difficult during the 2016 presidential campaign, as conservatives had nearly twenty-five years of practice demonizing Hillary Clinton.[42] As such, no amount of hyperbole was off-limits. In his RNC acceptance speech, he linked Clinton to nearly every major military and foreign policy blunder of the past two decades, concluding, "This is the legacy of Hillary Clinton: death, destruction and weakness."[43] Despite his electoral victory, "crooked Hillary" still makes regular appearances in his Twitter posts, usually to observe what he believes to be the unfairness that Clinton is not also under investigation by the FBI Special Counsel—an investigation he has referred to as the "single greatest witch hunt in American history."[44] "Lock her up!" remains in the repertoire of chants one might hear from the crowd at a Trump rally.

While Islam, gangs, and immigrants play their part in Trump's narrative of victimhood, the main adversary of Trump and his electorate remains the news media. Targeting the press enables Trump to laud his putatively unreported victories without ceding the moral high ground of victimhood. Claims of "fake news" enable him to disavow comments and actions that draw public scrutiny and undermine his critics' ability to engage in reality-referencing.[45] A survey of Republicans revealed that four out of ten agree with Trump that the press is "the enemy of the people."[46] He has referred to the press as the "very crooked media" and asserted that they have "committed a lot of atrocities when you look."[47] His frequent finger-pointing at the press covering his rallies is greeted with reflexive boos, insults, and obscenities by the crowd. At one rally Trump drew attention to "the very dishonest media, those people right up there with all the cameras [pointing] . . . and I mean truly dishonest people in the media and the fake media, they make up stories."[48] Drawing clear battle lines between the press and people, he referred to the media as a collective of "sick people" because they do not want to "make our country great again, and I honestly believe they don't."[49] These examples illustrate how Trump navigates between two contradictory representations of his electorate. On the one hand, his audience has made America great again and are therefore victorious, triumphant, and strong. They have eviscerated their enemies and taken back the country. On the other hand, his audience is victimized by a powerful cabal of dishonest journalists who continually thwart their efforts. While his demonization of the media serves a variety of purposes, including scapegoating and disavowal, his comments are also vital if he is to continue to cultivate audiences' affective investment in their own marginalization.

Alongside Trump's perpetual rival is the impenetrable obstacle: "the Wall." Although some of Trump's campaign promises were abstractions, a menacing wall that would stretch the length of America's southern border with Mexico was materially quantifiable and distinct. Though not yet built, the wall serves as a metonymic object that stands in for the Trump administration's "America First" agenda and testifies to Trump's skill as a builder.[50] When he announced his candidacy, he boasted, "I will build a great wall—and nobody builds walls better than me, believe me—and I'll build them very inexpensively. I will build a great, great wall on our southern border, and I will make Mexico pay for the wall. Mark my words."[51] While the call to build the wall energizes his supporters, the pragmatics of such a grand gesture have proved difficult for the administration.[52] As a result of funding and logistical difficulties, Trump's description of the wall has varied widely.[53] Is it a wall or a fence? Will it cover all 1,954 miles of the border, or sections designated as priorities by the border patrol? How much will it cost? Will Mexico pay for it? If so, how? Such tedious questions about policy specifics and implementation have proved somewhat burdensome and ultimately serve to dissipate the affective discharge of such a bold demand. This in no way denies that his supporters desire the wall; to be sure, they do. But rather I suggest that it is the demand for the wall itself that matters more than the tiresome details concerning how it will be ultimately achieved. For the wall to serve as an impenetrable object, its achievement must be perpetually deferred yet seem possible enough to warrant the demand. There must be an obstacle or group that is inimical to its completion. In Freud's words, "The suffering entailed by neuroses is precisely the factor that makes them valuable to the masochistic trend."[54] In other words, the wall must remain a source of frustration, a roadblock that can then serve as the raison d'être for the Trump electorate; a group already constituted through their shared pain. Put even another way, if the wall *was* built, the moral masochist would be denied the extended gratification entailed in making the demand.

Trump's rhetoric on the subject of "the wall" provides precisely this form of enjoyment. That is to say that he speaks of the wall as both possible and perpetually deferred. At the 2018 CPAC convention, Trump remarked:

> You're getting the wall. Don't worry. I heard some—getting the wall. Had a couple of these characters in the back say, oh, he really doesn't want the wall. He just used that for campaigning. I said, are you—can you believe it? You know, I say every time I hear that, the wall gets ten feet higher, you know that. Every single time. Okay. Now, we're going to have the wall. Or they're not going to have what they want. We have a problem. We need more Republicans. We have a group of people that vote against us in a bloc.[55]

In this passage, Trump vacillates between absolute guarantees that the wall will be built and doubts that they have enough support to make the wall a reality. "Build that wall" is qualified by a secondary demand, "We need more Republicans."[56] He seems to also demonstrate awareness that his opponents believe that the wall is nothing more than an empty campaign slogan. Upon relaying this critique, Trump promises a wall that is even bigger than first imagined: "ten feet higher" added every time his opponents test him. Paradoxically, the demand becomes somehow more impossible, more grandiose, even as it promises to become a material reality. If the demand is denied, he offers his supporters a secondary form of enjoyment: revenge. If Trump does not get what *he* wants, his opponents will not get what *they* want. And while this threat is much more characteristic of sadism, his statement reminds the audience that their perpetually deferred demand is thwarted by a ceaselessly frustrating rival. Elsewhere, Trump uses this paradox to disavow responsibility for making the wall a reality by ceding agency to his opponents. After claiming that the wall will be built, he adds this caveat: "Democrats in Congress who oppose a border wall and stand in the way of border security: You are putting all of America's safety at risk. You're doing that. You're doing that."[57] Again, the wall is both inevitable and yet also held prisoner by his opponents. In this way, the demand never loses its affective charge.

POLITICAL SADISM

Freud observed that sadism and masochism are frequently located in the same subject, entailing the possibility of vacillations between roles; hence his merging of the terms: *sadomasochism.* While Freud found sadism primarily in men and masochism in women, scholars have pointed out that his case studies for female masochism were all derived from his study of men. At any rate, the categories are not exclusive, and their structures of gratification are somewhat similar. For example, masochism can be understood as sadism turned inward. Conversely, sadism represents the externalization of the death drive—that which threatens to eviscerate the subject—onto others. Introducing the literary works of the *Marquis de Sade,* John Yankowski points out that "cruelty is an expression of the death impulse; it is the translation into physical terms of the emotion of hate."[58] In other words, where Eros works to preserve the ego, the death drive "seeks to destroy that which would imperil the ego."[59] The sadist forgoes relationships in which castration is a possibility in favor of relational configurations where the submission of another permits that "what might happen to the subject passively" can be "done actively to others."[60] Submission by others alleviates any guilt that might inhibit the sadist's enjoyment.

Much like the earlier discussion of masochism, sadism also underwrites a political-rhetorical perversion that is characterized by a speaker's transgressive fantasies of violence, cruelty, and humiliation of others without compunction or remorse. Violence need not serve a particular end; the subject may reference the norms against such fantasies and indulge them nonetheless. While political sadism is not an exclusively male phenomenon, it is a perversion that countersigns hypermasculine political movements, fascist and terrorist organizations, and cults that demand submission and obedience from their subjects. Political sadism is organized around masculine rhetorics of control, domination, and enjoyment in the suffering of one's opponent. It can be characterized in a fashion similar to Jasbir Puar's exploration of *debilitation,* the sovereign right to designate certain bodies as available for injury that manifests as the slow wearing-down of vulnerable populations.[61] The *right to maim,* Puar argues, is overdetermined by the demands of white fragility to be compensated for its superficial injuries. Similarly, the political sadist invents an enemy with superlative capacities in order to facilitate the ongoing debilitation of vulnerable populations.

It should come as no surprise to the reader that there is no shortage of examples wherein Trump indulges his affinity for political sadism. One need look no further than his 2016 campaign rallies to find shocking footage of protestors beaten and bloodied by his supporters and gleeful cheers for expressions of political violence. Rather than condemning such behavior, Trump told his supporters, "Knock the crap out of them . . . I promise you, I will pay for the legal fees."[62] Mere mentions of Hillary Clinton were reflexively greeted by the popular chant "lock her up!" which mirrors a masculine rape/bondage fantasy of a powerful rival forced into total submission. Discussions of immigrants or foreigners invited the audience to boo and yell obscenities, while fantasies of revenge were cheered and applauded. But it matters not merely that Trump's political affect can be characterized as sadistic; it is that certain tropes of cruelty garnered enjoyment and served particular political ends.

Here I offer two ways of organizing Trump's statements of cruelty. First, Trump identifies an abject out-group for whom the audience should feel no guilt about punishing. This trope can best be characterized as *justified cruelty.* Here, Trump makes use of plural possessive pronouns to draw essential distinctions between the identity of the dominant in-group and the submissive out-group. Foreign Others (China, Mexico, Islam) are cast as inimical to *our* wealth, *our* safety, and *our* sovereignty. For instance, in one form or another he repeats the mantra "We're going to bring back our jobs, bring back our wealth, and we are going to bring back our dreams, and we are going to bring back, once again our sovereignty as a nation."[63] Adopting the credo "America First," the collective pronoun "our" is relatively narrow in scope when defining who might benefit from America's power.[64] The nation's internal and external enemies share a common nefarious characteristic: they are takers. He warns, "They will repeal your tax cuts, they will put judges in that you wouldn't believe, they'll take away your Second Amendment, which we will never allow to happen, they'll take away your Second Amendment. Remember that. They will take away."[65] In addition to wealth, jobs, and rights, Trump points out that "they're trying to take away our culture. They are trying to take away our history."[66] Here, "our" narrows again to include only those supporters of both an unbridled Second Amendment and those who identify with both American exceptionalism and Confederate nostalgia. The in-group (mostly white, mostly male) is pitted against "they," a virtually indistinguishable horde of "takers" who desire nothing more than to dispossess "us" of "our" birthright entitlements. These in-group/out-group distinctions occasion a kind of justified cruelty against those whose very identities are inimical to the national interest.

Agonistic group distinctions serve as the basis for legitimate yet also enjoyable acts of revenge. For instance, Trump often boasts about law enforcement's capacity to revisit cruelty upon criminals and undocumented immigrants. At the same time, he often speaks about criminals and undocumented immigrants as deserving of legal and extralegal violence, punishments he seems eager to administer. Sharing a likeness to the racial mythology of the Black rapist, Trump talks of illegal immigration as an "infestation" of "animals" and "predators" who target innocent victims (typically white women).[67] For instance, he notes that "the predators and criminal aliens who poison our communities with drugs and prey on innocent young people, these beautiful, beautiful, innocent young people will, will find no safe haven anywhere in our country. And you've seen the stories about some of these animals."[68] After highlighting violent crimes committed by undocumented immigrants, Trump promises his audience revenge: "These families, the deaths of their loved ones will not have been in vain. I promised them."[69] Pointing out their lack of humanity, he assures his audience that "they cut them up into little pieces. These are animals. We are getting them out of here. We're throwing them in jails, and we're throwing them out of the country. We're liberating our towns."[70] Elsewhere he brags that "people that treat us badly, we treat them much *worse than they could ever imagine*. That's the way it has to be. That's the way it has to be."[71] For Trump, the inhumanity of America's enemies alleviates the government of any legal or moral responsibility for protecting due process or human rights. Furthermore, the nation's response to cruelty must be asymmetrical and merciless. While he can vividly imagine the cruelty of foreign "predators," he boasts that his cruelty is beyond even their imagination. Yet, he testifies that it is this cruelty that liberates the nation, much like a foreign military freeing an occupied nation from oppression. But revenge is not only efficacious, it is righteous.

Trump expresses satisfaction whenever criminals receive their just deserts. For instance, he shares his personal fantasy of turning the tables on those who might wish him harm. At one rally, Trump chained out a personal revenge fantasy by comparing himself to Charles Bronson's character in the 1974 film *Death Wish*. In that film, Bronson played Paul Kersey, a man who goes on a vigilante killing spree following the rape and murder of his wife and daughter. It is important to note that Bronson's character sought revenge not only on the attackers but also on the entire criminal element in New York City. Trump described a hypothetical revenge scenario in which someone attacked him while he carried a concealed weapon:

> I have a license to carry in New York, can you believe that? Somebody attacks me, can you imagine somebody says "there's Trump, he's easy pickin's" what you say? [Gun gesture]. What was the famous movie, remember? Where his wife was hurt so badly and killed . . . Charles Bronson right? The late great Charles Bronson. Death Wish! Remember that? Oh, we're gonna cut you up sir . . . uh, uh, uh, bing [making gun noise]. One of the great movies. You can't make that movie because it's not political correct. But could you image with Trump, somebody says ah, all these big monsters aren't around, he's easy pickin's, Shing [makes gun gesture]. This is about self-defense plain and simple.[72]

With a lighthearted smile, Trump mimics gun sounds and gestures as he delights in a glamorous portrayal of vigilante violence. His portrayal of "plain and simple" self-defense is in no way reluctant or solemn but rather delights in pleasures of righteous violence. And while this example is a bit tongue-in-cheek, it is consistent with his general expressions of pleasure when discussing the myriad ways in which our law enforcement agencies, or vigilantes, might exact a retributive "eye for an eye" justice against suspected criminals.

The second kind of cruelty expressed by Trump, more characteristic of classical sadism, is violence for the enjoyment of power. In other words, Trump often relishes the overwhelming potential of the nation to inflict violence upon others. For him, American power seems to be premised on the ability to impose its will capriciously and without justification. Displaying toughness garners the respect of the nation's enemies and, consequently, portends their submission to its will. When discussing MS-13, he observes, "We have tough people. I'll tell you what, when you deal with MS-13, the only thing they understand is toughness. They don't want anything. All they understand is toughness. If that ICE agent or border patrol agent is tougher than them, they respect him. We have the toughest guys you've ever seen. We got tough. They don't respect anything else. And they shouldn't be in our country."[73] This passage is indicative of Trump's fascination with toughness and brutality as characteristics that engender the respect and admiration of a sadistic rival. According to Trump, toughness is defined by the capacity to make others submit to one's will. Their respect and admiration of toughness alleviates any guilt that might interfere with the enjoyment of enacting violence against a submissive subject. Hence, he relished that "our ICE goes in there they [sic] grab by the neck, they throw them in the Paddy Wagon, they get them the hell out of our country."[74] That is to say that the key attribute of America's toughness is illustrated by the complete domination of an enemy. In this fantasy, MS-13 members are physically dominated, stripped of legal and bodily protections, and exiled from the polity. In this scenario, these once powerful gang members are rendered vulnerable to the whims of stronger, superior men. To be grabbed by the neck, incarcerated, and stripped of due process is to be superlatively powerless.

Trump also boasts about the monstrous cruelty of the nation's border patrol. In the passage below, Trump dispenses with humane treatment of suspected criminals with the dismissive label of "political correctness." Often asserting that Democrats coddle criminals and restrain the brutal powers of law enforcement, Trump distinguishes himself by taking pride in transgressing our formal laws and tacit norms against police brutality. In this extended quotation, Trump muses on his vision of a hypermasculine, "politically incorrect," model of law enforcement:

> We are dismantling and destroying the bloodthirsty criminal gangs, and well, I will just tell you in, we're not doing it in a politically correct fashion. We're doing it rough. Our guys are rougher than their

guys. I asked one of our great generals, "how tough are our people? How tough are they?" He said, "sir, you don't want to know about it." Then I saw one guy come out, a customs officer who is a monster. I said, "so general, you think I could take that guy in a fight?" He said, "Mr. President, sir I don't even want to think about it." I said "you're right, actually." We have tough people. Our people are tougher than their people. Our people are tougher and stronger and meaner and smarter than the gangs.[75]

Trump's gleeful tone belies the abject brutality entailed by "doing it rough." A far cry from President George W. Bush's call for "compassionate conservatism," Trump's vision of a meaner and more monstrous America relaxes our collective prohibitions against the extralegal use of force. This is not to suggest that Trump's predecessors are not responsible for policies that lead to similar acts of brutality, but rather that the difference is in terms of enjoyment. What distinguishes Trump as a political sadist is his lack of caveat, moral justification, or reluctance to use force only when necessary. His political sadism is marked by his willingness to openly transgress the norms against human rights abuses and state-sanctioned violence against noncitizens. Here we find an unapologetic endorsement of primal masculine violence devoid of any sense of ambivalence or redemption. While violence may also be demonstrative of America's power, it is primarily warranted for its own sake.

There are countless other examples that one could draw from to demonstrate Trump's sadism; however, these passages illustrate a larger pattern of discourse in which the president extolls the pleasures of humiliating and physically dominating the nation's enemies. The appeal of political sadism is that it dispenses with perfunctory expressions of morality that often accompany the use of force or any form of guilt that might arise and inhibit one's ability to derive pleasure from violence. His embrace of the will-to-power liberates his audience from the strictures of empathy. Political sadism foregrounds the nation's subjugation of any and all challengers but, most importantly, takes pleasure in the submissive admiration of those subjected to violence. Sadism also eradicates the symbolic threat of castration and emasculation presented by the nation's rivals. As such, with the tables turned, those who were once "laughing at us" will be made to suffer a much worse, unimaginable fate. Trump's rhetoric attempts to *re*-masculinize the nation by enacting fantasies of dominance and subjugation on inferior, dark-skinned men. Trump's rhetoric even forsakes redemption as the end of white masculine violence for a primal violence that is its own end. Physical abuse, torture, family separation, unlawful incarceration, and similar acts of cruelty are not only possible in this world; they are mandatory.

A MONSTROUS AMERICA

Trump's rhetoric of victimhood and revenge represent an abject form of white masculinity that is constituted through hierarchal relationships of domination, control, and violence. While Trump positions his audience as subservient, feminine, and subjugated, his vision of state power is "tough," "mean," "monstrous," and not "politically correct"—capable of inflicting unimaginable suffering on those who violate America's sovereignty, wealth, and safety. Trump offers to take the reins of power on his public's behalf and, in exchange for their obedience, offers to inflict pain on their enemies. But Trump's enactment of political sadomasochism is symptomatic of the larger structural forces at work in the cultural psyche of white men. Although it is easy to scapegoat Trump for igniting the perverse desires of his audience, he is but one pathway by which the affective intensities of white men are directed into perverse political forms. In response to a forty-year effort to paint white men as victims of social and economic change, Trump simply channels white male ressentiment and melancholia into a form of political agency organized around justified cruelty. He addresses his audience as if they were agentless victims of cultural trauma, thus affirming their identity as aggrieved subjects who are owed retribution and compensation. His attacks on political correctness remove the stigma and guilt associated with the perverse entailments of white identity politics, including, if necessary, violence. As Trump's America is a graveyard of rusted factories occupied by foreign armies, the nation does not have the luxury of kindness and civility in achieving its liberation.

Trump's personal kinks and political perversions remain a constant source of speculation in the news media. Titillating tales of hush money paid to Playboy models, spankings by porn stars, watersports in Russian hotel rooms, and the like speak to the perverse enjoyment of the news media and its anti-Trump spectators. Trump's opponents have seized on his perverse masculinity and his transparent overcompensation to suggest that he is an aberration of contemporary white masculinity.[76] Protestors have generated countless images of Trump as queer, womanly, transgender, and emasculated in an effort to call out his grotesque enactment of white masculinity. Images include that of Trump as a submissive in a BDSM relationship with Russian president and "leather daddy" Vladimir Putin, Trump kissing Putin, Trump carrying Putin's child, Trump as a castrated eunuch, and so on. Trump's opponents engage in problematic efforts to combat his personal and political perversity by suggesting that his performance of masculinity is abnormal and that he in no way reflects contemporary white manhood. These portrayals rely on the commonsense logic of homophobia and transphobia to exonerate and wrest white masculinity from its perversions. My concern here is that efforts to fight Trump's perversity fail to address its underlying appeal. That is to say, presenting Trump as deviant belies how his rhetoric and identity performances align with hegemonic white masculinity. Thus, although political sadomasochism is perverse, it is not an extreme abnormality. Instead, it reflects the broader structures of enjoyment that have become sutured to white masculinity as an identity constituted through logics of domination and submission. Suffering has become the *sine qua non* of entry into white male identity politics. Trump's political perversity is not simply an aberration; instead, it represents an intensification of white masculinity's demand politics. His rhetoric hails a subject who can at times find investment in their own suffering and at others derive gratification from the suffering of others.

CONCLUSION

Return to Charlottesville

IN SPIKE LEE'S 2018 film *BlacKkKlansman,* Black police detective Ron Stallworth (played by John David Washington) and his Jewish partner Flip Zimmerman (Adam Driver) infiltrate the Colorado Springs chapter of the Ku Klux Klan, in the process thwarting a violent attack against a group of Black college activists. Based on the real Detective Stallworth's autobiographical account of foiling the KKK in the 1970s, the film shows how Stallworth developed an over-the-phone persona that Zimmerman acted out in person in order to trick the likes of David Duke and infiltrate the organization. In the spirit of 1970s blaxploitation cinema, Stallworth heroically outsmarts white supremacists and wins the support and admiration of his fellow police officers. As audiences reach the film's dénouement, he and his girlfriend Patrice Dumas (Laura Harrier) debate whether the two have a future together—Patrice still a committed activist and Stallworth still a police detective. Suddenly, there is an unsettling knock on Stallworth's door. Attentive to the possibility of retribution, the two pull their guns and face the anonymous visitor at the door. Guns pointed at the camera, the two float down the hallway toward an ominous threat in a brief interlude of cinematic surrealism. There is a fire in the distance that the camera, upon closer inspection, reveals to be a burning cross. The atmosphere of hopeful jubilation engendered by KKK's defeat is dashed by the hardnosed realism of racism's endurance.

But the film does not end there. Before the credits appear and the audience begins to gather their things and exit the theater, the camera cuts to footage of the 2017 Unite the Right rally in Charlottesville. The images are uncannily familiar. Nazi salutes. Police protecting marchers chanting "Jews will not replace us!" White supremacists violently assaulting counterprotestors with improvised weapons. A homicidal driver careening their vehicle into the crowd. Screams of anguish and abject terror. Chaos in the streets. Cries for help. The nation's president refusing to condemn, in his words, these "fine people." Onlookers in disbelief. The audience is delivered from a fantasy of racial transcendence to the brutal reality of their racist present. In the here-and-now, there are neither myths of racial progress nor warm platitudes from which a white audience might draw to restore their faith in liberal democracy. Those vile racists cleverly thwarted by Stallworth and Zimmerman are not hermitically sealed in some screen fiction; they live in your neighborhood, attend your church, work in your office, and represent your interests in elected bodies. Quieted by the experience of cinematic whiplash, the audience is led to a terrifying conclusion: we have done this all before and we will do this all again. Of course, this is not news to audiences of color. Instead, Spike Lee confronts his white audience with the cruel reality that the KKK, Nazis, and other white supremacists have a voice in contemporary white America—one that reaches all the way to the top elected official in the nation.

In August 2018, Unite the Right organizers sought to mark the one-year anniversary of the events in Charlottesville by organizing a march in Washington, DC. This time, a small band of marchers were vastly outnumbered by swarms of protestors who effectively shouted down their message and swiftly ended the march without incident. As if to yet again confirm Marx's adage that history repeats, "first as tragedy, then as farce," the group's attempt to march on Washington wilted and relegated supporters back to the dark recesses of the manosphere, at least for the time being.[1] But I am less sanguine that this fragile peace will hold. Nor am I convinced that what we are witnessing is some sort of aberration in white masculinity that will wither when white men come to their senses with the hindsight of history. Revisiting Charlottesville, we are reminded more of the logistical difficulties of organizing hate groups offline than the disinfecting qualities of public light. Of course, men who marched unapologetically and with no fear of recourse in 2017 found themselves less organized and employable in 2018. Although reflective of some changes in public sentiments, much of the work to unsettle and resist white supremacy in the Trump era takes place in diffuse political movements such as antifascism (Antifa) and Black Lives Matter.

Since the march at Charlottesville, there have been a number of other significant public reckonings for white men wherein the rhetoric of victimhood has both shown its ugly face and been repudiated. For instance, in October 2017 film producer Harvey Weinstein was fired and expelled from the Academy of Motion Picture Arts and Sciences following over eighty separate allegations of sexual abuse, rape, and harassment.[2] The shocking details of Weinstein's crimes and the courageousness of the women who came forward to share their stories helped promulgate the #MeToo social media campaign to both publicize sexual harassment perpetrated by powerful men and cultivate empathy among the survivors. The #MeToo movement was originally founded by Tarana Burke as an effort to raise awareness and build connections between survivors of assault, particular women of color. In sharing their stories, survivors were afforded the opportunity to join social support networks, empathizes with others, and build solidarity to oust serial abusers and check white male power. The #MeToo movement is a fitting response to the networks of entitlement, power, and impunity outlined in this book—networks that prevent men from being held accountable for their actions, from Weinstein to Trump. As Michelle Rodino-Colocino writes, "Whereas Trump's cruelty seeks to legitimize and actualize white supremacist patriarchal power, Me Too's and #MeToo's mobilization of empathy counters the othering, distancing, and ultimately, the unequal relations of power that sexual assault symptomatizes and reinforces."[3] Here we see the emergence of a counternetwork, afforded by social media, that works against its masculine media ecology. Despite serving as a vector for men's rights networks, #MeToo seized Twitter to aggregate disparate women's voices and create a counternetwork, underwritten by empathy, to expose structures of impunity and build networks of support. #MeToo demonstrates the degree to which mediated forms are at times constraining and, at others, malleable. The hashtag became a powerful point of identification that enabled survivors to swarm the entrenched networks of white male power without fear of reprisal. Networked media need not nourish narratives of victimization but instead create new pathways and conduits by which the marginalized can challenge the powerful.

The emergence of counternetworks is necessary if we are to provide an effective antidote to the poisonous intoxicant that is white male victimhood. Men's rights networks will neither cede power willingly nor lose adherents by virtue of negative publicity. Perhaps no other event exemplifies the character of white male backlash than the 2018 Supreme Court confirmation hearing of Justice Brett Kavanaugh. Professor Christine Blasey Ford testified that Kavanaugh sexually assaulted her in 1982. Kavanaugh and his congressional supporters responded with fiery incredulity to the accusations, painting the Justice as an all-American guy who had been victimized by a movement that had accumulated too much power. The confirmation hearing transformed into a public trial of the #MeToo movement that ostensibly shifted the burden of proof onto the victims of sexual assault and further insulated the powerful from accountability. Kavanaugh portrayed himself as a victim of a "political hit job" on the part of a vast network of conspirators determined to take down the powerful "by any means necessary."[4] In his statement to Congress, he exclaimed, "This confirmation process has become a national disgrace. The Constitution gives the Senate an important role in the confirmation process. But you have replaced 'advice and consent' with 'search and destroy.'"[5] President Trump rushed to his aid by imploring, "Think of your son. Think of your husband. Think—I've had many false accusations. I've had it all the—I've had so many—and when I say it didn't happen, nobody believes me. But it's me. It's my job description."[6] Trump blamed Ford for besmirching Kavanaugh's character, commenting, "This woman had no clue what was going on. No clue. And yet she made the most horrible charges against a number one in his class at Yale, perfect human being, great father, great husband. This is a great person."[7] It is perhaps fitting that the only public apology Trump has issued in office to this point has been to Kavanaugh and his family. The Kavanaugh hearing provided an opportunity for white men to make the case that the #MeToo movement was premised not on empathy but on vindictiveness—a conspiracy hell-bent on destroying the lives and careers of hardworking white men. The hearings helped cast doubt on the claims of survivors and built sympathy for those who assert that they have been falsely accused. This moment demonstrated that white men's networks will fight tooth and claw to retain their privileges and evade scrutiny for their treatment of women and the vulnerable. Victimhood remains a refuge for white men to, when cornered, turn the tables on the marginalized when they demand justice. Furthermore, white male victimhood serves as the occasion for recuperating a moment in time when white men were not subject to such extraordinary scrutiny. Yet, the nourishment and solidarity cultivated by the #MeToo movement offers a model of how marginalized groups can form networks capable of transforming broader cultural narratives. Though not a panacea, marginalized networks demand a different model of justice that includes both collective support for survivors and accountability for the perpetrators.

Despite the backlash politics of the moment, men must be held accountable. They must *also* hold themselves and each other accountable. The call to transform white masculinity, and masculinity writ large, has also materialized from within. For instance, the Gillette razor company launched a #MeToo-inspired advertising campaign that asked men to take the lead in addressing toxic masculinity. In the television commercial, the narrator explains, "You can't hide from it. You can't laugh it off, making the same old excuses," such as "boys will be boys."[8] The ad presents scenes in which men demonstrate empathy and intervene to stop fellow men from bullying, catcalling, and harassing women. The narrator concludes, "It's only by challenging ourselves to do more, that we can get closer to our best." Although we should be skeptical of a multibillion dollar company such as Proctor & Gamble using progressive messages to brand their products, the message is nonetheless one that men need to hear. Predictably, some men pushed back. They posted videos of themselves burning their razors and vowing to boycott the company for impugning men's character. On YouTube, the ad received twice as many dislikes as likes.[9] But the message of accountability is remarkable because it provides men the opportunity to divest in privilege while reclaiming masculinity as a source of empathy and a commitment to justice.

This form of masculinity is exemplified by actor Terry Crews, who revealed that he, too, was a survivor of sexual assault. His public statements address a common sense of vulnerability that provide space for men to acknowledge the role that toxic masculinity plays in impeding men's ability to empathize and change their behavior. Explaining why he felt compelled to speak out, Crews observed,

> I'd actually just read a comment someone made on Twitter about one of Weinstein's accusers. It went something like: She's just looking for attention and a payday. It really affected me. I couldn't stop thinking about it. I remember going to my phone and I started writing. And I couldn't stop. What it became was this sixteen-tweet missive from me. I just remember having to say what I felt. I was really angry because these women were being discounted. These women were being discarded. Their pain was just—it was nothing. I wanted to join in. I wanted to say something. I wanted to support. But I did have to let these women know they weren't alone. And that I understood. My whole mission was to give them strength. Don't accept the shame that people are giving you. Because that's what it was. They were being shamed. They were being victimized again. I just couldn't stand for it.[10]

Crews's comments provide a positive model of ally-ship with those who have been harassed, assaulted, dismissed, and silenced. For Crews, listening to the voices of survivors compelled him to speak out without consideration for his own reputation or the possibility of reaping credit for his actions. His remarks speak to a kind of justice that privileges healing, redemption, and solidarity.

In addition to the networked power of men—both on- and offline—efforts to disrupt the victimhood narrative must construct a model of justice that does not simply focus on individual perpetrators but instead addresses the systematic, structural, and psychical dimensions of white melancholia. Crews's bold yet remarkably straightforward remarks suggest the possibility that men can address their accumulated privileges without seeing themselves as powerless. As a Black man and survivor of assault, Crews is likely in a unique position to speak about empathy and victimization. There is something uniquely promising about his expressions of solidarity. In other words, divesting from masculine privilege means developing a productive politics that does not simply absolve ourselves of culpability by expelling the predators in our midst without considering the structural conditions—both political and symbolic—that will invariably propel us, again and again, toward new moments of reckoning.

Of course we know that simply voting Trump out of office or exiling doomsday preppers and men's rights activists back to their home turf will bring us no closer to unraveling the politics of white male victimhood. This is why I argue that the death drive is central if we are to understand white men's investment in victimhood and, consequently, develop a convincing portrait of accountable masculinity. Above all, it explains that the traumatic loss that characterizes the subject can be sutured to ideological belief structures that invite the subject to invest in and restage loss under the misguided belief that there was some object or object-relation that could be recovered. What all aggressive forms of white male identity politics share in common is that they offer seemingly coherent explanations for white men's suffering. In other words, the rhetoric of victimhood asserts that alienation is neither an effect of subjectivity nor capitalism's iron grip on the drives (i.e., Marcuse's performance principle). Instead, the threat is external to these conditions—projected onto caricatures of man-hating feminists, illegal immigrants, and big government. Implored to ruminate on specific loss, white men are misdirected from the psychical and economic structures that leave them wanting. Such a politics can never follow through with specific mandates or well-defined courses of action lest it reveals its own emptiness. Assuming white men could simply legislate away their list of grievances, they would still be left disappointed. After defeating their foes, it's not difficult to imagine one muttering to themselves: "Is that it?" Assuming one were able to "Make America Great Again," as abstract as that is, they would then be deprived the jouissance of demanding that America be made great again. One would be forced to find new foes, impenetrable objects, and moments in the past to which one can return without ever achieving satisfaction.

Despite the inescapability of the death drive, it is important to note that what we are observing in the current iteration of the crisis of white masculinity is a particular enlistment of our compulsions toward a political end. Freud argued that traumatic loss grips the subject, demanding that they invariably return to and restage loss because this experience is the closest the subject ever gets to the hypothetical object—despite its impossibility or nothingness. One can merely repeat the process through which the object is lost; they can never recover that which never existed. This is the very structure of subjectivity. The problem is that subjects are frequently mislead, often by ideological structures, to believe what was lost mattered and, if recovered, could make them whole (again). In other words, the men's rights network, in all its forms, demands that its adherents take a particular orientation toward the loss of a privileged object—channeling the very experience that constitutes subjectivity toward some illusory sense of satisfaction. The illusion engendered by this demand is that it can free anyone of dissatisfaction. As Marcuse insists, the harnessing of the drives toward some greater political project—be it capitalism, nationalism, religion, or heteronormativity—only pushes us further away from freedom. The death drive, then, is what makes us vulnerable to political projects that tell us otherwise, that we can recover and restore ourselves to a period before the experience of loss. This is not possible, because it is the initial sacrifice we make when we enter language—the sacrifice of an undifferentiated world without objects or subjects—that makes subjectivity possible. Put differently, it is the drive to repeat this experience of loss that renders us desiring subjects. Despite the promises of a new world to come, each chapter in this book has illustrated that no recuperative project of white masculinity can reach past the very thing that predicates its own existence.

Take, for instance, the political project of nostalgia that is so central to contemporary men's rights narratives. Nostalgia demands a return to a historical moment in which the subject enjoyed an unmediated and uninterrupted relationship with the hypothetical object. As McGowan writes, nostalgia "permits us to avoid seeing the necessity of the link between enjoyment and loss." Instead, "the false image of enjoyment that nostalgia portrays is the source of its widespread appeal. As subjects, we constantly turn ourselves toward both our individual past and our collective cultural history in an attempt to find what we have lost."[11] The problem is that the subject is predicated on loss, and they never experienced the pure satisfaction promised by politics. Only politics can commandeer the drives by deluding the subject into believing that repetition achieves anything beyond its own enjoyment. What this suggests about white masculine victimhood is that its proponents sell their audience on the impossible idea that loss serves some greater political purpose, that one's suffering has meaning, or that one's suffering can be accounted for by some external threat. Herein is the optimism that motivates this project: the weakness of a politics of nostalgia or righteous suffering is that it cannot afford to admit the existence of the death drive. This is why McGowan asserts that an acknowledgment of the death drive disabuses us of the notion that primary loss is external to the self and that a disavowal of loss will bring the subject any close to satisfaction. He explains that "a psychoanalytic politics of the death drive produces a thoroughgoing critique of ideology in all the forms that it takes up."[12] This is also why Lee Edelman invites a queer embrace of the death drive to indict the logic of futurism that is pervaded by heterosexual culture's valorization of the child and the reproductive subject as ideal citizens. Delinked from the ideological confines of reproductive futurism, queerness partakes in the senseless compulsion of the drives while insisting on the unproductivity of loss.[13] Freedom, then, is found in the intrinsic and nonproductive enjoyment of the drives.

On first glance, a politics premised on the pointless and forbidden enjoyment of the death drive seems too esoteric and abstract to constitute a viable alternative future. Yet, I suggest that the necessary failure of white masculinity to provide a sense of mastery offers subjects the opportunity to divest from the doctrine of productive suffering. Crews's public statements exemplify this divestment and leave us with a sense that masculinity could be something other than what it has been in the past and what it will be in the future. Victimhood is a powerful narcotic that in many ways defers a series of necessary social reckonings that perhaps would have helped us renegotiate the gendered division of labor; allowed the concept of masculinity to accommodate racial, sexual, and emotional diversity; and disarticulated success at any price and backbreaking labor from what it means to be a man, and to view gains by others as positive-sum victories for social progress. In search of a positive identity, white men were steered away from the idea that their unearned advantages might help others reach their level of achievement and instead toward the notion that their privileges were private property and that groups demanding equality ultimately seek to steal those privileges.

This version of white masculinity stands at the edge of oblivion— willing to burn it all down rather than let others share their dwindling reserves of prosperity. If the case studies I have offered in this book teach us anything, it is that glorification of white male suffering has made it increasingly difficult for some white men to see that they have an interest in common with others. Men's consciousness-raising began as an effort to build the kind of solidarity occluded by the masculine mystique but has sputtered into a perverse contest of psychic wounds and incoherent cries of reverse discrimination. The doomsday prepper, the mass shooter, the Red Pill enthusiast, the gun activist, and the white man shouting the call to "Make America Great Again" are all trapped and isolated from others, including themselves, by their endless repetition of loss. These men are no closer to reaching liberation now than they were a generation ago. If social change is experienced as trauma, we are stuck between the untenability of the status quo and the inability to imagine a future of peaceful coexistence. It is in this tension where the apocalyptic imagination takes shape.

Are, then, white men consigned to ceaselessly externalize the death drive onto others? One way of addressing this question is to ask another question: have the rallying cries of white masculine victimhood actually helped improve men's lives? Although I cannot speak to the personal feelings of white men, I can certainly surmise that many men in the white working class are less likely to earn more and be financially secure than the previous generation.[14] This trend of downward mobility will continue if wages fail to keep pace with inflation, companies continue to move overseas, the tax base shrinks and tax burdens are shifted away from the wealthy, union membership dwindles, and the list goes on. Yet, in the Trump era, economic problems such as these are perpetually recast as identity troubles—takers, racial Others, foreigners, criminals, and other worthless adversaries are the *real* reason you suffer, they are told. The problem is that men's rights advocates *are* correct about one thing: white men do suffer along with the rest of society. They are led astray, however, by a promise of mastery and coherence that no one can provide. And while they clearly retain an objective material advantage relative to others, they *are* treated as disposable, but it is often by the very people they are told have their best interests at heart. It is no surprise that many misguided white men are drawn to fantasies of national renewal and the illusory promises of a return to better days. Perhaps it is in the recognition of mutual suffering—different in degree yet common in cause—that might pull some back from the brink.

Furthermore, I wish to emphasize that it's not that the death drive is inherently bad—after all, the death drive is an inevitable and necessary component of our symbolic existence. Instead, the central concern of this book has been the way in which white men are *invited to respond* to the death drive. There might be productive embraces of the death drive that do not hurl us all toward collective oblivion. One productive embrace (enjoyment) of the death drive is that it is a necessary accompaniment to Eros (the subject is never free of tension between these two forces). Marcuse asks a similar question: "Does Eros, in spite all the evidence, in the last analysis work in the service of the death instinct, and is life really only one long 'detour to death'? But the evidence is strong enough, and the detour is long enough to warrant the opposite assumption. Eros is defined as the great unifying force that preserves all life."15 Freud observed that the constancy principle dictates that the psyche maintains a minimum of tension between Eros and Thanatos to keep from reaching its final discharge—or at the very least, the tension necessarily vacillates within the subject. At any rate, this book suggests that there may be more productive enjoyments of the death drive that accompany Eros, and, further, that Eros loses meaning without the tension produced by the death drive. In the end, what I have observed is a deflection outward into political projects that harness the drives for effect beyond repetition itself, manifesting in cruelty, scapegoating, and melancholia.

White masculinity could be something else. Strength could be defined by how one cares for others, demonstrates empathy and emotional reciprocity. Masculinity could mean openness rather than fear of a wide range of experiences. It could mean investing in love and creativity while divesting from domination and toil. It could be composed of a variety of gender performances that span across a spectrum rather than a binary. It could be detached from idealized hard bodies that unfortunately remain differently raced, sexed, and abled. It need not be defined by achievement, work, sexual performance, income, or the size of a gun. At any rate, whatever another version of white masculinity might come to be is dependent on the available rhetorical resources for white men to make sense of and act on their own inevitable feelings of vulnerability. Of one thing I am certain: there must be something better.

NOTES

NOTES TO INTRODUCTION

1. Perriello and Lithwick, "Only One Side."
2. Heim, "How a Rally.'"
3. Kelly, "The Man-Pocalypse."
4. See Kimmel, *Angry White Men.*
5. Johnson, "Masculine Victimhood."
6. Rodino-Colocino, "The Great He-Cession."
7. See Kellner, *Guys and Guns Amok,* and Gibson, *Warrior Dreams.*
8. Freud, *The Ego and the Id.*
9. Stuart Murray argues that Thanatos is an animating feature of Foucault's biopolitics. In one sense, a politics of death is a necessary counterpart of the state's imperative to "making live," or the dictate that life by preserved in the name of death. In another sense, death escapes capture by the biopolitics apparatus by being a space beyond the life world that cannot be regulated and controlled. See Murray, "Thanatopolitics," and Foucault, *The Birth of Biopolitics.*
10. See McCall, *Viewer Discretion Advised.*
11. See Robinson, *Authenticity Guaranteed* and "Feminized Men."
12. Because of its depiction of white masculinity—including themes of homoeroticism, violence, and castration anxiety—*Fight Club* has received significant scholarly attention. See Gunn and Frentz, "Psychosis," and Ashcraft and Flores, "'Slaves with White Collars.'"
13. Gunn and Frentz, "Psychosis," 288. For more on *Rambo* and masculinity, see Enloe, *The Morning After*; Jeffords, *The Remasculinization of America*; Jeffords, *Hard Bodies*; Morag, *Defeated Masculinity*; and Tasker, *Spectacular Bodies.*

14. The term *male autarky* is borrowed from Barbara Spackman's analysis of virility, misogyny, and homosexual panics in fascist Italy. See Spackman, *Fascist Virilities*, and Sedgwick, *Between Men*.
15. King, "It Cuts Both Ways."
16. Kristeva, *The Power of Horror*.
17. King, "It Cuts Both Ways," 371.
18. King, "It Cuts Both Ways," 370.
19. Freud, "Mourning and Melancholia." See also Creed, "Dark Desires."
20. Robinson, *Marked Men*, 6.
21. Kimmel, *Manhood in America*.
22. Faludi, *Stiffed*.
23. Faludi, *Stiffed*, 35.
24. Gibson, *Warrior Dreams*.
25. Rodino-Colocino, "The Great He-Cession."
26. Connell, *Gender and Power*; Connell, *Masculinities*; Hanke, "The 'Mock-Macho' Situation"; and Trujillo, "Hegemonic Masculinity."
27. Mowitt, "Trauma Envy"; and Brown, *States of Injury*.
28. McCann, "Therapeutic and Material <Victim> hood."
29. McCann, "Therapeutic and Material <Victim> hood," 386.
30. Anker, *Orgies of Feeling*.
31. Coontz, "Masculine Mystique."
32. Friedan, *The Feminine Mystique*, 521.
33. Key texts include Sawyer, "On Men's Liberation" (1970); Farrell, *The Liberated Man* (1974); Fasteau, *The Male Machine* (1975); Goldberg, *The Hazards of Being Male* (1975) and *The New Male* (1979); Nichols, *Men's Liberation* (1975); David and Brannon, *The Forty-Nine Percent Majority* (1976); and Pleck and Sawyer, *Men and Masculinity* (1974).
34. Robert Connell, *Masculinities*; Raewynn Connell, *Gender and Power*.
35. See Jeffords, *Hard Bodies*.
36. Bean, *Post-Backlash Feminism*.
37. Faludi, *Backlash*.
38. Blake, "Mad Men."
39. Gingrich-Philbrook, "'Good Vibration' or Domination?" 21.
40. See Gibson, *Warrior Dreams*; Lipsitz, *Possessive Investment*; Klein, *The Bully Society*; and Agger and Luke, *Gun Violence*.
41. Kellner, *Guys and Guns Amok*, 90.
42. Kellner, *Guys and Guns Amok*, 92.
43. Kellner, *Guys and Guns Amok*, 24.
44. Kelly, "The Rage Network."
45. Elam, "Violent Bitch Month."
46. Southern Poverty Law Center, "Male Supremacy."
47. Southern Poverty Law Center, "Male Supremacy."
48. Southern Poverty Law Center, "Male Supremacy."
49. Brooks, "The Jordan Peterson Moment."
50. Seitz-Wald, "Alex Jones."
51. Malone, "Breitbart."
52. Southern Poverty Law Center, "Misogyny."
53. Connell, *Masculinities*, 228.

54. For more on the psychology of projection and introjection see Melanie Klein, *Collected Works*; and Sánchez-Pardo, *Death Drive*.
55. Gunn and Beard, "On the Apocalyptic Columbine," 199; and "On the Apocalyptic Sublime."
56. See Lamy, *Millennium Rage*; and Mitchell, *Dancing at Armageddon*.
57. See Alcoff, *The Future of Whiteness*.
58. Freud, *Beyond the Pleasure Principle*.
59. Copjec, *Desire*, 46.
60. Copjec, *Desire*, 47.
61. Marcuse, *Eros and Civilization*, 27.
62. See Holowchak and Lavin, *Repetition*; and Teresa De Lauretis, *Freud's Drive*.
63. Freud, *Beyond the Pleasure Principle*.
64. Silverman, *Male Subjectivity*.
65. Silverman, *Male Subjectivity*, 58.
66. Silverman, *Male Subjectivity*, 58.
67. See Radstone, *Sexual Politics*.
68. See King, *Washed in Blood*.
69. See Alexander, *Trauma*; Cavedon, *Cultural Melancholia*; Kaplan, *Trauma Culture*; and Caruth, *Unclaimed Experience*.
70. LaCapra, *Writing History*.
71. LaCapra, *Writing History*, 46.
72. Freud, "Mourning and Melancholia."
73. Butler, "Melancholy."
74. Butler, "Melancholy," 23.
75. Butler, "Melancholy," 30.
76. See Lundberg, "Enjoying God's Death," 402; See also Lacan, *The Other Side of Psychoanalysis*.
77. Savran, *Taking It Like a Man*. Claire Sisco King and Joshua Gunn similarly argue that victimization and feminization are often conflated. To that end, they argue that the gaze and compulsive repetition alike do not validate but instead undermine the subject's need for mastery (the subject is treated as an object). See King and Gunn, "On a Violence Unseen."
78. Freud, "Masochism."
79. King and Gunn, "On a Violence Unseen," 206.
80. Marcuse, *One-Dimensional Man*.
81. Marcuse, *Eros and Civilization*, 216.
82. Michel Foucault points out that the so-called liberation of sex and sexual discourse is the very means by which sexuality is subjected to new regimes of power. We might consider, then, the type of productive power that might govern sexuality if it were not harnessed by the repressive apparatus of capitalism but took some other form that dispenses with the need to suture civilization to domination. See Foucault, *Sexuality*.
83. Carroll, *Affirmative Reaction*, 6.
84. Gunn, "Perversion," 163.
85. Black, *Rhetorical Questions*, 10.
86. Lacan, *Fundamental Concepts*.
87. Lundberg, *Lacan*, 113.
88. Matheson, *Desiring the Bomb*, 16.

89. See Biesecker, "Mourning."
90. Black, "The Second Persona," 113.
91. Levine, *Forms*.
92. Miller, "Genre."
93. Campbell and Jamieson, *Form and Genre*.
94. Levine, *Forms*, 6.
95. Felski, *Critique*.
96. Burke, *Counter-Statement*, 31.
97. Felski, *Critique*, 12–13.
98. McLuhan, *Understanding Media*, 127.
99. Couldry, *Media Rituals*, 16.
100. I borrow the term *networked media* from Damien Pfister, who argues that the term better captures the affordances of connectivity than terms such as *digital media*. See Pfister, *Networked Media*.
101. Ott, "Twitter"; Ott and Dickinson, *Twitter Presidency*; and Gunn "On Social Networking."
102. See Murray and Ouellette, eds., *Reality TV*; Ouellette, "The Trump Show"; and Cloud, "The Irony Bribe."
103. See Butler, *Bodies*; and Sobchack *Carnal Thoughts*.
104. See Andrejevic, "Jouissance."

NOTES TO CHAPTER 1

1. Carroll, "Men's Soaps."
2. Lynn Spigel, *Make Room for TV*.
3. Corner, "Performing the Real: Documentary Diversions."
4. Kelly, "Strange/Familiar," and Murray, "Documentary and Reality TV."
5. Rademacher and Kelly, "Storage Wars."
6. Ouellette and Hay, *Better Living*.
7. Goffman, *Everyday Life*, 70.
8. Fox, "Big Brother."
9. Dubrofsky and Ryalls, "The Hunger Games," 395.
10. Andrejevic, *Reality TV*; and Dubrofsky and Hardy, "Performing Race."
11. Boylorn, "As Seen On TV."
12. Edwards, "'Reality Game Shows," 227.
13. Vale, "American Survivalists."
14. Feuer, "The Preppers Next Door"; Martin, "Disaster-Preparedness Economy"; and Murphy, "Barackalypse."
15. *The Economist*, "I Will Survive"; Jacobs, "NYC Firefighter"; and Stewart, "Post-apocalypse."
16. O'Connor, "Suburban Preppers."
17. Brady, "Three Million 'Preppers'"; and Eells, "'Doomsday Preppers.'"
18. Michaud, "One in Seven."
19. Hawkins, and O'Malley Greenberg, "Doomsday Investing"; The National Geographic Channel, "Doomsday Preppers Survey."
20. PrepperCon, "About Us."

21. Matheson, "'Jade Helm 15.'"
22. Watts, "Postracial Fantasies."
23. See Quarles, *The Ku Klux Klan*.
24. See Stern, *A Force Upon the Plain*.
25. Rose, *One Nation Underground*.
26. Wojcik, *The End of the World*.
27. William, *Warrior Dreams*.
28. Kellner, *Guys and Guns Amok*, 97.
29. Mitchell, *Dancing at Armageddon*.
30. See Quinby, *Anti-Apocalypse*.
31. See Darsey, *The Prophetic Tradition*; Hall, *Apocalypse*; and Morris and Wander, "Ghost Dance."
32. See Derrida, "Apocalyptic Tone."
33. See Brummett, *Contemporary Apocalyptic Rhetoric*; and O'Leary, *Arguing the Apocalypse*.
34. Ducat, *The Wimp Factor*, 231.
35. Nichols, *Introduction to Documentary*, 37.
36. Erik Lacitis, "Preppers Do Their Best."
37. National Geographic Society, "Global."
38. Lacitis, "Preppers."
39. Passy, "Hobby."
40. See Bloom, *Gender on Ice*. For an exploration of President Roosevelt's influence on popular conceptions of frontier masculinity see Leroy G. Dorsey, *We Are All Americans*.
41. Dubrofsky and Hardy, "Hunger Games," 396.
42. Boylorn, "As Seen On TV," 423.
43. Goffman, *Everyday Life*, 22.
44. Goffman, *Frame Analysis*.
45. By "hysterical" I mean the clinical sense of a subject who becomes the object of a desire that s/he believes the other desires, sometimes characterized by emotional excess or attention-seeking behavior. Historically wielded against women by the psychiatric establishment, the construction of hysteria is profoundly gendered and used to medicalize and discipline the feminine. See Meyer, Fallah, and Wood, "Madness."
46. Meyer, Fallah, and Wood, "Madness," 219.
47. Meyer, Fallah, and Wood, "Madness," 220.
48. Kimmel, *Manhood in America*, 319.

NOTES TO CHAPTER 2

1. See Futrelle, "Men's-Rights Activism."
2. Woods and Hahner, *Make America Meme Again*, 40.
3. See Castells, *Networks*.
4. Peter Wright, "Men Who Sit at the Screens."
5. Wright, "Screens."
6. Wright, "Screens."

7. Wright, "Screens."
8. This description of anonymous, stateless, collective action mirrors Michael Hardt and Antonio Negri's theory of the "multitude." See Hardt and Negri, *Multitude*.
9. Wright, "Screens."
10. See Fisher, "Narration."
11. Levine, *Forms*, 113.
12. Wright, "Screens."
13. For work on the rhetoric of feminist consciousness-raising, see Campbell, "Oxymoron" and "Consciousness-Raising"; Dubriwny, "Consciousness-Raising"; Sowards and Renegar, "Third Wave Feminism."
14. Riley, Klumpp, and Hollihan, "Angry White Guys."
15. Fraser, "Rethinking."
16. Noble, *Algorithms*.
17. Hu, *Cloud*, 11
18. Campbell, "Oxymoron," 79.
19. Kellner and Pierce, *Herbert Marcuse*, 58.
20. Anker, *Orgies*, 3.
21. u/PK_atheist, "Newcomers."
22. Married Man Sex Life, "What is the Red Pill?"
23. u/TPV Vanguard, "Flavour."
24. For instance, so-called pickup artist Daryush Valizadeh, who goes by Roosh V, is the most well known as a proponent of sex tourism on his blogs www.rooshv.com and rooshvforum.com and in fourteen books that includes titles such as *Bang Estonia, Don't Bang Latvia,* and *Bang Lithuania.* Pickup artists have a prominent presence on the web, particularly on Reddit (see r/seduction), a community that grew after the publication of Neil Strauss's book *The Game* (New York: Regan Books, 2005), a quasi-ethnographic study of the pickup artist subculture, and Erik Von Markovik's VH1 reality show *The Pickup Artist* (2007–8).
25. Tomassi, "Ownership."
26. While the terms *beta* and *alpha* are used quite frequently, the moderators of r/TheRedPill argue that they are labels of a spectrum of behavior, rather than biological categories. Hence, they attempt to steer conversation threads away from declarations about the behavior of "real alphas" and "betas." u/SoftHarem writes, "Stop labeling each other alphas and betas, they're terms we use to classify particular behaviors and help demonstrate good versus bad behavior. Nobody is intrinsically an 'alpha,' some people just have more alpha traits than others. Stick to constructive criticism and drop the stupid out-alpha talk. It's not seddit folks, this conversation has become a caricature of itself." See u/SoftHarem, "The Basics Explained."
27. u/NeoreactionSafe, "System."
28. u/TRP Vanguard, "The Red Pill."
29. u/TRP Vanguard, "The Red Pill."
30. Married Man Sex Life, "What is the Red Pill?"
31. Furioso, "The Blue Pill World." Emphasis mine.
32. u/Green Piller, "Blue Pill Peterson."
33. Givens, "A Red Pill Message."
34. Anonymous, "About/Meta."

35. Included in this list would also be websites such as Breitbart News and Infowars who routinely produce their own jeremiads about the risk that feminism poses to Western civilization. I excluded them from analysis here only because their content does not exclusively pertain to advancing the men's rights movement.
36. Elam, "MHRM Overview."
37. A Voice for Men, "Mission."
38. u/PK_Atheist, "Welcome."
39. u/TPR Vanguard, "Five Stages."
40. u/redpillschool, "Where Anger Leads."
41. u/apollostatus, Response to u/redpillschool "Where Anger Leads."
42. Robert Brockaway, "Walk Away."
43. Mgtow.com, "About."
44. Mgtow.com, "About."
45. Mgtow.com, "The History of M.G.T.O.W."
46. Mgtow.com, "The History of M.G.T.O.W." Emphasis original.
47. Mgtow.com, "The History of M.G.T.O.W."
48. Mgtow.com, "Hypergamy."
49. Marcuse, *Eros,* 199.
50. McGowan, *Enjoying,* 35.

NOTES TO CHAPTER 3

1. Quoted in Clark-Flory, "Involuntary Celibates."
2. See u/manofire, "Prostitution."
3. See u/icepickethegod, "Elliot Rodgers [sic] Manifesto."
4. Mezzofiore, "'Incel Rebellion.'"
5. BBC News, "Toronto Suspect."
6. Bever, "Christopher Cleary."
7. PUAHate.com was shut down in August 2014. However, a Scribd user named Matthew Keys has made available a number of cached threads in which Rodger participated. They are available at https://www.scribd.com/lists/4516330/Elliot-Rodger-Online-Posts.
8. Rodger, "Elliot Rodger: PUAHate.com Posts (10)."
9. Rodger, "Elliot Rodger: BodyBuilding.com (7)."
10. Wilson, "Violent Misogyny."
11. Rodger, "My Twisted World."
12. Though it was commonly invoked by Second Wave feminists, the phrase the "personal is political" first appeared in Carol Hanisch's 1969 essay of the same name. The phrase denotes the feminist doctrine that women's personal, often invisible suffering in the home is a political experience that might engender a feminist consciousness. See Hanisch, "The Personal."
13. Burke, *Philosophy,* 191.
14. Burke, *Philosophy,* 191.
15. On the rising fascist and other right-wing movements in the US and Europe, see Berlet and Lyons, *Right-Wing Populism*; Finchelstein, *From Fascism*; and Mazower, "Fascism Revisited?"

16. See Paxton, *Fascism*.
17. I borrow the term *inborn dignity* from Burke's thematic reading of *Mein Kampf*. He argues that Hitler appealed to a secular, natural-born superiority of Volk. He argues that "after the defeat of Germany in the World War, there were especially strong emotional needs that this compensatory doctrine of an *inborn* superiority could gratify." See Burke, *Philosophy*, 202.
18. Bellassai, "The Masculine Mystique."
19. Kaufman, "Men's Violence"; and Theweleit and Ehrenreich, *Male Fantasies*.
20. Woodley, *Fascism*, 218.
21. Spackman, *Fascist Virilities*, 51.
22. See Marcuse, *One-Dimensional Man*.
23. See Mosse, *The Image of Man*.
24. Paxton, *Fascism*.
25. Kimmel, *Angry White Men*, 18.
26. See Colón, "Beta Testing Fascism"; and Nagle, "The Lost Boys."
27. Solon, "'Incel.'"
28. See Baker, "Incel Movement."
29. Rodger, "My Twisted World," 2.
30. In his examination of the "scapegoat mechanism," Kenneth Burke identifies a similar pattern at work in narratives of victimage, guilt, and redemption. While Burke's analysis of guilt-victimage-redemption helps identify a common pattern that can be traced in Rodger's manifesto (particularly his emphasis on inborn dignity and purification), it is too general of a pattern to be of any interest if applied here. Instead, it provides backing for this chapter's specific inquiry into the dark appeal of recursive trauma and fantasies of persecution and omnipotence—both of which implicitly draw from a fascist imaginary. See Burke, *Permanence*, 16; and Burke, *The Philosophy of Literary Form*.
31. Rodger, "My Twisted World," 107.
32. Rodger, "My Twisted World," 1.
33. Rodger, "My Twisted World," 1.
34. See Merchant, *Death*; and Smith, *Virgin Land*.
35. Rodger, "My Twisted World," 65.
36. Rodger, "My Twisted World," 133.
37. On the cultural mythology of the frontiersman, see Slotkin, *Regeneration*.
38. Rodger, "My Twisted World," 84.
39. Rodger, "My Twisted World," 117.
40. See Dellamora, *Masculine Desire*; and Carnes, *Secret Ritual*.
41. Buescher and Ono, "Civilized Colonialism."
42. Rodger, "My Twisted World," 133.
43. Rodger, "My Twisted World," 88.
44. Rodger, "My Twisted World," 117.
45. Rodger, "My Twisted World," 117.
46. Rodger, "My Twisted World," 117.
47. Rodger, "My Twisted World," 135.
48. See Bercovitch, *Jeremiad*; Murphy, "'Shame and Sorrow.'"
49. Rodger, "My Twisted World," 104.
50. Rodger, "My Twisted World," 59.
51. Rodger, "My Twisted World," 108.

52. Rodger, "My Twisted World," 118.
53. See McGuire, "Elliot Rodger's."
54. Rodger, "My Twisted World," 135.
55. Rodger, "My Twisted World," 135.
56. Rodger, "My Twisted World," 137.
57. Rodger, "My Twisted World," 136.
58. Rodger, "My Twisted World," 137.
59. Atwood, quoted in "Famous Feminist Quotes."
60. See Irigaray, *This Sex Which Is Not One.*
61. Marcuse, *Eros,* 216.

NOTES TO CHAPTER 4

1. The photo is available at https://www.facebook.com/VirginiaOpenCarry/
2. See Giffords Law Center to Prevent Gun Violence, "Open Carry."
3. Milburn, "Open Carry Activists."
4. Valentine, "Tallying the Costs of Open Carry."
5. DeLuca, "Unruly Arguments."
6. Cameron, *Sexual Politics,* 154.
7. King, "Arming Desire," 89.
8. See DeLuca, "Unruly Arguments."
9. For more on the relationship between gun ownership, militias, and slavery, see Dunbar-Ortiz, *Loaded;* Winkler, *Gunfight;* and Hadden, *Slave Patrols.*
10. Bloom and Martin, *Black Against Empire;* and Rhodes, *Black Panthers.*
11. According to Statistica.com, "The statistic shows the number of mass shootings in the United States between 1982 and February 2018, by race and ethnicity of the shooter(s). Between 1982 and February 2018, 56 out of 97 mass shootings were initiated by white shooters. The Las Vegas strip massacre in 2017 had the highest number of victims between 1982 and 2018, with 58 people killed, and over 500 injured." See "U.S.: Mass Shootings by Race 1982–2018."
12. See DeLuca and Peeples, "Public Screen."
13. For more on the state of US gun laws governing open and concealed carry, see Meltzer, "Open Carry."
14. Melzer, *Gun Crusaders.*
15. Matheson, "'What Does Obama Want of Me?'"
16. Arkin and Popken, "Fake 'Crisis Actors.'"
17. Collins, "The Second Amendment."
18. Lundberg, "Equivalential Chains."
19. Lundberg, "Enjoying God's Death."
20. Brummett, *Style,* 152. Emphasis mine.
21. Similarly, early studies on the rhetoric of social movements found that confrontation was a way to constrain the state's response to movement demands. In part, confrontation baits the state into showing its oppressive nature to the general public. See Scott and Smith, "Confrontation."
22. Reigstad, "Controversy."
23. Modesti, "Home Sweet Home," 209.

24. See Slotkin, *Gunfighter Nation*.
25. Bailey, "Guns."
26. These image events offer a sharp contrast to the democratic liberalism that Robert Hariman and John Lucaites locate in contemporary photojournalism. Rather than structuring adherence to the civic rituals of democratic culture, open carry images suggest either that liberalism is a mask for a more brutish state of nature or that liberalism is predicated on the threat of justified violence. For more on the visual rhetoric of iconic images, see Hariman and Lucaites, *No Caption Needed*.
27. Nevadacarry, "Nevada Carry."
28. Larson, "This Militia Group."
29. See Frum, "The Chilling Effects."
30. Larson, "This Militia Group."
31. Krieg, "Cleveland Police."
32. Stuart, "Black Gun Owners"; and Suen, "Trump Supporters."
33. See Lipsitz, *Possessive Investment*; Nakayama and Krizek, "Whiteness"; and Dyer, *White*.
34. Silverman, *Male Subjectivity*, 62.
35. King, "Arming Desire," 87–88.
36. National Public Radio, "Open Carry Activists."
37. Rodino-Colocino, "He-Cession."
38. Kimmel, *Angry White Men*.
39. Kelly, "Cooking Without Women."
40. Rademacher and Kelly, "Storage Wars."
41. Zadrozny, "Gun Control."
42. Sally Robinson argues that protests against the phoniness of consumer culture often decry shopping and conspicuous consumption as signs of inauthenticity and, thus, the feminization of public life. See Robinson, *Authenticity Guaranteed*.
43. Sharp, "Roy Moore."
44. Savransky, "Roy Moore."
45. See Ott, Aoki, and Dickinson, "Ways of (Not) Seeing Guns."
46. See Anderson, *Cowboy Imperialism*; Starrs, *Cowboy Ride*; and Wright, *The Wild West*.
47. Roy Moore, quoted n Jamie Ducharme, "Roy Moore."
48. See Aleiss, *White Man's Indian*; Carter, *Myth*; Rollins, *Hollywood's West*.
49. Kristen Hoerl uses the term *selective amnesia* to denote how public memories are composed of textual fragments that are carefully chosen or reshaped for their ideological alignment with hegemonic narratives. See Hoerl, "Selective Amnesia."
50. López, *Dog Whistle Politics*.
51. McCrummen, Reinhard, and Crites, "Woman Says."
52. See Buescher and Ono, "Civilized Colonialism."

NOTES TO CHAPTER 5

1. Trump, "RNC."
2. Begala, "Midnight."
3. Trump, "RNC."

4. Johnson, "Masculine Victimhood," 241.
5. Terrill, "The Post-Racial," 501.
6. Michael Lee argues that while the content may vary, populism is an argumentative form that positions a virtuous public against a powerful enemy who aims to dispossess the people of their wealth and democratic representation. While the argument here does not pivot on a theory of populist reason, structurally speaking, Trump's rhetoric does borrow this frame to establish that the aggrieved character of his audience. See Lee, "Populist Chameleon." Populism can also be conceived of as a political discourse of marginality that can be taken up by groups who share no specific material linkage or allegiance to a marginalized class. See Laclau, *On Populist Reason.*
7. Dana L. Cloud argues that the media culture of fact-checking the president is largely counterproductive in relation to the affective intensities generated within his base of supporters. See Cloud, *Reality Bites.*
8. For more on the masculine investments generated by revenge cinema, see Kelly, "Feminine Purity."
9. See Cloud, "The Irony Bribe"; Ouellette, "The Trump Show"; and Murray and Ouellette, *Reality TV.*
10. Phillips, "'The Safest Hands," 88.
11. Lockwood, "All Stripped Down," 45; See also Noys, *Death*; and Aaron, *Spectatorship.*
12. Stuckey, "American Elections," 676.
13. Stuckey, "American Elections," 677.
14. Gunn, "Political Perversion."
15. For an exploration of the affective charge of cruelty in the Trump era, see Levina and Silva, "Cruel Intentions."; Levina, "Cruelty"; and Silva, "Love-Cruelty."
16. The American Psychiatric Association issued a statement calling for professional psychiatrists to refrain from offering analysis of Trump's mental fitness for office. The APA's Goldwater Rule (Section 7 of the Principles of Medical Ethics) states that it is unethical to offer professional psychiatric diagnosis for people they have not examined. The rule was created in 1964 after *Fact* magazine published the results of a survey of 1,189 psychiatrists who believe candidate Barry Goldwater was psychologically unfit to be president. See Chasmar, "American Psychiatric Association."
17. Rushe, "Trade U-Turn."
18. See Azarian, "Trump Supporters"; Khazan, "Trump"; and Ehrenfreund, "Learned."
19. Diamond, "Donald Trump."
20. By persona, I mean the character of the audience constructed by the rhetor as opposed to a physically present and empirical verifiable audience. This concept of audience draws from Edwin Black's "second persona," or an ideal audience constructed within a text—the clue to their identity manifest in specific textual cues and rhetorical choices. See Black, "The Second Persona."
21. Parker, Corasaniti, and Berenstein, "Voices."
22. See Freud, "Beaten."
23. Freud, "Masochism," 164.
24. Savran, *Taking It Like a Man,* 35–36.

25. See Stekel, *Sadism*; Stekel argues that sadism and masochism are more about enacting fantasies of control than about sexual gratification.

26. Girard, *Things Hidden.*

27. Trump, "RNC."

28. Trump, "Presidential Announcement."

29. Trump, "Presidential Announcement."

30. Trump, "Presidential Announcement."

31. Trump, "Presidential Announcement."

32. Trump, "Presidential Announcement."

33. Trump, "RNC."

34. Trump, "Presidential Announcement."

35. Trump, "Inauguration Speech."

36. Trump, "Inauguration Speech."

37. Trump, "RNC."

38. Johnson, "Victimhood," 240.

39. Trump, "Conference."

40. Trump, "Phoenix."

41. Trump, "Phoenix."

42. See Anderson, "Presidential Pioneer"; and Campbell, "Hating Hillary."

43. Trump, "RNC."

44. This statement appeared in a January 10, 2018, Tweet from Donald Trump at https://twitter.com/realDonaldTrump/status/951109942685126656.

45. For more on the concept of reality-referencing, see Triece, *Tell It Like It Is.*

46. Riotta, "New Poll Finds."

47. Trump, "Conference."

48. Trump, "Phoenix."

49. Trump, "Phoenix."

50. Trump, "Inaugural."

51. Trump, "Presidential Announcement."

52. Nixon, "Trump's Border."

53. The *New York Times* published list of quotes from Trump from 2015 to 2018 that show the evolution of Trump's border-wall proposal as new logistical challenges emerge. See Ron Nixon and Qiu, "Trump's Evolving."

54. Freud, "Masochism," 165.

55. Trump, "Conference."

56. Trump, "Conference."

57. Trump, "Phoenix."

58. Yankowski, "Introduction," 20.

59. Yankowski, "Introduction," 20.

60. Yankowski, "Introduction," 21.

61. Puar, *The Right to Maim.*

62. Clio, "Legal Fees."

63. Trump, "Ohio."

64. Trump, "RNC."

65. Trump, "Conference."

66. Trump, "Phoenix."

67. See Stracqualursi, "Trump Re-Ups." References to undocumented immigrants as "animals" can be found in Trump, "Phoenix," "Conference," and "Ohio." Infesta-

tion metaphors have a long racist history in anti-immigration rhetoric. See Cisneros, "Contaminated Communities."

68. Trump, "Ohio."
69. Trump, "Phoenix."
70. Trump, "Phoenix."
71. Trump, "Conference."
72. Trump made these remarks at a May 19, 2018, rally in Nashville, Tennessee. A video clip of these remarks can be found at https://www.youtube.com/watch?v=Svzcox2QBow. A special thanks to Paul Johnson for pointing out this passage to me.
73. Trump, "Conference."
74. Trump, "North Dakota."
75. Trump, "Ohio."
76. I develop this argument further through an analysis of homophobic anti-Trump protest art that seeks to emasculate or "out" Trump's abhorrent expressions of white masculinity. See Kelly, "Emasculating Trump."

NOTES TO CONCLUSION

1. Marx, *The 18th Brumaire*, 13.
2. *BBC News*, "Harvey Weinstein."
3. Rodino-Colocino, "Me Too."
4. Brett Kavanaugh, quoted in Phillips, "'Statement to Congress."
5. Kavanaugh, quoted in Phillips, "Statement to Congress."
6. Trump, "Mississippi."
7. Trump, "Mississippi."
8. Smith, "Backlash."
9. Smith, "Backlash."
10. Terry Crews, quoted in Dockterman, "Read Terry Crews."
11. McGowan, *Enjoying*, 40.
12. McGowan, *Enjoying*, 35.
13. Edelman, *No Future*.
14. See Chetty et al., "The Fading American Dream."
15. Marcuse, *Eros*, 26–27.

BIBLIOGRAPHY

Aaron, Michael. *Spectatorship: The Power of Looking On*. New York: Wallflower Press, 2007.

Agger, Ben, and Timothy W. Luke. *Gun Violence and Public Life*. New York: Routledge, 2015.

Alcoff, Linda Martín. *The Future of Whiteness*. New York: John Wiley & Sons, 2015.

Aleiss, Angela. *Making the White Man's Indian: Native Americans and Hollywood Movies*. Westport, CT: Greenwood, 2005.

Alexander, Jeffrey C. *Trauma: A Social Theory*. New York: John Wiley & Sons, 2013.

Anderson, Karrin Vasby. "Presidential Pioneer or Campaign Queen? Hillary Clinton and the First-Timer/Frontrunner Double Bind." *Rhetoric & Public Affairs* 20, no. 3 (2017): 525–38.

Anderson, Mark. *Cowboy Imperialism and Hollywood Film*. New York: Peter Lang, 2007.

Andrejevic, Mark. "The Jouissance of Trump." *Television & New Media* 17, no. 7 (2016): 651–55.

———. *Reality TV: The Work of Being Watched*. Lanham, MD: Rowman & Littlefield, 2004.

Anker, Elisabeth Robin. *Orgies of Feeling: Melodrama and the Politics of Freedom*. Durham, NC: Duke University Press Books, 2014.

Arkin, Daniel, and Ben Popken. "How the Fake 'Crisis Actors' Conspiracy Took Off on Social Media after Florida School Shooting." *NBC News*, February 21, 2018.

https://www.nbcnews.com/news/us-news/how-internet-s-conspiracy-theorists-turned-parkland-students-crisis-actors-n849921.

Azarian, Bobby. "An Analysis of Trump Supporters Has Identified 5 Key Traits." *Psychology Today,* December 31, 2017. https://www.psychologytoday.com/blog/mind-in-the-machine/201712/analysis-trump-supporters-has-identified-5-key-traits.

Bailey, Chelsea. "Since 1968, Guns Have Killed More Americans Than All U.S. Wars Combined." *NBC News,* October 4, 2017. https://www.nbcnews.com/storyline/las-vegas-shooting/more-americans-killed-guns-1968-all-u-s-wars-combined-n807156.

Baker, Peter. "The Woman Who Accidentally Started the Incel Movement." *Elle Magazine,* March 1, 2016. http://www.elle.com/culture/news/a34512/woman-who-started-incel-movement/.

BBC News. "How the Harvey Weinstein Scandal Unfolded." January 10, 2019. https://www.bbc.com/news/entertainment-arts-41594672.

Bean, Kelly. *Post-Backlash Feminism: Women and the Media since Reagan-Bush.* Jefferson, NC: McFarland, 2007.

Begala, Paul. "Trump's Midnight in America." *CNN,* July 22, 2016. https://www.cnn.com/2016/07/22/opinions/trumps-midnight-in-america-begala/index.html.

Bellassai, Sandro. "The Masculine Mystique: Antimodernism and Virility in Fascist Italy." *Journal of Modern Italian Studies* 10, no. 3 (2005): 314–35.

Bercovitch, Sacvan. *The American Jeremiad.* Madison: University of Wisconsin Press, 2012.

Berlet, Chip, and Matthew N. Lyons. *Right-Wing Populism in America: Too Close for Comfort.* New York: Guilford, 2018.

Bever, Lindsey. "Christopher Cleary Threatened to Kill 'as Many Girls as I See' Because He Is a Virgin, Police Say." *Washington Post,* January 22, 2019. https://www.washingtonpost.com/crime-law/2019/01/22/man-cited-his-virginity-reason-he-planned-kill-many-girls-he-could-police-say/?utm_term=.231cdb6647f0.

Biesecker, Barbara A. "No Time for Mourning: The Rhetorical Production of the Melancholic Citizen-Subject in the War on Terror." *Philosophy & Rhetoric* 40, no. 1 (2007): 147–69.

Black, Edwin. *Rhetorical Questions: Studies of Public Discourse.* Chicago: University of Chicago Press, 1992.

———. "The Second Persona." *Quarterly Journal of Speech* 56, no. 2 (1970): 109–19.

Blake, Mariah. "Mad Men: Inside the Men's Rights Movement—and the Army of Misogynists and Trolls It Spawned." *Mother Jones,* January/February 2015. https://www.motherjones.com/politics/2015/01/warren-farrell-mens-rights-movement-feminism-misogyny-trolls/2/.

Bloom, Joshua, and Waldo E. Martin Jr. *Black Against Empire: The History and Politics of the Black Panther Party.* Berkeley: University of California Press, 2016.

Bly, Robert. *Iron John: A Book about Men.* Cambridge, MA: Da Capo Press, 2004.

Boylorn, Robin M. "As Seen On TV: An Autoethnographic Reflection on Race and Reality Television." *Critical Studies in Media Communication* 25, no. 4 (2008): 413–33.

Brady, Tara. "Fill the Pool with Fish and Stockpile the Guns: Up to Three Million 'Preppers' in the U.S. are Prepared for the End of the World." *Daily Mail*, February 11, 2012. https://www.dailymail.co.uk/news/article-2099714/Meet-preppers-Up-3-MILLION-people-preparing-end-world-know-it.html.

Brooks, David. "The Jordan Peterson Moment." *New York Times*, January 25, 2018. https://www.nytimes.com/2018/01/25/opinion/jordan-peterson-moment.html.

Brown, Wendy. *States of Injury*. Princeton: Princeton University Press, 1995.

Brummett, Barry. *A Rhetoric of Style*. Carbondale: Southern Illinois University Press, 2008.

Buescher, Derek T., and Kent A. Ono. "Civilized Colonialism: Pocahontas as Neocolonial Rhetoric." *Women's Studies in Communication* 19, no. 2 (1996): 126–53.

Burke, Kenneth. *Permanence and Change: An Anatomy of Purpose*. 3rd edition. Berkeley: University of California Press, 1984.

———. *The Philosophy of Literary Form*. 3rd edition. Berkeley: University of California Press, 1974.

———. *Counter-statement*. 1st edition. Berkeley: University of California Press, 1968.

Butler, Judith. *Bodies That Matter: On the Discursive Limits of Sex*. New York: Routledge, 2011.

———. "Melancholy Gender/Refused Identification." In *Constructing Masculinities*, edited by Maurice Berger, Brian Wallis, and Simon Watson. New York: Routledge, 2012.

Cameron, Deborah. *On Language and Sexual Politics*. New York: Routledge, 2006.

Campbell, Karlyn Kohrs. "Consciousness-Raising: Linking Theory, Criticism, and Practice." *Rhetoric Society Quarterly* 32 (2002): 45–64.

———. "The Discursive Performance of Femininity: Hating Hillary." *Rhetoric & Public Affairs* 1, no. 1 (1998): 1–19.

———. "The Rhetoric of Women's Liberation: An Oxymoron." *Quarterly Journal of Speech* 59 (1973): 74–86.

Campbell, Karlyn Kohrs, and Kathleen Hall Jamieson. *Form and Genre: Shaping Rhetorical Action*. Falls Church, VA: The Speech Communication Association, 1978.

Carnes, Mark Christopher. *Secret Ritual and Manhood in Victorian America*. New Haven, CT: Yale University Press, 1989.

Carroll, Hamilton. *Affirmative Reaction: New Formations of White Masculinity*. Durham, NC: Duke University Press, 2011.

———. "Men's Soaps: Automotive Television Programming and Contemporary Working-Class Masculinities." *Television & New Media* 9 (2008): 263–83.

Carter, Matthew. *Myth of the Western: New Perspectives on Hollywood's Frontier Narrative*. Edinburgh: Edinburgh University Press, 2015.

Caruth, Cathy. *Unclaimed Experience: Trauma, Narrative, and History.* Baltimore: Johns Hopkins University Press, 2016.

Castells, Manuel. *Networks of Outrage and Hope: Social Movements in the Internet Age.* New York: John Wiley & Sons, 2015.

Cavedon, Christina. *Cultural Melancholia: US Trauma Discourses Before and After 9/11.* Boston: Brill, 2015.

Chasmar, Jessica. "American Psychiatric Association Calls for End to 'Arm Chair' Psychiatry amid Trump Speculation." *Washington Times,* January 10, 2018. https://www.washingtontimes.com/news/2018/jan/10/american-psychiatric-association-calls-end-arm-cha/.

Chetty, Raj, David Grusky, Maximilian Hell, Nathaniel Hendren, Robert Manduca, and Jimmy Narang. "The Fading American Dream: Trends in Absolute Income Mobility since 1940." NBER Working Paper No. 22910. Cambridge, MA: National Bureau of Economic Research, 2016.

Cisneros, J. David. "Contaminated Communities: The Metaphor of 'Immigrant as Pollutant' in Media Representations of Immigration." *Rhetoric & Public Affairs* 11, no. 4 (2008): 569–601.

Clark-Flory, Tracy. "Inside the Terrifying, Twisted Online World of Involuntary Celibates." *Salon,* May 27, 2014. https://www.salon.com/2014/05/27/inside_the_terrifying_twisted_online_world_of_involuntary_celibates/.

Clio, Chang. "If You Beat Up a Protester at Trump's Rally, He'll Cover Your Legal Fees." *The New Republic,* February 1, 2016. https://newrepublic.com/minutes/128896/beat-protester-trumps-rally-hell-cover-legal-fees.

Cloud, Dana L. "The Irony Bribe and Reality Television: Investment and Detachment in The Bachelor." *Critical Studies in Media Communication* 27 (2010): 413–37.

———. *Reality Bites: Rhetoric and the Circulation of Truth Claims in U.S. Political Culture.* Columbus: The Ohio State University Press, 2018.

Collins, Laura J. "The Second Amendment as Demanding Subject: Figuring the Marginalized Subject in Demands for an Unbridled Second Amendment." *Rhetoric & Public Affairs* 17, no. 4 (2014): 737–56.

Colón, John Michael. "Beta Testing Fascism: How Online Culture Wars Created the Alt-Right." *In These Times,* June 27, 2017. http://inthesetimes.com/article/20275/online-culture-wars-created-the-alt-right-nagle-kill-all-normies.

Connell, Raewynn W. *Masculinities.* New York: Polity, 2005.

Connell, Robert. *Gender and Power: Society, the Person, and Sexual Politics.* Palo Alto: Stanford University Press, 1987.

Coontz, Stephanie. "Yes, I've Folded Up My Masculine Mystique, Honey." *The Sunday Times of London,* February 24, 2013. http://www.thesundaytimes.co.uk/sto/newsreview/article1219753.ece.

Copjec, Joan. *Read My Desire: Lacan Against the Historicists.* New York: Verso, 2015.

Corner, John. "Performing the Real: Documentary Diversions." *Television & New Media* 3, no. 3 (2002): 255–69.

Couldry, Nick. *Media Rituals: A Critical Approach.* New York: Routledge, 2003.

———. "Playing for Celebrity: Big Brother as Ritual Event." *Television and New Media* 3, no. 3 (2002): 205–26.

Creed, Barbara. "Dark Desires: Male Masochism in the Horror Film." In *Screening the Male: Exploring Masculinities in Hollywood Cinema,* edited by Steven Cohan and Ina Rae Hark, 118–33. New York: Routledge, 1993.

Darsey, James. *The Prophetic Tradition and Radical Rhetoric in America.* New York: New York University Press, 1999.

De Lauretis, Teresa. *Freud's Drive: Psychoanalysis, Literature and Film: Psychoanalysis, Literature and Film.* New York: Springer, 2008.

Dellamora, Richard. *Masculine Desire: The Sexual Politics of Victorian Aestheticism.* Chapel Hill: University of North Carolina Press, 1990.

DeLuca, Kevin M. "Unruly Arguments: The Body Rhetoric of Earth First!, Act Up, and Queer Nation." *Argumentation and Advocacy* 36, no. 1 (1999): 9–21.

DeLuca, Kevin Michael, and Jennifer Peeples. "From Public Sphere to Public Screen: Democracy, Activism, and the 'Violence' of Seattle." *Critical Studies in Media Communication* 19, no. 2 (2002): 125–51.

Diamond, Jeremy. "Donald Trump Could 'Shoot Somebody and Not Lose Voters.'" *CNN,* January 24, 2016. https://www.cnn.com/2016/01/23/politics/donald-trump-shoot-somebody-support/index.html.

Dockterman, Eliana. "Read Terry Crews' TIME Person of the Year Interview 2017" *Time,* December 6, 2017. http://time.com/5049671/terry-crews-interview-transcript-person-of-the-year-2017/.

Dorsey, Leroy G. *We Are All Americans, Pure and Simple: Theodore Roosevelt and the Myth of Americanism.* Tuscaloosa: University of Alabama Press, 2013.

Dubriwny, Tasha N. "Consciousness-Raising as Collective Rhetoric: The Articulation of Experience in the Redstockings' Abortion Speak-Out of 1969." *Quarterly Journal of Speech* 91, no. 4 (2005): 395–422.

Dubrofsky, Rachel E., and Antoine Hardy. "Performing Race in Flavor of Love and The Bachelor." *Critical Studies in Media Communication* 25, no. 4 (2008): 373–92.

Dubrofsky, Rachel E., and Emily D. Ryalls. "The Hunger Games: Performing Not-Performing to Authenticate Femininity and Whiteness." *Critical Studies in Media Communication* 31, no. 5 (2014): 395–409.

Ducat, Stephen. *The Wimp Factor: Gender Gaps, Holy Wars, and the Politics of Anxious Masculinity.* Boston: Beacon Press, 2004.

Ducharme, Jamie. "Roy Moore Told a Black Man That America Was Great During Slavery." *Time,* December 7, 2017. http://time.com/5056590/roy-moore-america-great-slavery/.

Dunbar-Ortiz, Roxanne. *Loaded: A Disarming History of the Second Amendment.* San Francisco: City Lights Books, 2018.

Dyer, Richard. *White: Essays on Race and Culture.* New York: Routledge, 1997.

Edelman, Lee. *No Future: Queer Theory and the Death Drive.* Durham, NC: Duke University Press, 2004.

Edwards, Leigh H. "'What a Girl Wants': Gender Norming on Reality Game Shows," *Feminist Media Studies* 4, no. 2 (2004): 226–28.

Eells, Josh. "'Doomsday Preppers: The Survivalists Next Door." *Men's Journal,* March 2013. http://www.mensjournal.com/magazine/doomsday-preppers-the -survivalists-next-door-20130212.

Ehrenfreund, Max. "I Asked Psychologists to Analyze Trump Supporters. This Is What I Learned." *Washington Post,* October 15, 2015. https://www.washingtonpost. com/news/wonk/wp/2015/10/15/i-asked-psychologists-to-analyze-trump -supporters-this-is-what-i-learned/?noredirect=on&utm_term=.f1f8426a89f6.

Faludi, Susan. *Backlash: The Undeclared War Against American Women.* New York: Broadway Books, 2006.

———. *Stiffed: The Betrayal of the American Man.* Reprint edition. New York: Harper Perennial, 2000.

"Famous Feminist Quotes That Keep Fuelling the Debate." *The Telegraph,* September 21, 2015. https://www.telegraph.co.uk/film/suffragette/famous_feminist_quotes/.

Felski, Rita. *The Limits of Critique.* Chicago: University of Chicago Press, 2015.

Feuer, Alan. "The Preppers Next Door." *New York Times,* January 26, 2013. http:// www.nytimes.com/2013/01/27/nyregion/the-doomsday-preppers-of-new-york. html?pagewanted=alland_r=0.

Finchelstein, Federico. *From Fascism to Populism in History.* Berkeley: University of California Press, 2017.

Fisher, Walter R. "Narration as a Human Communication Paradigm: The Case of Public Moral Argument." *Communication Monographs* 51, no. 1 (1984): 1–22.

Foucault, Michel. *The Birth of Biopolitics: Lectures at the Collège de France, 1978—1979.* New York: Picador, 2010.

———. *The History of Sexuality: Volume 1.* New York: Random House, 1978.

Fox, Ragan. "'You Are Not Allowed to Talk About Production': Narratization on (and off) the Set of CBS's Big Brother." *Critical Studies in Media Communication* 30, no. 3 (2013): 189–208.

Fraser, Nancy. "Rethinking the Public Sphere: A Contribution to the Critique of Actu- ally Existing Democracy." *Social Text* 25/26 (1990): 56–80.

Freud, Sigmund. *Beyond the Pleasure Principle.* Translated by James Strachey. New York: W. W. Norton & Company, 1990.

———. "The Economic Problem of Masochism." In *General Psychological Theory,* edited by Phillip Rieff, translated by James Strachey, 191–204. New York: Collier, 1963.

———. *The Ego and the Id.* Translated by James Strachey. Norton, 1962.

———. "Mourning and Melancholia." In *The Standard Edition of the Complete Psycho- logical Works of Sigmund Freud,* translated by James Strachey, 243–58. Volume 14. London: The Hogarth Press, 1964.

———. 'A Child is Being Beaten: A Contribution to the Study of the Origin of Sexual Perversions." In *The Standard Edition of the Complete Psychological Works of Sigmund Freud, Volume XVII (1917–1919): An Infantile Neurosis and Other Works*, translated by James Strachey, 175–6. Volume 17. London: The Hogarth Press, 1964.

Friedan, Betty. *The Feminine Mystique*. New York: W. W. Norton & Company, 2001.

Frum, David. "The Chilling Effects of Openly Displayed Firearms." *The Atlantic*, August 16, 2017. https://www.theatlantic.com/politics/archive/2017/08/open-carry -laws-mean-charlottesville-could-have-been-graver/537087/.

Furioso, Relampago. "Why Everything in the Blue Pill World Is a Lie." *Return of Kings*, December 6, 2016. http://www.returnofkings.com/105093/why-everything-in-the -blue-pill-world-is-a-lie.

Futrelle, David. "Men's-Rights Activism Is the Gateway Drug for the Alt-Right." *New York Magazine*, August 17, 2017. https://www.thecut.com/2017/08/mens-rights -activism-is-the-gateway-drug-for-the-alt-right.html.

Gibson, James William. *Warrior Dreams: Violence and Manhood in Post-Vietnam America*. Reprint edition. New York: Hill & Wang, 1994.

Gingrich-Philbrook, Craig. "'Good Vibration' or Domination?: Stylized Repetition in Mythopoetic Performance of Masculinity." *Text & Performance Quarterly* 14, no. 1 (1994): 21–45.

Girard, René. *Things Hidden since the Foundation of the World*. Translated by Stephen Bann and Michael Metteer. Palo Alto: Stanford University Press, 1987.

Givens, Tom. "A Red Pill Message to a Blue Pill World." *A Voice for Men*, April 27, 2011. https://www.avoiceformen.com/men/ mens-issues/a-red-pill-message-to-a-blue-pill-world/.

Goffman, Erving. *Frame Analysis: An Essay on the Organization of Experience*. Cambridge, MA: Harvard University Press, 1974.

———. *The Presentation of Self in Everyday Life*. New York: Penguin Books, 1990.

Gunn, Joshua. "On Political Perversion." *Rhetoric Society Quarterly* 48, no. 2 (2018): 161–86.

———. "On Social Networking and Psychosis." *Communication Theory* 28, no. 1 (2018): 69–88.

Gunn, Joshua, and David E. Beard. "On the Apocalyptic Columbine." *Southern Communication Journal* 68, no. 3 (2003): 198–216.

———. "On the Apocalyptic Sublime." *Southern Communication Journal* 65, no. 4 (2000): 269–86.

Gunn, Joshua, and Thomas Frentz. "Fighting for Father: Fight Club as Cinematic Psychosis." *Western Journal of Communication* 74, no. 3 (2010): 269–91.

Hadden, Sally E. *Slave Patrols: Law and Violence in Virginia and the Carolinas*. Cambridge, MA: Harvard University Press, 2001.

Hanisch, Carol. "The Personal Is Political." In *Notes from the Second Year: Women's Liberation, Major Writings of the Radical Feminists*, edited by Shulamith Firestone and Anne Koedt, 76–78. New York: Radical Feminism, 1970.

Hanke, Robert. "The 'Mock-Macho' Situation Comedy: Hegemonic Masculinity and Its Reiteration." *Western Journal of Communication* 62, no. 1 (1998): 74–93.

Hardt, Michael, and Antonio Negri. *Multitude: War and Democracy in the Age of Empire.* New York: Penguin, 2005.

Hariman, Robert, and John Louis Lucaites. *No Caption Needed: Iconic Photographs, Public Culture, and Liberal Democracy.* Chicago: University of Chicago Press, 2011.

Hawkins, Asher, and Zack O'Malley Greenberg. "Doomsday Investing." March 12, 2009. https://www.forbes.com/forbes/2009/0330/054-doomsday-investing.html#a3a1c4044ad0.

Heim, Joe. "How a Rally of White Nationalists and Supremacists at the University of Virginia Turned into a 'Tragic, Tragic Weekend.'" *Washington Post,* August 14, 2017. https://www.washingtonpost.com/graphics/2017/local/charlottesville-timeline/.

Hoerl, Kristen. "Selective Amnesia and Racial Transcendence in News Coverage of President Obama's Inauguration." *Quarterly Journal of Speech* 98, no. 2 (2012): 178–202.

Holowchak, M. Andrew, and Michael Lavin. *Repetition, the Compulsion to Repeat, and the Death Drive: An Examination of Freud's Doctrines.* Lanham, MD: Lexington Books, 2017.

Hu, Tung-Hui. *A Prehistory of the Cloud.* Cambridge, MA: MIT Press, 2015.

Irigaray, Luce. *This Sex Which Is Not One.* Ithaca, NY: Cornell University Press, 1985.

Jacobs, Harrison. "Why this NYC Firefighter is Prepping for the End of the World." *Business Insider,* November 26, 2014. https://www.businessinsider.com/a-doomsday-prepper-explains-why-prepping-is-a-lot-more-sensible-than-you-think-2014-11.

Jeffords, Susan. *Hard Bodies: Hollywood Masculinity in the Reagan Era.* New Brunswick, NJ: Rutgers University Press, 1994.

Johnson, Paul Elliott. "The Art of Masculine Victimhood: Donald Trump's Demagoguery." *Women's Studies in Communication* 40, no. 3 (2017): 229–50.

Kaplan, E. Ann. *Trauma Culture: The Politics of Terror and Loss in Media and Literature.* New Brunswick, NJ: Rutgers University Press, 2005.

Kaufman, Michael. "The Construction of Masculinity and the Triad of Men's Violence." In *Beyond Patriarchy: Essays by Men on Pleasure, Power, and Change,* edited by Michael Kaufman, 1–29. New York: Oxford University Press, 1987.

Kellner, Douglas. *Guys and Guns Amok: Domestic Terrorism and School Shootings from the Oklahoma City Bombing to the Virginia Tech Massacre.* New York: Routledge, 2008.

Kellner, Douglas, and Clayton Pierce. *Philosophy, Psychoanalysis and Emancipation: Collected Papers of Herbert Marcuse. Volume 5: Herbert Marcuse Collected Papers.* New York: Routledge, 2010.

Kelly, Casey Ryan. "Cooking Without Women: The Rhetoric of the New Culinary Male." *Communication and Critical/Cultural Studies* 12, no. 2 (2015): 200–204.

———. "Feminine Purity and Masculine Revenge-Seeking In Taken (2008)." *Feminist Media Studies* 14, no. 3 (2014): 403–18.

———. "The Man-Pocalpyse: Doomsday Preppers and the Rituals of Apocalyptic Manhood." *Text and Performance Quarterly* 36, no. 2–3 (J2016): 95–114.

———. "The Rage Network: Toxic Masculinity in Digital Space." In *Networking Argument: Selected Papers for the 19th Biennial Conference on Argumentation,* edited by Carol Winkler. London: Taylor & Francis, forthcoming.

Khazan, Olga. "Why Did People Vote for Trump?" *The Atlantic,* April 23, 2018. https://www.theatlantic.com/science/archive/2018/04/existential-anxiety-not-poverty-motivates-trump-support/558674/.

Kimmel, Michael. *Angry White Men: American Masculinity at the End of an Era.* New York: Nation Books, 2015.

———. *Manhood in America: A Cultural History.* London: Oxford University Press, 2012.

King, C. Richard. "Arming Desire: The Sexual Force of Guns in the United States." In *Open Fire: Understanding Global Gun Cultures,* edited by Charles Fruehling Springwood, 87–97. New York: Bloomsbury, 2007.

King, Claire Sisco. "It Cuts Both Ways: Fight Club, Masculinity, and Abject Hegemony." *Communication & Critical/Cultural Studies* 6, no. 4 (2009): 366–85.

———. *Washed in Blood: Male Sacrifice, Trauma, and the Cinema.* New Brunswick, NJ: Rutgers University Press, 2011.

King, Claire Sisco, and Joshua Gunn. "On a Violence Unseen: The Womanly Object and Sacrificed Man." *Quarterly Journal of Speech* 99, no. 2 (2013): 200–208.

Klein, Jessie. *The Bully Society: School Shootings and the Crisis of Bullying in America's Schools.* New York: New York University Press, 2012.

Klein, Melanie. *The Collected Works of Melanie Klein.* London: Karnac Books, 2017.

Krieg, Gregory. "Cleveland Police Union Asks for Suspension of 'Open Carry' in Wake of Baton Rouge, ahead of RNC." *CNN,* July 18, 2016. https://www.cnn.com/2016/07/17/politics/cleveland-police-baton-rouge-security-open-carry/index.html.

Kristeva, Julia. *The Power of Horror: An Essay on Abjection.* New York: Columbia University Press, 1982.

Lacan, Jacques. *The Four Fundamental Concepts of Psychoanalysis.* New York: W. W. Norton & Company, 1998.

LaCapra, Dominick. *Writing History, Writing Trauma.* Baltimore: Johns Hopkins University Press, 2000.

Lacitis, Erik. "Preppers Do Their Best to Be Ready for the Worst." *Seattle Times,* May 14, 2012. https://www.seattletimes.com/seattle-news/preppers-do-their-best-to-be-ready-for-the-worst/.

Laclau, Ernesto. *On Populist Reason.* New York: Verso, 2007.

Lamy, P. *Millennium Rage: Survivalists, White Supremacists, and the Doomsday Prophecy.* New York: Springer, 2013.

Larson, Peter. "This Militia Group Walked Around the RNC with AR-15s, AK-47s, and G3s." *Vice,* July 18, 2016. https://www.vice.com/en_us/article/zn8xv9/this-militia-group-walked-around-the-rnc-with-ar-15s-ak-47s-and-g3s.

Lee, Michael J. "The Populist Chameleon: The People's Party, Huey Long, George Wallace, and the Populist Argumentative Frame." *Quarterly Journal of Speech* 92, no. 4 (2006): 355–78.

Levina, Marina. "Whiteness and the Joys of Cruelty." *Communication & Critical/Cultural Studies* 15, no. 1 (2018): 73–78.

Levina, Marina, and Kumarini Silva. "Cruel Intentions: Affect Theory in the Age of Trump." *Communication and Critical/Cultural Studies* 15, no. 1 (2018): 70–72.

Levine, Caroline. *Forms: Whole, Rhythm, Hierarchy, Network.* Princeton: Princeton University Press, 2015.

Lipsitz, George. *Possessive Investment in Whiteness.* Philadelphia: Temple University Press, 1998.

Lockwood, Dean. "All Stripped Down: The Spectacle of 'Torture Porn.'" *Popular Communication: The International Journal of Media and Culture* 7, no. 1 (2009): 40–48.

López, Ian Haney. *Dog Whistle Politics: How Coded Racial Appeals Have Reinvented Racism and Wrecked the Middle Class.* London: Oxford University Press, 2015.

Lundberg, Christian. "Enjoying God's Death: The Passion of the Christ and the Practices of an Evangelical Public." *Quarterly Journal of Speech* 95, no. 4 (2009): 387–411.

———. *Lacan in Public: Psychoanalysis and the Science of Rhetoric.* Tuscaloosa: University Alabama Press, 2012.

———. "On Being Bound to Equivalential Chains." *Cultural Studies* 26, no. 2–3 (2012): 299–318.

Malone, Clare. "Trump Made Breitbart Great Again." *FiveThirtyEight.com,* August 18, 2016. https://fivethirtyeight.com/features/trump-made-breitbart-great-again/.

Marcuse, Herbert. *Eros and Civilization: A Philosophical Inquiry into Freud.* Boston: Beacon Press, 1974.

———. *One-Dimensional Man: Studies in the Ideology of Advanced Industrial Society,* Boston: Beacon Press, 1964.

Martin, Andrew. "Hurricane Sandy and Disaster Preparedness Economy." *New York Times,* November 10, 2012. https://www.nytimes.com/2012/11/11/business/hurricane-sandy-and-the-disaster-preparedness-economy.html?mtrref=www.google.com&gwh=06C749A3350FDEA99D5A8F08B2AE1A07&gwt=pay&assetType=REGIWALL.

Marx, Karl. *The 18th Brumaire of Louis Bonaparte.* Rockville, MD: Wildside Press, 2008.

Matheson, Calum Lister. *Desiring the Bomb: Communication, Psychoanalysis, and the Atomic Age.* Tuscaloosa: University of Alabama Press, 2018.

———. "'What Does Obama Want of Me?' Anxiety and Jade Helm 15." *Quarterly Journal of Speech* 102, no. 2 (2016): 133–49.

Mazower, Mark. "Fascism Revisited? A Warning about the Rise of Populism." *Financial Times,* April 11, 2018. https://www.ft.com/content/6d57a338-3be9-11e8-bcc8 -cebcb81f1f90.

McCall, Jeffrey. *Viewer Discretion Advised: Taking Control of Mass Media Influences.* Lanham, MD: Rowman & Littlefield, 2007.

McCann, Bryan J. "Therapeutic and Material <Victim> Hood: Ideology and the Struggle for Meaning in the Illinois Death Penalty Controversy." *Communication and Critical/Cultural Studies* 4, no. 4 (2007): 382–401.

McCrummen, Stephanie, Beth Reinhard, and Alice Crites. "Woman Says Roy Moore Initiated Sexual Encounter When She Was 14, He Was 32." *Washington Post,* November 9, 2017. https://www.washingtonpost.com/investigations/ woman-says-roy-moore-initiated-sexual-encounter-when-she-was-14-he-was- 32/2017/11/09/1f495878-c293-11e7-afe9-4f60b5a6c4a0_story.html.

McGowan, Todd. *Enjoying What We Don't Have: The Political Project of Psychoanalysis.* Lincoln: University of Nebraska Press, 2013.

McGuire, Patrick. "Elliot Rodger's Online Life Provides a Glimpse at a Hateful Group of 'Anti-Pick-up Artists.'" *Vice,* May 26, 2014. https://www.vice.com/en_us/article/ znwz53/elliot-rodgers-online-life-provides-a-glimpse-at-a-hateful-group-of-pick- up-artists.

McLuhan, Marshall. *Understanding Media: The Extensions of Man.* Cambridge, MA: MIT Press, 1994.

Meltzer, Jonathan. "Open Carry for All: Heller and Our Nineteenth-Century Second Amendment." *Yale Law Journal* 123 (2014/2013): 1486.

Melzer, Scott. *Gun Crusaders: The NRA's Culture War.* New York: New York University Press, 2012.

Merchant, Carol. *The Death of Nature: Women, Ecology, and the Scientific Revolution.* Reprint edition. New York: HarperOne, 1990.

Meyer, Michaela D. E., Amy M. Fallah, and Megan M. Wood. "Gender, Media, and Madness: Reading a Rhetoric of Women in Crisis Through Foucauldian Theory." *Review of Communication* 11, no. 3 (2011): 216–28.

Mezzofiore, Gianluca. "The Toronto Suspect Apparently Posted About an 'Incel Rebellion.' Here's What That Means." *CNN,* April 25, 2018. Accessed April 28, 2018. https://www.cnn.com/2018/04/25/us/incel-rebellion-alek-minassian-toronto -attack-trnd/index.html.

Michaud, Chris. "One in Seven Thinks End of World Is Coming: Poll." *Reuters,* May 1, 2012. http://www.reuters.com/article/2012/05/01/us-mayancalendar-poll -idUSBRE8400XH20120501.

Milburn, Forest. "Open Carry Activists Plan Rally to Arm Teachers with Guns in Santa Fe, a Month After Deadly School Shooting." *Dallas Morning News,* June 11, 2018. https://www.dallasnews.com/news/2018/06/11/open-carry-activists-plan -rally-to-arm-teachers-with-guns-in-santa-fe-a-month-after-deadly-school -shooting/.

Miller, Carolyn R. "Genre as Social Action." *Quarterly Journal of Speech* 70, no. 2 (1984): 151–67.

Mitchell, Richard G. *Dancing at Armageddon: Survivalism and Chaos in Modern Times.* Chicago: University of Chicago Press, 2002.

Modesti, Sonja. "Home Sweet Home: Tattoo Parlors as Postmodern Spaces of Agency." *Western Journal of Communication* 72, no. 3 (2008): 197–212.

Moore, Robert, and Douglas Gillette. *King, Warrior, Magician, Lover: Rediscovering the Archetypes of the Mature Masculine.* San Francisco: HarperOne, 1991.

Mosse, George L. *The Image of Man: The Creation of Modern Masculinity.* London: Oxford University Press, 1998.

Mowitt, John. "Trauma Envy." *Cultural Critique,* no. 46 (2000): 272–97.

Murphy, John M. "'A Time of Shame and Sorrow': Robert F. Kennedy and the American Jeremiad." *Quarterly Journal of Speech* 76, no. 4 (1990): 401–14.

Murphy, Tim. "Preppers Are Getting Ready for the Barackalypse." *Mother Jones,* January/February 2013. https://www.motherjones.com/politics/2012/12/preppers-survivalist-doomsday-obama/.

Murray, Stuart. "Thanatopolitics: On the Use of Death for Mobilizing Political Life." *Polygraph: An International Journal of Politics and Culture* 18 (2006): 191–215.

Murray, Susan. "'I Think We Need a New Name For It': The Meeting of Documentary and Reality TV." *Reality TV: Remaking Television Culture,* edited by Susan Murray and Laurie Ouellette, 65–81 New York: New York University Press, 2008.

Nagle, Angela. *Kill All Normies: Online Culture Wars from 4Chan and Tumblr to Trump and the Alt-Right.* Washington, DC: Zero Books, 2017.

———. "The Lost Boys." *The Atlantic,* December 2017. https://www.theatlantic.com/magazine/archive/2017/12/brotherhood-of-losers/544158/.

Nakayama, Thomas K., and Robert L. Krizek. "Whiteness: A Strategic Rhetoric." *Quarterly Journal of Speech* 81, no. 3 (1995): 291–309.

National Geographic Channel. "Doomsday Prepper Survey." Accessed August 29, 2019. http://images.nationalgeographic.com/wpf/media-live/file/Doomsday_Preppers_Survey_-_Topline_Results.pdf.

National Geographic Society. "National Geographic Brings Viewers on Immersive, Global Expeditions." December 6, 2018. https://www.nationalgeographicpartners.com/press/2018/12/national-geographic-brings-viewers-on-immersive-global-expeditions/.

Nevadacarry. "Nevada Carry: The NRA Are a Bunch of Loser Cucks." *Nevada Carry* (blog), January 22, 2018. http://nevadacarry.blogspot.com/2018/01/the-nra-are-bunch-of-loser-cucks.html.

Nichols, Bill. *Introduction to Documentary.* Bloomington: Indiana University Press, 2001.

Nixon, Ron. "Trump's Border Wall Could Waste Billions of Dollars, Report Says." *New York Times,* August 7, 2018. https://www.nytimes.com/2018/08/06/us/politics/trump-border-wall-report.html.

Nixon, Ron, and Linda Qiu. "Trump's Evolving Words on the Wall." *New York Times,* February 14, 2018. https://www.nytimes.com/2018/01/18/us/politics/trump -border-wall-immigration.html.

Noble, Safiya Umoja. *Algorithms of Oppression: How Search Engines Reinforce Racism.* New York: New York University Press, 2018.

Noys, Benjamin. *The Culture of Death.* London: Berg Publishers, 2005.

O'Connor, Rod. "These Suburban Preppers are Ready for Anything." *Chicago Magazine,* April 27, 2015. https://www.chicagomag.com/Chicago-Magazine/May-2015/ Suburban-Survivalists/.

"Open Carry." *Giffords Law Center to Prevent Gun Violence* (blog). Accessed June 11, 2018. http://lawcenter.giffords.org/gun-laws/policy-areas/guns-in-public/ open-carry/.

"Open Carry Activists Bear Arms in the Streets—and Chipotle." *NPR.org,* June 6, 2016. https://www.npr.org/2014/06/06/319552462/open-carry-activists-bear-arms -in-the-streets-and-chipotle.

"Open Carry Activists Plan Rally to Arm Teachers with Guns in Santa Fe, a Month after Deadly School Shooting." *Dallas News,* June 11, 2018. https://www. dallasnews.com/news/guns/2018/06/11/open-carry-activists-plan-rally-arm -teacherswith-guns-santa-fe-month-after-deadly-school-shooting.

Ott, Brian L. "The Age of Twitter: Donald J. Trump and the Politics of Debasement." *Critical Studies in Media Communication* 34, no. 1 (2017): 59–68.

Ott, Brian L., Eric Aoki, and Greg Dickinson. "Ways of (Not) Seeing Guns: Presence and Absence at the Cody Firearms Museum." *Communication & Critical/Cultural Studies* 8, no. 3 (2011): 215–39.

Ott, Brian L., and Greg Dickinson. *The Twitter Presidency: Donald J. Trump and the Politics of White Rage.* New York: Routledge, 2019.

Ouellette, Laurie. "The Trump Show." *Television & New Media* 17, no. 7 (2016): 647–50.

Ouellette, Laurie, and James Hay. *Better Living through Reality TV: Television and Post-Welfare Citizenship.* Malden, MA: Wiley-Blackwell, 2008.

Parker, Ashley, Nick Corasaniti, and Erica Berenstein. "Voices from Donald Trump's Rallies, Uncensored." *New York Times,* December 21, 2017. https://www.nytimes. com/2016/08/04/us/politics/donald-trump-supporters.html.

Passy, Charles. "'Doomsday Preppers' Turn the Apocalypse into a Hobby." *Wall Street Journal,* February 8, 2012. https://blogs.wsj.com/speakeasy/2012/02/07/ doomsday-preppers-turn-the-apocalypse-into-a-hobby/.

Paxton, Robert O. *The Anatomy of Fascism.* New York: Knopf Doubleday, 2007.

Perriello, Tom, and Dahlia Lithwick. "There Is Only One Side to the Story of Charlottesville." *Slate,* August 13, 2017. http://www.slate.com/articles/news_and_politics/ politics/2017/08/tom_perriello_on_the_charlottesville_protests.html.

Pfister, Damien Smith. *Networked Media, Networked Rhetorics: Attention and Deliberation in the Early Blogosphere.* University Park: Pennsylvania State University Press, 2014.

Phillips, Amber. "'I Have Never Sexually Assaulted Anyone': Brett Kavanaugh's Opening Statement to Congress, Annotated." *Washington Post,* September 26, 2018. https://www.washingtonpost.com/politics/2018/09/26/i-have-never-sexually -assaulted-anyone-brett-kavanaughs-testimony-congress-annotated/.

Phillips, Kendall R. "'The Safest Hands Are Our Own': Cinematic Affect, State Cruelty, and the Election of Donald J. Trump." *Communication and Critical/Cultural Studies* 15, no. 1 (2018): 85–89.

"Preparing for the Apocalypse: I Will Survive." *The Econonmist,* December 17, 2014. https://www.economist.com/christmas-specials/2014/12/17/i-will-survive.

PrepperCon. "About Us." *PrepperCon* (blog), July 15, 2016. https://preppercon.com/ about-us/.

"Prostitution—r/TheRedPill." Reddit. Accessed April 20, 2018. https://www.reddit. com/r/TheRedPill/comments/2a0vxo/prostitution/.

Puar, Jasbir K. *The Right to Maim: Debility, Capacity, Disability.* Durham, NC: Duke University Press Books, 2017.

Rademacher, Mark A., and Casey Kelly. "'I'm Here to Do Business. I'm Not Here to Play Games.' Work, Consumption, and Masculinity in Storage Wars." *Journal of Communication Inquiry* 40, no. 1 (2016): 7–24.

Radstone, Susannah. *The Sexual Politics of Time: Confession, Nostalgia, Memory.* New York: Routledge, 2007.

Reigstad, Leif. "The Great Texas 'Come and Take It' Controversy." *Texas Monthly,* October 12, 2016. https://www.texasmonthly.com/the-daily-post/great-texas-come -take-controversy/.

Rhodes, Jane. *Framing the Black Panthers: The Spectacular Rise of a Black Power Icon.* Champagne: University of Illinois Press, 2017.

Riley, Patricia, James F. Klumpp, and Thomas A. Hollihan. "The Dark Side of Community and Democracy: Militias, Patriots and Angry White Guys." In *Argument in a Time of Change: Definitions, Frameworks, and Critiques,* edited by James F. Klumpp, 202–7. Annandale, VA: National Communication Association, 1997.

Riotta, Chris. "43% of Republicans Say Trump Should Be Able to Shut Down News Outlets, New Poll Finds." *Independent,* August 7, 2018. https://www.independent. co.uk/news/world/americas/us-politics/donald-trump-republicans-press-media- enemy-of-american-people-news-trust-ipsos-poll-a8481686.html.

Robinson, Sally. *Authenticity Guaranteed: Masculinity and the Rhetoric of Anti-Consumerism in American Culture.* Amherst: University of Massachusetts Press, 2018.

———. "Feminized Men and Inauthentic Women: Fight Club and the Limits of Anti-Consumerist Critique." *Genders,* May 1, 2011. https://www.colorado.edu/ gendersarchive1998-2013/2011/05/01/feminized-men-and-inauthentic-women -fight-club-and-limits-anti-consumerist-critique.

———. *Marked Men: White Masculinity in Crisis.* New York: Columbia University Press, 2000.

Rodger, Elliot. "My Twisted World." May 22, 2014. https://www.documentcloud.org/ documents/1173808-elliot-rodger-manifesto.html.

Rodino-Colocino, Michelle. "The Great He-Cession: Why Feminists Should Rally for the End of White Supremacist Capitalist Patriarchy." *Feminist Media Studies* 14, no. 2 (2014): 343–47.

———. "Me Too, #MeToo: Countering Cruelty with Empathy." *Communication and Critical/Cultural Studies* 15, no. 1 (2018): 96–100.

Rollins, Peter. *Hollywood's West: The American Frontier in Film, Television, and History.* Lexington: University Press of Kentucky, 2005.

Rose, Kenneth D. *One Nation Underground: The Fallout Shelter in American Culture.* New York: New York University Press, 2001.

Rushe, Dominic. "Trump Said to Be Reviewing Trans-Pacific Partnership in Trade U-Turn." *Guardian,* April 12, 2018. http://www.theguardian.com/world/2018/apr/12/trump-trans-pacific-partnership-trade-deal-reversal.

Sánchez-Pardo, Esther. *Cultures of the Death Drive: Melanie Klein and Modernist Melancholia.* Durham, NC: Duke University Press Books, 2003.

Savage, William W. *The Cowboy Hero: His Image in American History & Culture.* Norman: University of Oklahoma Press, 1979.

Savran, David. *Taking It Like a Man: White Masculinity, Masochism, and Contemporary American Culture.* Princeton: Princeton University Press, 1998.

Savransky, Rebecca. "Roy Moore Pulls Out Gun While Speaking at Rally." *The Hill,* September 26, 2017. http://thehill.com/homenews/senate/352410-roy-moore-pulls-out-gun-while-speaking-at-rally.

Scott, Robert L., and Donald K. Smith. "The Rhetoric of Confrontation." *Quarterly Journal of Speech* 55, no. 1 (1969): 1–8.

Sedgwick, Eve Kosofsky. *Between Men: English Literature and Male Homosocial Desire.* New York: Columbia University Press, 1985.

———. *Tendencies.* Durham, NC: Duke University Press, 1993.

Seitz-Wald, Alex. "Alex Jones: Conspiracy Inc." *Salon.com,* May 2, 2013. http://www.salon.com/2013/05/02/alex_jones_conspiracy_inc/.

Sharp, John. "Roy Moore Flashing Gun at Rally Not a Crime, Police Say after Complaint." *AL.com,* September 27, 2017. https://www.al.com/news/mobile/index.ssf/2017/09/fairhope_police_receive_compla.html.

Silva, Kumarini. "Having the Time of Our Lives: Love-Cruelty as Patriotic Impulse." *Communication and Critical/Cultural Studies* 15, no. 1 (2018): 79–84.

Silverman, Kaja. *Male Subjectivity at the Margins.* New York: Routledge, 1992.

Slotkin, Richard. *Gunfighter Nation: The Myth of the Frontier in Twentieth-Century America.* Norman: University of Oklahoma Press, 1992.

———. *Regeneration through Violence: The Mythology of the American Frontier, 1600–1860.* Norman: University of Oklahoma Press, 2000.

Smith, Henry Nash. *Virgin Land: The American West as Symbol and Myth.* Cambridge, MA: Harvard University Press, 2007.

Smith, Tovia. "Backlash Erupts after Gillette Launches a New #MeToo-Inspired Ad Campaign." *NPR.org,* January 17, 2019. https://www.npr.org/2019/01/17/685976624/backlash-erupts-after-gillette-launches-a-new-metoo-inspired-ad-campaign.

Sobchack, Vivian. *Carnal Thoughts: Embodiment and Moving Image Culture.* Berkeley: University of California Press, 2004.

Solon, Olivia. "'Incel': Reddit Bans Misogynist Men's Group Blaming Women for Their Celibacy." *Guardian,* November 8, 2017. http://www.theguardian.com/technology/2017/nov/08/reddit-incel-involuntary-celibate-men-ban.

Southern Poverty Law Center. "Male Supremacy." Accessed April 9, 2018. https://www.splcenter.org/fighting-hate/extremist-files/ideology/male-supremacy.

———. "Misogyny: The Sites." *Southern Poverty Law Center,* March 1, 2012. https://www.splcenter.org/fighting-hate/intelligence-report/2012/misogyny-sites.

Sowards, Stacey K., and Valerie R. Renegar. "The Rhetorical Functions of Consciousness⊠raising in Third Wave Feminism." *Communication Studies* 55, no. 4 (2004): 535–52.

Spackman, Barbara. *Fascist Virilities: Rhetoric, Ideology, and Social Fantasy in Italy.* Minneapolis: University of Minnesota Press, 1996.

Spigel, Lynn. *Make Room for TV: Television and the Family Ideal in Postwar America.* Chicago: University of Chicago Press, 2013.

Starrs, Paul F. *Let the Cowboy Ride: Cattle Ranching in the American West.* Baltimore: Johns Hopkins University Press, 2000.

Stekel, Wilhelm. *Sadism and Masochism: The Psychology of Hatred and Cruelty.* New York: Liverright, 1929.

Stewart, D.C. "Finally, a Home Where You Can Enjoy the Post-Apocalypse." *Discover Magazine,* June 2012. http://discovermagazine.com/2012/jun/02-finally-home-where-you-can-enjoy-post-apocalypse.

Stracqualursi, Veronica. "Trump Re-Ups 'Infestation' Rhetoric in Immigration Debate." *CNN,* July 3, 2018. https://www.cnn.com/2018/07/03/politics/trump-ms13-illegal-immigration-rhetoric/index.html.

Stuart, Tessa. "Black Gun Owners on Facing a Racist Double Standard." *Rolling Stone,* July 14, 2016. https://www.rollingstone.com/culture/culture-news/black-gun-owners-speak-out-about-facing-a-racist-double-standard-75081/.

Stuckey, Mary E. "American Elections and the Rhetoric of Political Change: Hyperbole, Anger, and Hope in U.S. Politics." *Rhetoric and Public Affairs* 20, no. 4 (2017): 667–94.

Suen, Brennan. "Trump Supporters Are Using Fox's Contrived New Black Panther Scandal From 2010 To Defend His 'Rigged Election' Claim." *Media Matters for America,* October 21, 2016. https://www.mediamatters.org/fox-friends/trump-supporters-are-using-foxs-contrived-new-black-panther-scandal-2010-defend-his.

Terrill, Robert E. "The Post-Racial and Post-Ethical Discourse of Donald J. Trump." *Rhetoric & Public Affairs* 20, no. 3 (Fall 2017): 493–510.

"The Great Texas 'Come and Take It' Controversy." *Texas Monthly,* October 12, 2016. https://www.texasmonthly.com/the-daily-post/great-texas-come-take -controversy/.

Theweleit, Klaus, and Barbara Ehrenreich. *Male Fantasies, Vol. 1: Women, Floods, Bodies, History.* Translated by Chris Turner, Stephen Conway, and Erica Carter. Minneapolis: University of Minnesota Press, 1987.

"Toronto Suspect Praised 'Incel' Killer." *BBC News,* April 25, 2018. http://www.bbc.com/news/world-us-canada-43883052.

Triece, Mary E. *Tell It Like It Is: Women in the National Welfare Rights Movement.* Columbia: University of South Carolina Press, 2013.

Trujillo, Nick. "Hegemonic Masculinity on the Mound: Media Representations of Nolan Ryan and American Sports Culture." *Critical Studies in Mass Communication* 8, no. 3 (1991): 290–308.

Trump, Donald. "Donald Trump Ohio Rally Speech: Read Full Transcript." *Time,* July 26, 2017. http://time.com/4874161/donald-trump-transcript-youngstown-ohio/.

———. "Donald Trump's Presidential Announcement Speech." *Time,* June 16, 2015. http://time.com/3923128/donald-trump-announcement-speech/.

———. "Full Text: 2017 Donald Trump Inauguration Speech Transcript." *Politico,* January 20, 2017. https://www.politico.com/story/2017/01/full-text-donald-trump -inauguration-speech-transcript-233907.

———. "Full Text: Donald Trump 2016 RNC Draft Speech Transcript." *Politico,* July 21, 2016. http://politi.co/2ApcBDB.

———. "President Donald Trump Delivers Remarks at a Make America Great Again Rally." Southaven, Mississippi." *Federal News Service,* October 2, 2018. Retrieved from Nexis Uni.

———. "President Trump Delivers Remarks Fargo North Dakota, Jun 27 2018," *CSPAN. org,* June 27, 2018. https://www.c-span.org/video/?447664-1/president-trump -delivers-remarks-fargo-north-dakota&live&start=605.

———. "President Trump Ranted for 77 Minutes in Phoenix. Here's What He Said." *Time,* August 22, 2017. http://time.com/4912055/donald-trump-phoenix-arizona -transcript/.

———. "Remarks by President Trump at the Conservative Political Action Conference." *The White House,* February 23, 2018. https://www.whitehouse.gov/briefings -statements/remarks-president-trump-conservative-political-action-conference -2/.

"Trump Supporters Are Using Fox's Contrived New Black Panther Scandal from 2010 to Defend His 'Rigged Election' Claim." *Media Matters for America,* October 21, 2016. https://www.mediamatters.org/blog/2016/10/21/trump-supporters-are -using-fox-s-contrived-new-black-panther-scandal-2010-defend-his-rigged -election/214038.

"U.S.: Mass Shootings by Race 1982–2018." *Statista.* Accessed June 24, 2018. https:// www.statista.com/statistics/476456/mass-shootings-in-the-us-by-shooter-s-race/.

Vale, Paul. "Survivalism in America is a Big Deal." *Huffington Post,* April 27, 2015. https://www.huffingtonpost.co.uk/2015/04/27/american-survivalists-meet-at-the -first-ever-preppercon-to-view-underground-bunkers-and-armored-vehicles_n_ 7151810.html.

Valentine, Matt. "Tallying the Costs of Open Carry." *The Atlantic,* January 31, 2016. https://www.theatlantic.com/politics/archive/2016/01/open-carry-laws/436665/.

Watts, Eric King. "Postracial Fantasies, Blackness, and Zombies." *Communication and Critical/Cultural Studies* 14, no. 4 (2017): 317–33.

Wilson, Jason. "What Do Incels, Fascists and Terrorists Have in Common? Violent Misogyny." *Guardian,* May 4, 2018. http://www.theguardian.com/commentisfree/ 2018/may/04/what-do-incels-fascists-and-terrorists-have-in-common-violent -misogyny.

Winkler, Adam. *Gunfight: The Battle over the Right to Bear Arms in America.* New York: W. W. Norton & Company, 2011.

Wojcik, Daniel N. *The End of the World as We Know It: Faith, Fatalism, and Apocalypse in America.* New York: New York University Press, 1999.

Woodley, Daniel. *Fascism and Political Theory: Critical Perspectives on Fascist Ideology.* New York: Routledge, 2009.

Woods, Heather Suzanne, and Leslie A. Hahner. *Make America Meme Again: The Rhetoric of the Alt-Right.* New York: Peter Lang, 2019.

Wright, Peter. "Men Who Sit at the Screens." *A Voice for Men,* March 17, 2017. https:// www.avoiceformen.com/mens-rights/activism/men-who-sit-at-the-screens/.

Wright, Will. *The Wild West: The Mythical Cowboy and Social Theory.* Thousand Oaks, CA: Sage, 2001.

Yankowski, John S. "Introduction." In *The Complete Marquis de Sade, Vol. 1,* 15–26. Los Angeles: Holloway House, 2008.

Zadrozny, Brandy. "Gun Control Group Moms Demand Action Asking Kroger to Ban Guns in Stores." *The Daily Beast,* August 18, 2014. https://www.thedailybeast.com/ articles/2014/08/18/gun-control-group-moms-demand-action-asking-kroger-to -ban-gun-in-stores.

INDEX

www.ingramcontent.com/pod-product-compliance
Lightning Source LLC
Chambersburg PA
CBHW020352270326
41926CB00007B/396